An Empire of Schools

An Empire of Schools

Japan's Universities and the Molding of a National Power Elite

Robert L. Cutts

Foreword by
Chalmers Johnson

An East Gate Book

M.E. Sharpe
Armonk, New York
London, England

An East Gate Book

Library of Congress Cataloging-in-Publication Data

Cutts, Robert L., 1945–
An empire of schools : Japan's universities and the molding of a national power elite /
Robert L. Cutts : foreword by Chalmers Johnson.
p.   cm.
"An East Gate book."
Includes Index.
ISBN 1-56324-843-3 (alk. paper)
1. Education, Higher—Social aspects—Japan—Case studies.
2. Elite (Social sciences)—Japan—Case studies.
3. Nationalism and education—Japan—Case studies.
4. Tōkyō Daigaku.
I. Title.
LA1318.C88   1996
378.521′35—dc21
96-49365
CIP

Printed in the United States of America

∞

BM (c)   10   9   8   7   6   5   4   3   2   1
BM (p)   10   9   8   7   6   5   4   3   2   1

*This book is dedicated to all of the Japanese people,
one of whom is my beloved wife, Eiko*

*and to my father, machinist's mate and gunner's assistant
on board the USS Dobbin, anchored just off Battleship Row
on that fateful Sunday.*

Contents

Foreword

Most of the great controversies surrounding Japan in the United States and other English-speaking countries originate in the peculiar pretensions of American academic social science. Questions such as Who actually rules in Japan? Is Japan a democracy? and When will the Japanese and American forms of capitalism converge? are thought to be difficult only because what American "theory" asserts the answers ought to be clashes with ordinary reality experienced on the ground in Japan. Because the Americans tried to impose their own socioeconomic system on Japan after World War II and because, during the cold war, the two nations became military allies, American ideology insists that the older country is or is in the process of becoming a clone of the United States.

Take democracy, for example. "The Japanese may tell the world they are a Western democracy," writes Robert Cutts. "But this invites judgment of far more than their electoral political system. . . . The implication is that Japanese society ought to perform like a student of America. But these judgments can't help but make hypocrites of both sides. The Japanese never asked for democracy and never said they wanted to be like anyone else at all. And the same judgments make it very hard for outsiders to understand that the real social purposes of Japan's institutions—its own brand of elitism, the academic ladder that leads to it, and what it defines as democratic function—are to meet demands very, very different from those Western societies face. Insistence on hanging foreign explanations and adjectives on modern Japan like ill-fitting suits (which is something, regrettably, even Japanese 'spokesmen' to the outer world constantly do) just makes everyone uncomfortable."

Japan needs to be taken on its own terms, not as an example or specimen of some alleged universal category. Just because Japan has political parties, civil servants, banks, labor unions, antitrust regulators—and universities—does not for a moment mean that Japan has the same institutions as other societies. Nowhere is this more true than in Japan's centrally directed system of public schools and universities and its parallel, for-profit world of extracurricular academies and cram schools.

Robert Cutts's study of the University of Tokyo deals not just with the pinnacle of the Japanese educational system but, above all, with the social system of which it is a part. He stresses that Japan's educational system originated from above, from the state, and not from within Japanese society, that Japan's "institutionalized child abuse," as he calls the years of cramming for tests to enter the university, works, in the sense that it does what its creators want it to do and the dropout rate is a fraction of that in places like the United States. The University of Tokyo does *not* play the same role in producing a Japanese establishment as, for example, Oxford and Cambridge do in Britain, he points out. The University of Tokyo is also not a great intellectual center nor does it house a particularly distinguished faculty. It is, instead, a gatekeeper for identifying a particular kind of talent, which the university then influences only slightly. Japan's unique reliance on educational testing at every level of the system produces the world's best " 'quick studies' in absorbing vast masses of new and unfamiliar information, whether originating in Japan or in the West, and organizing it quickly to solve problems."

Japan's modern education system, dating from the Meiji era, is the key to a number of Japanese characteristics that seem contradictory to the Western mind. It produces extremely competitive people who are nonetheless devoted to cooperating with one another in most social contexts; it legitimates hierarchies among a people who are also very egalitarian in their ultimate beliefs; it is more democratic than the American educational system, in that it gives more ordinary citizens higher levels of valuable skills, but it lets down the exceptionally gifted; and it does not prepare people to "question authority" (as the American university bumper sticker has it) but rather to adjust to it. This book is about much more than the Japanese educational system, important as that is. It also explains why Japanese leadership has seemed paralyzed in the face of the political and economic flaws that have become apparent in post–cold war Japan.

Robert Cutts is the ideal Japan hand. He does not come to his study of Todai with preconceived "theoretical" propositions about the functions of universities in advanced industrial democracies or of the relationship between education and democracy. His methods are empirical and inductive, not formal and deductive. He has worked in Japan for some three decades as a businessman and journalist. He wrote one of the first major analyses in English of how the Japanese construction industry is rigged to keep out foreign competition (*California Management Review,* summer 1988), and his essay on cartels and *keiretsu* is familiar to hundreds of business school students (*Harvard Business Review,* July–August 1992). He is currently at work on a major analysis of Japan's famous general trading companies.

In this book, Cutts accomplishes three important things. First, he explains the interconnectedness and unity of the socialization process across all levels of the Japanese educational system and demonstrates that not just those admitted to Todai but all Japanese have a stake in the maintenance and functioning of the system. Second, Cutts suggests that Japan is not a political democracy so much as an economy masquerading as one, and that the Japanese citizen role has been reduced to an individual's contributions to the economy. Third, he shows how the educational process in Japan produces more or less identical, nationalistic leaders for the whole system, ranging from aristocratic elites to the lowliest functionaries, and how they are taught to believe that their positions are legitimated by a peculiarly Japanese form of democratic consciousness.

These are important achievements. They reinforce a growing need for the United States to stop assuming that Japan is "just like us." The United States needs to staff its diplomatic and analytical offices with people who know something about Japan and who realize that adjusting to and influencing Japan requires extensive cultural and linguistic knowledge. There are other good books on aspects of Japanese education, but this is the first to begin to point to the implications of this educational system for political and economic relations with other friendly countries.

Chalmers Johnson
Japan Policy Research Institute

Preface

As American–Japanese relations today, pilotless and largely rudderless, increasingly deteriorate in their wanderings toward deepening rivalry, conflict—and probably, however eventually, toward war—it seems to me a shame, as well as perhaps a reason, that very few persons have tried to explain to either side the real *people* who exist on the other.

There are almost countless books, essays, interviews, and articles that attempt to explain Japanese institutions, economy, and culture. But there are very few that ask in a consistent way what the Japanese people of *today,* not of the famous postwar period, believe in and want from life. We have all suffered from that shortage.

To Americans, who think themselves attuned to the nuances, traditions, and foibles of their cultural next-of-kin on what seems almost an intimate basis (the pride of the French, the reserve of the Britons, the passion of the Italians, the stoicism of the Russians, etc.), the Japanese persona has remained a peculiar enigma, as uniform, orderly, and discrete as the ranks of labeled soup cans on a food store aisle: cream of engineer, bouillon of businessman, consommé of bureaucrat, adolescent and noodle.

This book is a bold attempt to open all the cans and pour them out, to take a taste of each and even a sip of the many blends, as appetizing or as unappealing as each may be, that result from life in Japan today. If we are bound to share again the fate of a flourishing enmity with the Japanese, as now seems almost inescapable on a nation-to-nation basis, we might as well get to know them this time as individuals, too: smell the sweat of their labors, taste the bread of their convictions, walk the Japanese kilometer in their shoes. I attempt to paint no admiring, nor damning, portrait here, though reasons enough exist for both interpretations, as they doubtless do in American society. I am merely convinced that if we don't ask this time what more the Japanese are made of than their labels, then we really are certain to be led down that 54-year-old path of damnation across the Pacific again.

I propose an answer to "what" the Japanese are in terms of their education. Because education, more than anything else, makes all Japanese what they are. The United States holds Japan's school system in great esteem for its obvious accomplishments, and wonders what America can learn and how it might emulate the nationwide academic achievement. It is something that is impossible to do—not merely because the Japanese educational system is an amalgam of such famously unnatural pressures that in the latest, 1993–94 school year, one Japanese student was being driven to commit suicide every three days (a figure actually lower, proportionately, than in America). But mainly because we do not in the least understand what the system itself really is, let alone how to evaluate comparatively its human results, or even whether it is accomplishing the true purposes of education as we think of them. It is much as when we admire a beautiful predatory animal like the cheetah, for its speed, grace, and efficiency—yet turn away so as not to watch the achievement of the natural ends of these qualities, the tearing and devouring of living flesh.

When Americans look at the supposed harmony, politeness, respect, earnestness, and tenacity of the Japanese educational system, they are led to believe what they are seeing at work are the long-dominant strains of an elegant, intellectual, Confucian moral tradition which values piety, devotion, self-improvement, self-discipline, and a personal dedication to learning throughout the society. Yet it was one of Japan's earliest, most esteemed modern educators himself who pointed out that "Confucianism is a school of both politics and morality." Indeed seven of every ten pages of the revered Confucian texts that early-Meiji scholar Yukichi Fukuzawa himself examined, he found, "concern politics: how to govern a nation and how to bring peace to the world; and moral teaching occupies only the remaining 30 percent."

Just so: When Americans look at schooling in Japan, they are not looking at an educational system at all. They are looking primarily at a political system, a primary and crucial stage of government with goals congruent foremost to nationalist purpose. They are, these Americans, examining the first, and most important, 10 percent of an entire national social system without which the remaining 90 percent could not function—and which, without the existence of that other 90 percent, could not possibly achieve its intended ends of serving that society.

The national educational system, bluntly, exists to prepare the Japanese to take their roles in the institutions and the economic machinery of their state, not to prepare them to think about the world around them. All the tests, all the grades, all the hours of study are the honing of fine parts of an immense human machine.

There *is* no real Japanese educational system, nor Japanese university, as this book will explain. There is only the Japanese system, of which education, from kindergarten to graduate school, is one closely calibrated component. There are good teachers here and there; stimulating classes and a genuine love of learning in corners and seminar rooms scattered all throughout this vast conglomerated set of institutions, of course. But all the training, knowledge, self-discipline, and obedience, in the end, are there only to support the ever-growing glory and power of the nation.

And the success of this effort, as Japan rises ever closer to the top economic rank among nations, is what is now forming a great, dark, lengthening shadow of crisis across the country itself, across Asia, and across the world.

I am indebted to many for help with this project. In particular, four men—Chalmers Johnson, Karel Van Wolferen, Yoshiya Abe, and William Wetherall—helped me to see old patterns in completely new ways, and advised me through some or all of the four years I have taken to complete this work. To Ivan Hall, Leon Hollerman, Mark Schreiber, and Barbara Mori I also owe a debt of inspiration. To Toshi Tokunaga Cooper I owe more than is repayable, for assistance, encouragement, insight, and unfailing friendship. Katsuyuki Arai was an able and appreciated assistant in research and translation. Bernd Langer helped me to get this project off on the right foot, and advised me throughout its duration. My wife, Eiko, was unfailingly patient and supportive through the long days and the demanding work, on two continents, that this took. For all errors, and for all purely subjective interpretations, however, I bear sole responsibility.

January 1996
Shimo-Ogawa, Ibaraki Prefecture

An Empire of Schools

1

If There Is a God, He Went to Todai

There is no world-class university in Japan. There never has been.
—distinguished faculty member,
University of Tokyo[1]

Japan's educational system is the most comprehensive, efficient, and successful, as well as possibly the most admired, in the world today. At the same time, it is failing the nation.

It is successful because it continues to produce the largest and most capable, cultured, compatible, and self-assured class of social elites on earth.

It is failing because it cannot stop. Year after year it imposes on men and women a suffocatingly nationalist, single-track concept of what the "ideal Japanese" should be and tries to hold them to it with overpowering bonds of social obligation.

How this can be so—that any system of learning could produce such a marvelous paradigm of self-evidently democratic, capitalist, and social success as modern Japan and, at the same time, such an ethical, cultural, and intellectual straitjacket as seemingly to mute the creativity of a nation of 124 million people—is a major question for Western societies. To consider it requires that we do some learning ourselves.

We have to begin by backing away from measuring Japan's internal successes or failures by our own social yardsticks because they may not apply. By backing up still farther, we can see that the Japanese may think much more broadly about "education" than we do. In formal organization, and in everyday life, Japan uses education as the defining landscape of society itself. In a sense, all Japanese are both students and teachers, all their lives.

In fact, education could in a sense be called Japan's national religion. Like any establishment religion it is intended to instill in people beliefs, values, and character, including national character. And like any established religion, it ultimately rests on elements of overweening moral, and often enough secular, control. That is why the Japanese seem so subdued, so homogeneous, and so bound up in conforming to "being Japanese." It's what they are zealously educated to be, at home, in school, and in life.

And that is why Japan's thousand-plus universities and four-year and two-year colleges, clustered around the greatest of them all, the University of Tokyo—Todai—are analogous in their impact on Japanese society to temples of the True Faith. Ultimately they are, even for those who never attend them, the arbiters of one's enduring contentment here on earth.

Contentment on earth seems more or less assured if one is a graduate of the University of Tokyo. In one recent national cabinet, for example, not only were the prime minister and his chief cabinet secretary graduates, but so were the foreign and finance ministers, the posts and telecommunications minister, the director general of the Defense Agency, and the respective chairmen of the Executive Council and the Policy Research Council —roughly a quarter of the cabinet.

Moreover, for every cabinet-level ministry or agency, there is an administrative vice-minister, appointed from the ranks of the elite career bureaucracy. And during the tenure of that same particular cabinet, eighteen of these twenty civil servant elites were Todai alumni also, as were, it happens, twelve of the fourteen sitting associate justices of the nation's Supreme Court.[2]

To be equitable, we should note that Todai (the name is a contraction of *Tokyo* and *daigaku,* Japanese for "university") educates leadership candidates at the opposite end of the political spectrum as well. During the same cabinet's tenure, both the chairman and the deputy chairman of the Central Executive Committee of the Japan Communist Party—which has a small number of Diet, or parliament, members in both Japan's Upper and Lower Houses—were graduates of the university. Though ideological temperaments may differ, no doubt the social atmosphere is congenial for them in the Diet chambers: more than 21 percent of all 763 members were at the time fellow Todai alumni.[3]

But that bastion of Japanese capitalism, the business world, is still more familiar territory for Todai men. The chairmen of Japan's three most prestigious business groups, the Federation of Economic Organizations, the Federation of Employers' Associations, and the Japan Chamber of Commerce and Industry, all happened to be University of Tokyo alumni during the same administration. And a full 15 percent of all managers of all 1,865 corporations listed on the Tokyo Stock Exchange were, too. So typical is their presence in the executive suite, in fact, that the *Japan Economic Journal* profiled the new crop of corporate presidents promoted in 1989 with the "picture of a 'typical' new chief executive officer or president as a flexible and well-respected fifty-nine-year-old University of Tokyo graduate who has worked for one company all his life."[4] Among Japan's largest corporations, one out of every six executives is a Todai graduate.

Every year, the Ministry of Finance (which supervises the central bank, the national, regional, and local commercial banking systems, the National Tax Agency, and the stock market) takes in more than 75 percent of its entering career elites from the graduating class of Todai. The Ministry of International Trade and Industry in 1995 took the same percentage of its new fast-trackers from Todai, and the Home Ministry and the National Police Agency were not far behind, with 72 percent each. But most of the rest of the ministry recruits come from Kyoto University (Kyodai, another former imperial college for elites), from the two top private universities of Keio and Waseda, or from another elite national school in Tokyo, Hitotsubashi. Lesser government agencies scramble, competing with private industry, for the remainder of the graduates of these "Big Five," and other schools just below them on the ladder of Japan's 490 public and private universities.

Corporations begin recruiting, often furtively, among these Todai, Kyodai, Keio, Waseda, and Hitotsubashi seniors a full year before their graduation. Competition for this handful of Golden Grads is so tight that businesses have been known to sign young candidates months before they receive their degrees, then sequester them in mountain lodges on paid vacations during the regular recruiting "season," so no competitors can find and lure them away with sweeter bids.

This stunning performance of Todai in the production of elites might justifiably be compared to that of Oxford and Cambridge in England, which—at the same time that the above-mentioned administration was in office—accounted for nearly half the members of the House of Commons, half of Lords and two-thirds of Margaret Thatcher's cabinet. Yet Todai's is much the more impressive score when you compare numerically: While Oxbridge at that time granted degrees to an average of just below 7 percent of all Britain's undergraduates yearly,[5] the University of Tokyo produces only just over half of one percent of all of Japan's university, college, and junior-college graduates each year.

Still more interesting, unlike the case of Oxbridge graduates in England, this impressive record says very little either about the academic quality of the education at the University of Tokyo or of the class status of the students who go there. Neither factor is decisive in opening for Todai men (and 85 percent of its graduates are men) the ladders to elite ranks in Japan's government, economy, and society. Instead, what their astonishing preponderance at the top of the Japanese power structure illustrates is how thoroughly "the Todai system" dominates Japan. It is an influence so enthralling in the society and in the educational system that it justifies coining a term all their own for Japan's network of 65,724 schools, colleges, and universities: "The Socio-Educational System." Or perhaps even, the Academic Archipelago.

To see the relationship between power in Japan and the Todai system, again we need some new perspectives. Whom would we think of as the elites in Western societies? Are they holders of high office, captains of industry, blazer-clad grads of the Ivy League? Are they defined by Old Wealth or ostentatiously New Money? Is a Los Angeles high-school principal an elite? Would the label apply to a junior-college dean in Iowa? What about the president of Harvard—or his son? Beyond a few stereotypes Americans, for example, are reluctant to talk much about who really has elite status because it leads them to the idea of rule by class—a distinctly uncomfortable thought for democratic America. It's an uncomfortable thought for meritocratic Japan, too. That's why it's hard even for thoughtful Japanese to point beyond an obvious first tier of powerful government and business executives (who, by the way, themselves thoroughly believe that they won their jobs on personal worth, not status) to those whom they would call elites.

But an awareness of an elite status that is much broader in Japan is pervasive. Perhaps so much so that it is impossible to predict exactly to whom it might apply—or how. A student who graduated this spring from the most prestigious faculty of Todai, the law school, is not considered by anyone to be an elite. But it is understood by all who know what school he's from that he is almost certain to become one. A senior teacher in a high school would hardly be classed as an elite in the United States. But in Japan, the deference and attention paid him by students, their families, and members of the community who know his profession—and the influence he may have to open doors to certain colleges and jobs for their children and relatives—amounts to informal acknowledgment of his status as a veritable community elder: one whose position demands careful respect.

Conversely, the eldest son of a Japanese billionaire industrialist or entrepreneur is by no means socially accepted as an elite, nor even as a person likely to become one. He must, over many years, prove himself worthy of that recognition on his own. And this subjectivity applies high and low. Fifteen of the 23 prime ministers Japan has had since World War II have been graduates of one of Japan's Top Five universities (ten of them from Todai). Except for one, Kakuei Tanaka, all have attended at least semi-elite schools. In his career both in and out of the nation's highest office, Tanaka was by far the most powerful of all Japan's postwar politicians, even accruing the respect of the snobbish bureaucrats of the nation's higher civil service—the very definition of "elitist." But Tanaka was the son of a farmer, attended an engineering school, and made his fortune in construction (one of the most corrupt industries in Japan). For all those reasons he was never remotely imagined by any Japanese to be a genuine elite.

It's obvious, then, that behind the similarities of Japan to Western societies, there are important differences that prevent foreigners from safely assuming much at all about what the Japanese think of one another, or how the leaders they follow are selected. This should not shock anyone who recalls that Japan is a civilization more than two thousand years old, formed on the bases of Chinese linguistic, cultural, and technical traditions, Buddhist belief in reincarnation, indigenous worship of the sun and nature, and, more recently, a period of more than twelve generations of anachronistic feudal agrarianism and self-imposed isolation from all other cultures. What ought to surprise us, in fact, is how readily Westerners assume that Japanese should be just like them.

The Japanese may tell the world their country is a Western democracy. But this invites judgment of far more than their electoral political system by measures that are comfortable only to the people who originally drew up the sweeping social blueprints according to what "democracy" really means. The implication is that Japanese society ought to perform like a student of America. But these judgments cannot help but make hypocrites of both sides. The Japanese never asked for democracy and never said they wanted to be like anyone else. And the same judgments make it very hard for outsiders to understand that the real social purposes of Japan's institutions —its own brand of elitism, the academic ladder that leads to it, and what it defines as democratic function—are to meet demands that are different from those that Western societies face. Insistence on hanging foreign explanations and adjectives on modern Japan like ill-fitting suits (which is something, regrettably, even Japanese "spokesmen" to the outside world constantly do) just makes everyone uncomfortable.

If not democrats or freshmen Westerners then, what are the Japanese? Farmers, or industrialists? Spiritual, or materialistic? Aesthetes writing poetry to flowers, or Philistines laying waste to rain forests? What do they say and think about themselves, and what do they want for the world? What really emerges from their schools: humanists? Or robots?

Zenjiro Yano is a graduate of the University of Tokyo. All the hard years of his public-school preparation for Todai were to make him ready to meet the task with which the university itself was charged, under Article 1 of the Imperial University Order, dated 1886: "The purpose of the Imperial University shall be to provide instruction in the arts and sciences and to inquire into the abstruse principles of learning in accordance with the needs of the state."[6]

When he finally entered, he pursued goals at Todai that were completely different, in line with Article 1 of the Fundamental Law of Education, dated 1947: "The goal of education is the full development of personality, the training of a mentally and physically sound people, and the creation of a love of truth and justice . . . and the independence of spirit to contribute to a peaceful nation and society."[7] Yano symbolizes the way in which the Japanese people, and their relation to education and leadership, have been once again caught brutally in the abrupt turning of the pages of Japan's history.

The son of a fabric dyer, Yano as a bright lad had been advised by his high-school teacher to take the exams given by the preparatory schools that led to the seven Imperial Universities, the acknowledged training grounds for Japan's elites. "My father didn't care much about learning, but he told me to give it a try."

Yano was one of the lucky one in ten who passed the exams, and he made it to and through prep school and was admitted to Todai—in 1945. The Americans landed on Okinawa, Yano was drafted, and it was not until 1946 that he actually entered the hallowed halls. "At Todai there was no food, my parents had lost our house to the bombing raids, and there was no heat anywhere that winter. It was very hard just to stay alive, just to find enough to eat. Our professors were not ready then to discuss any future for Japan. But I worried most about my future—I'm sorry to say I didn't trust in Japan's future much at all. When I was a schoolchild, a Todai future meant a guarantee of success. Now none of us even expected to find a job after graduation. I thought I might have to become a farmer."

Japan's future was reborn, of course, and neither Yano (who graduated in economics, went on to a career in the National Tax Administration Agency, and eventually sent three of his own sons to university) nor Todai itself starves now. But regardless of where education led the Japanese in the age of fascism, or what it has accomplished for postwar Japan, that collision of cross-purposes—whether learning should produce human resources equipped to serve the state, or independent, free-minded citizens—still reverberates. So too does the unresolved question of what an American-style "democratic" constitution imposed on Japan by the Occupation really means, a problem examined more closely below. Japanese now elect their political officials, and Yano, the Todai undergrad who raised his own vegetables to keep from starving, today watches Todai graduates drive the streets of Tokyo in Mercedes-Benzes. But the underpinning assumptions of life in Japan were swept away in 1945, and little has developed to satisfactorily replace them. That's why these two unanswered questions still frame the crisis of Japan's educational system, and the crisis of its national purpose, today.

The Jaws of History

To a point, as scholar Robert C. Marshall[8] points out, Japan really is what it claims to be: unique in history. Alone among the states that Western colonial powers attempted to swallow in the late nineteenth century, Japan survived, completely on its own initiatives and strength. It transformed its antique government and society from feudalistic structures to those of a modern nation-state, and did it from within, in less than two generations. Without allies, it managed to repel almost all of the worst Western intrusions upon its sovereignty as it quickly entered the community of advanced countries. And in less than forty years it became an industrial, military, and economic success that could and did defeat a Western power—tsarist Russia, in 1905—on the latter's own military terms.

The national educational system was a major engine of this revolution. Japan's modern-era government was founded in 1868, as the age of *shogun* and *samurai* was swept away with a broad and brutal stroke of the broom of history. Young Turks from the warrior caste in western Japan gained control of the country, and in a truly phenomenal epic of history—the Meiji Restoration—turned it almost full-circle from its deadening focus on the past toward a modern future. These men grasped from the start that importing Western learning and technology quickly would be Japan's only salvation from the rapacious West itself. And they soon saw, still more cogently, that they could use Western technology only in the context of Western systems of government and economy. After careful study of European and American schools, they founded Japan's modern educational system by national writ in 1872. It called for universal education, with a division of learning into elementary school, middle school, and one university—Todai.

The foundations of the University of Tokyo itself reach back to a small government academy, created within the Tokugawa Shogunate and devoted to the study of foreign languages, whose job was translating and analyzing imported writings on the West: a sort of government intelligence agency. From the start, based on these studies of the West, Todai's mission was to support the imperative of national progress. Compulsory national education (three or four years) was longer in coming than was modern education itself. First stipulated only fourteen years after the statement of the national principle of a universal modern education (and at the same time that Todai was formally commanded to serve the "needs of state"), compulsory education was not actually enforced until the turn of the century. Of course in 1900 Japan was still very poor, and even the idea of a compulsory education had to be thrust on the population—large percentages of which rejected it outright, even violently.[9] This is worth remembering because this theme will be encountered again and again: The educational system that accomplished so much for Japan in its times of crisis was a national initiative, installed almost like conscription, from above by autocrats in Tokyo.

In fact, as some of Japan's most seminal social-reform thinkers began to voice novel and populist ideas about the rights of citizens as far back as the 1870s, it occurred to the imperial government (which was worried about domestic political enemies as well as foreign) that not only novel but dangerous ideas were loose in the land. To counter their influence, not just central power over the schools but central control of the curriculum would be useful. By 1881, then, it was formally determined that "moral training," a catchall emphasizing absolute loyalty to the Emperor and his government, would be the most important curricular item in all Japanese schools. All elementary-school teachers were on notice: Their first pedagogical imperative was loyalty to the state, both to hold it and to teach it. By the time of the 1886 decision to eventually adapt nationwide compulsory education, a special "normal school" system just for the training of teachers was envisioned—with its organization held comparable in purpose and dedication to those of the Imperial Army itself.[10]

One of Japanese history's most famous documents, the 1888 Imperial Rescript on Education issued by the Meiji Emperor, put the guiding philosophy frankly:

> Our Imperial Ancestors have founded Our Empire on a basis broad and everlasting and have deeply and firmly implanted virtue; Our subjects are united in loyalty and filial piety and have from generation to generation illustrated the beauty thereof. This is the glory of the fundamental character of Our Empire, and herein also lies the source of Our education.

If the verbiage is florid, that fit the intentions of its writers. Formally, the glory of the Emperor was the reason all Japanese went to school. One present-day Japanese commentator stresses that in its day the Rescript "was not merely a document but had the status of religious scripture, controlling people's thought and behavior."[11] That held everywhere in Japan, for fifty-eight years; there are many people in the senior generation alive today who can remember their school principals reading the Rescript aloud to ceremonial gatherings of whole student bodies at every national holiday. It made the purposes of both the society and the educational system blind obedience to an invisible Emperor, above the clouds, whose ministers on earth were national bureaucrats—and also, eventually, imperial generals.

And so in the hoariest of terms, the foundations were laid both for the miraculous, thirty-year industrial transformation of Japan through the spread of mass education, and for the great iniquity of state Shinto and its mass indoctrination of schoolchildren that held the Emperor was a god, and that the Imperial Army made war in his name. Private schools and colleges —some of them Christian—had been founded in abundance in Japan in these intervening decades, but all were powerless to resist the imperial prerogatives of indoctrination. From 1925 onward, military officers were assigned to the staffs of all boys' middle schools, high schools, and colleges. "They played an important role in militarizing education."[12] And thereby, in socializing the nation's young as well as the nation's academics and intellectuals—those who would have had the strongest voice to say "no"— to the final military imperatives of the Greater East Asia Co-Prosperity Sphere.

No one said "no" because the educational system did more than teach loyalty: It *rewarded* loyalty. Many of the bureaucrats who ran that system got their jobs by going through the schools themselves. In creating a great machine for mass education and nation-building skills, the early imperial government also made it a major gateway to power, status, and affluence in the new nation itself. This was done by forging two grand links, beyond mere education, between Japanese society and schools. The first was the gradual near-eradication of class as the major qualification for power jobs in the new government and economy. True, many of the first generation of autocrats, entrepreneurs, and peers of the new Japanese state were themselves former *samurai* or their lords, the *daimyo* (who had governed the old provinces of Japan, under the *shogun*). But, officially, the old class system that had stamped people almost permanently as warriors, farmers, craftsmen, or townspeople was swept away before the turn of the century. This eventually allowed commoners who showed personal and managerial excellence to move quickly into the jobs where the new state needed them most—providing only that they were male. The only place where young men from poor families could both qualify and prove themselves was, of course, in school. The educational system thus became the natural breeding ground, in this brave new society, for large generations of new elites.

Since the new pool of *potential* elites included theoretically everyone in school, a strenuous winnowing process was needed to choose the worthiest from among them all. And this process was the second important result of the nationalization of education in Japan: the entrance examinations. There seemed no better model for this winnowing process than the civil service meritocracy of ancient China—where state ministers of every grade earned their ranks by the passage of progressions of examinations. That model, of an implied or actual competition between every individual in the school system, fit the goals of Japan's national educational system in a modern context because the *material* taught and tested would not be Confucian classics, but modern know-how that would enable people to serve the state with advanced skills and knowledge no matter what level of schooling they achieved in the competition. And those who passed the highest exams would certainly be what the imperial government most needed as civil servants and business elites: "quick studies" in absorbing vast masses of new and unfamiliar information, whether originating in Japan or in the West, and organizing it quickly to solve problems.

Compulsory education concerned the first six years of school only; all further advance in Japan was based on competitive exams. Thus the system was installed—more or less along the lines of how it operates today. Those who, like Yano, passed the toughest exams were admitted to one of the seven Imperial Universities—including Todai—and were marked as automatic candidates for the highest government, commercial, and industrial posts. (In prewar days graduates of Todai Law School were simply inducted straight into the government—they didn't even have to take the civil service entry exams.) The serious private universities quickly learned the exam pattern and adopted it for admissions criteria too. This was probably in self-defense. With the school system and the exam system the only upward social path in Japan, and with education now compulsory, the problem quickly changed from selecting the very best to winnowing out all the rest.

The System That Keeps On Going

Even when their world is turned upside-down, societies no more than people change fundamental values rapidly—which really is what the Americans expected of the Japanese after August 1945. Westerners today will have to look closely at the needs and purposes of the society—if not of the state—to understand what is taught in Japanese universities now, and why people go to them.

Although about five times as many students go on to higher education in Japan today as under the prewar system, the school and examination systems have survived as the national selection mechanism for elite jobs and status—just as before the war, and despite efforts of the Occupation authorities to reform the content of education in Japan. There are three main reasons for this continuity:

- because the system had served national needs so well and so long;
- because its universalistic framework, offering a "fair" chance to every-one, fit with the egalitarian ideals of the new American autocrats; and
- because any big changes made in the elite access system in the late 1940s, when they were still possible, would have confused and an-gered the politically restive postwar population.

The old systems were also flexible enough to answer a new challenge that resulted from Japan's democratization and its economic reconstruction and takeoff: the popular demand and the national need for mass access to higher education. Annual entry to university before the war had never ex-ceeded a few tens of thousands of applicants. Today 94 percent of all Japanese students complete high school, and almost 1.1 million of them apply to college or university. About two-thirds are accepted—but only a third can be admitted to the most coveted schools, Japan's 490 four-year universities.[13] And the entrance exams still serve very well as the selection mechanism that the public accepts as the fairest.

There is one last reason. After the Americans had gone and for a long time afterward, the old educational system served the purposes of a new leadership hierarchy in Japan, which replaced the imperial government. This hierarchy includes the postwar, conservative bureaucratic and political leadership, intent on dominating the system and inculcating "moral educa-tion" into every young Japanese, and the corporate executive leadership that for forty-five years has expected the state to turn out ever-larger numbers of educated workers to fill the needs of accelerating economic expansion. "The corporations expected the [postwar] government to institute a man-power policy that would be of direct use to them: an educational system that would separate the elite from the general public and that would train people in the ability to carry out their assigned tasks faithfully."[14]

And so, the old bogeyman of nationalist purpose has never been van-quished from the educational system at all. "Training people" for conscien-tious execution of assigned tasks is the highly useful and overriding goal of a nation intent on building industrial economy and national power—just as it was in the Meiji period, the World War I era, the Roaring Twenties, the Great Depression, and finally the Great Pacific War.

Japan may have had to start all over in 1945. But its dominating position today in the global economic landscape was reached in about the same half-century as Japan's initial great leap to modern power. That helps us appreciate just how, and how well, the national government, economic, social, and educational systems have worked together since 1947 toward the national goals: a continuing—endlessly continuing—economic expansion.

This, then, is the "front half" of the Todai system, the formal half. A handful of elite universities, with Todai the bright, shining tower rising above them all, sit atop the entire national and private educational system like temples on an Aztec pyramid, reachable only via a narrow, unforgivingly steep staircase that leads straight from kindergarten to the top of the society. Examinations, and the years of cobralike intensity necessary to prepare for them, are virtually the only steps. Children as young as three years old attend cram schools and take simulated exams to pass entry tests to the right kindergartens, to get on the track to the top of the heap. Everyone—like it or not, needing it or not, intending to reach the top of that heap or not—is pressed through this human sieve. One in every five Japanese junior high-school students—and more than 10 percent of elementary-school pupils—suffer from some type of depression,[15] and the government itself admits that this is probably because of the pressures of "Exam Hell" —the national nickname for what is in fact the Todai system.

There is a "back half" to the Todai system too, as we shall see. But it's here in this meshing of the schools and the society that we can observe how Japanese elites are made, what really defines and motivates them, and what sends them into their roles.

Reflections in a Japanese Mirror

When asked, Japanese frequently tell Westerners that a common value of their society is "harmony." Just as when Americans say they are democratic, or egalitarian, it is at one level a common popular conceit that often melts quickly in the heat of political and everyday passion. But it has been endorsed as a public virtue by the institutions regulating Japanese social, legal, and economic affairs and enforced as a principle of Japanese authority, public and private. Anyone who has read even a shallow article explaining Japan's industrial "miracle" has been told that corporations strive for it, on the assembly line and as a managerial principle. Schools teach it with extreme seriousness. Everyone is touched by it, so it will help to know what the Japanese really mean by it.

Normally, bureaucracies at the top of the society, with meritocratic exam systems as the only access to jobs in them, would not produce cooperation but competition among the ambitious aiming for "the top." But Japan's modern social system grew from the older class structure imposed by the *shoguns,* which kept everyone rigidly in place. One was born a *samurai,* or a farmer, and seldom was permitted to change that station. In an agrarian society where land was scarce, prosperity depended on cooperation. Efforts such as artificial irrigation, bringing water from a single distant stream to spread among hundreds of acres of rice paddy, meant sharing work and sharing fruits: Bluntly, people living in villages either were "harmonious" or faced starvation. The same ethic of survival prevailed in cities and towns, among both high and low: Whether in warrior-caste or among merchant or craftsman communities, family loyalty and strict, obedient compliance were the overriding demands.

Couple this motivation with a strong enforcement system that vested most authority in heads of households and, above them, village elders, and it is easy to see how the Japanese grew up closely interdependent in small work groups, which could individually work with—or compete with—other groups. Both work and social ties were based on personal relationships in all these groups. People depended directly for their continuing well-being on keeping the goodwill of the group's leader, as well as of the others with whom they worked and lived each day. In modern Japan, they still do.

The modernization of the late 1800s, though, unleashed great social chaos. As industry grew, many sons and daughters left the farms to join not trades or merchant houses, but the industrial work force. They had to be educated and socialized to accept a strong vertical, as opposed to local, authority that would weave all the reforms together into a nation: thus the centrality of the imperial Rescript and the allegiance to the Emperor that was drilled into all teachers and all students. With the retention of the disciplines of the old educational system into the postwar and present-day periods, now in the name of the "survival" of Japan rather than of the Emperor himself, the influences on each generation of modern Japanese have been a blending of new and old. The same gigantic vortex remains, atomizing individuals through upward competition for the best jobs in the new hierarchies of industrialism and the state, together with a reinforcement of common purpose with "the group," to achieve universal goals. These imperatives of simultaneous, vertical, and horizontal responsibilities for everyone encourage both competition and cooperation at the same time.

Thus "harmony"—competing without showing it—is what the Japanese are *raised* to value. Individual competition is unavoidable and is intense, but is downplayed as a matter of personal and institutional propriety as much as possible. However demanding the exam system is for each student, the public considers it "objective," fair, and open to everyone. It is bad form for losers to weep, or for winners to preen, in public. And so personal academic competition in the classroom itself does not enter into it. Preparation for the exams is done largely outside the schools anyway, in the commercial cram courses known as *juku*—which one of every six elementary-school students and half of all middle-school students attend[16]—or under the instruction of a personal tutor (and the best tutors, of course, are considered to be Todai undergraduates moonlighting for pocket money).

But how does the same Japanese society that makes Nintendo and Sega video games for youths by the millions produce children willing to devote every last ounce of personal effort to beating their classmates in exams—yet showing (at least until recently) no aggression, jealousy, or despair in defeat? It goes back to the home, of course.

Commonly accepted concepts of child-rearing are different in Japan from what they are in America. Where American mothers generally consider their infants dependent, and thus in need of being raised to independence, Japanese mothers see the opposite. They see their infants as born without any awareness of the social ties they will need to survive in this densely interwoven world. And so the mother's job is to create in her child an abiding sense of dependence, first upon herself and later upon others whose groups the child will join.[17]

When the time comes, kindergartens and primary schools will continue to stress this dependence. Rather than supervise each child directly, teachers in the lower grades allow pupils to orient themselves and their activities to one another, without much interference or structuring from adults. Each is guided, rather, by the teachers' eliciting praise or comment from the other children in the group. Each child is socialized to respond to and cooperate with his or her classmates in getting things done together—whether in sharing out toys, cleaning up after lunch, or maintaining reasonable order in the classroom.

That is the beginning. The vertical discipline instilled by the schools comes a bit later. And so Japan grows, from the start, as a deeply dependent society on the most basic level. "If we look closely at the [social] developmental cycle," writes one sociologist who has studied Japanese children and schools at length, "we find at every stage from nursery school to early employment the same basic routines reiterated and the same social lessons repeated again and again. The very powerful emotional pressures for participation [in the group] normally associated in the West with the family are at work throughout the society."[18] And that is what the Japanese mean by harmony: You've got to go along to get along.

Patterns in acculturation are not really the point here, though. The point is that in a heterogeneous society of 124 million people, all ultimately divided into small groups, there are obviously a very large number of groups. Thus there is a need for a very large number of group leaders, who can elicit cooperation as naturally, and understand subordinates almost as intimately, as can a mother or father. Far below the lofty heights of national ministries and Fortune 500 corporations, the educational system must produce all these highly socialized leaders—small-scale elites—as well as all the subordinates who will be attuned to accept their intimate leadership. That is why the Todai system of channeling natural competitiveness at every level to impel individuals toward an ultimate ethic of self-discipline, obedience, and cooperative effort is so ingenious and so widespread throughout Japanese education. Even far short of the goal of entry to a top-ranked university and the realms of government and business beyond, its products—the vast majority of six hundred thousand college and university graduates each year, and of 1.7 million high-school graduates—will be ready to follow within any group. And to lead within any group, when their turn comes.

That is why there are truly so many elites in Japanese society: hundreds of thousands, even millions, of "leaders," all operating on basically the same assumptions of ethical principles, and all more or less accepting as personal obligations the same responsibilities for supervision of intimate relationships within the group, to accomplish a mission defined from above.

The system does not always work, as Japanese society is beginning to bear witness. And in any society—like those of the Western democracies—where internalization of industry's goals and government's goals are not accepted as the highest priorities of socialization by nearly the whole populace, it would not work at all. So what the Japanese educational system has to teach Westerners is necessarily circumscribed. But so far it has worked well enough in serving Japan's social, political, and economic goals that Westerners can measure its successes with true amazement—and perhaps even real praise.

What Is Learned—and What Is Not

Todai can be a good school, but generally it is a bad university. Much the same can be said of the other four elite universities at the top of the pyramid: Kyoto (Kyodai), Keio, Waseda, and Hitotsubashi.

The reasons vary. The most basic stems from the approach to education itself in Japan and the exam system that arose from it. Remember that schools in formative years of the educational system itself grew as training institutions in Japan—something distinct from liberal educational institutes. The system was pressured to produce as many graduates as possible competent in the crucial, technical skills needed by the economy and the government. There was little time and, politically, virtually no inclination left for discussion of the development of the intellectually independent Whole Man —even though the private universities had been founded on just this difference of goals with the national university system. What was wanted was the responsive man, the capable man, the dedicated man. The educational system overall was best served by rank didacticism and rote memorization of the teacher's output of knowledge. And it fit with the imperial government's Confucian values of the teacher as an unimpeachable, revered source of knowledge. No one was taught to raise questions, only to understand and commit to memory what was presented.

Generally, those systemics of teaching remain in the school system today. Whether in primary, middle, or high school, students are not expected to ask teachers questions, let alone raise challenges to concepts presented in such courses as Contemporary Society, Japanese History, and Politics and Economy. This is not only a question of intellectual docility: The very real pressures on the students are to pass examinations, and the strength of the social as well as academic pressures for simple absorption of information are hard for outsiders to comprehend.

This means the student "material" entering the universities today has been socialized, as well as educated, largely not to press intellectual inquiry but to accept all truths as given. Throughout most of their school lives, students have survived the rigors of the winnowing system by being alert to what they are expected to absorb and memorize from texts and lectures—to pass an exam. That is what, in the main, they have proved that they are good at: doing quick takes on the material, and pounding it into memory. Teachers rarely ask them for anything else.

In fact, in the elite private universities, teachers seldom seem to ask for much of anything. After surviving the exam grinder for eight years or more in high, middle, and even elementary school, college education in the liberal arts core seems to be largely a holiday. Students are allowed to sign up for large numbers of credits and then drop whichever courses they dislike— some of which require only a single classroom hour a week—at their discretion, to try them again later if they like. In the private schools very little academic work is required to graduate; it is assumed that if the student got this far on exam abilities, he or she has already shown the skills to adapt quickly, at whatever the chosen career turns out to be. That's the value employers will be most looking for.

This is not universally true at Todai. There are nine faculties at the school, the most prestigious being that of law—which still sends a huge proportion of its graduates into the elite civil service. These graduates in particular will face rigorous government examinations after Todai, leading to the prestigious ministry and agency jobs. And so they must do classwork and keep themselves sharp for the tests that are the last doorways to the hierarchies of status. Still, Todai students often find themselves in gigantic classes of 300, 400, or more, with lecturers required to speak over public address systems. Seminar courses are offered, but only in a limited number and only in the final two years of undergraduate study. Moreover, faculty members are seldom available for counseling. An additional pressure is often financial: Students come from all over Japan, and to pay tuitions and boarding fees totaling almost $20,000 a year they must often supplement money from their families with part-time jobs.

It also often seems, even at Todai Law, that the more important activities of the campus during these four years are really membership in the various activities clubs—music, sports, etc.—that will for the first time allow students to "network" across backgrounds and groups they have never had contact with before. The campus clubs can be a very serious business, requiring great dedication to the disciplines (such as mountaineering, soccer, skiing, etc.) they embrace, because here will be formed *gakubatsu* (literally, school faction) friendships that can prove very valuable later in life. As the average graduate, once he (or she) has begun employment, will be expected to confine professional as well as personal life to his immediate work group, he will have precious little chance later to form personal relationships with peers outside his company or ministry. This is one such chance, and through dedication to *these* groups, mutually advantageous friendships are formed here that often last for a lifetime.

But the real problems confronting the Todai system rise outside, rather than within, the ornate, feudal-era *Akamon* (Red Gate) that leads to the hallowed Bunkyo campus, out in the society that Todai has helped to form.

Japan, like America, is a society that prefers to believe it is classless, but, of course, it is not. Japanese public-opinion surveys consistently show that at any given time about 90 percent of those responding believe that they are all part of one homogeneous "middle class." And, just as in America, that public sentiment has its political uses. In the schools, which is to say in the first level of the society, it has its economic uses. But the tremendous disequilibrium created within the national economy by Japan's explosive growth alone has in fact begun dividing its people sharply into haves and have-nots. The Tokyo real-estate bubble alone created, within about eighteen months in the late 1980s, nearly 800,000 new millionaire households inside the greater Tokyo metropolis. Many more achieved that status as land values soared in successive waves in other urban regions. Though that bubble has long since burst, it created uncomfortable chasms of self-consciousness among those who had always assumed themselves equals in the same class—along the simple fault lines of who owned a city home versus who rented one—along which divisive echoes ring still. At Todai, the typical entering freshman now comes from a household averaging $73,000 in annual income, about 20 percent more than the average for other national universities.[19] Ten percent of all freshmen admitted come from families headed by grads;[20] few farmers' or fishermen's sons are found on its campuses today.

Almost all Japanese schoolchildren go through their young, formative years and lower school grades purposely segregated from any people or any ideas that are "different," that demonstrate the viability of nongroup, non-homogeneous ideas. That makes it difficult for young Japanese to grasp, other than as an academic abstraction, that there are different races and cultures to be found in the world, not to mention different cultures and values even among other Japanese. These concepts are left almost completely undisturbed through the years of secondary education as well; that is, in the years in which as much knowledge as will fit is crammed in for regurgitation in the college entrance exams.

The very university system itself, then, is founded upon the shared political dogma—what is referred to throughout this book as "Japanese nationalism" —that any real diversity among Japanese peoples and Japanese groups must remain unvalidated wherever possible, and certainly is not to be elevated to the focus of a sustained dialogue. This presents great problems for Todai, and the other schools, as universities. Liberal arts faculties are supposed to teach and discuss ideas. As we see today in American universities, the more closely those ideas touch on real problems in the society, the more raucous and conflicting is truly open discussion—which may lead to the expression of "politically incorrect" passions. Speech should be free, but within limits. Those limits are narrow indeed at the Japanese university.

This awkwardness in Japan is compounded immensely by the fact that even the ideas of class lie unarticulated. Japan has many classes: social outcasts, farmers, old-money industrialists, bureaucratic and educational elites. Students themselves form a class: a group systematically stripped of most constitutionally guaranteed rights to develop and perfect its own precious individual characteristics. But no one can admit that any of these are classes.

The national constitution is, in fact, at the heart of the problem. Before the war, classes were acknowledged to exist: There was an Imperial family and a peerage, overshining all; beneath them were aristocratic and political elites, extending down into the ranks of the imperial civil service, and the Imperial Army and Navy. Farmers formed a class; so did capitalists and laborers. The significance of the educational system was its virtue to those in lower classes: It removed the barriers that trapped them there and enabled real upward mobility. That has been the true "miracle" of modern Japanese society. But in the 1947 constitution that installed popular sovereignty and vested pluralistic democracy as the highest resort of authority in the state (cut whole, of course, from American cloth) the Occupation completely paved over Japan's genuine social history. Thus, the Occupation removed discussion of this social history from the "politically correct" agenda and sealed it off in a realm of official nonrecognition from which it cannot emerge.

The Japanese, no less than the Americans or the Russians, must deal with the truths and resolve the contradictions of their own history; a great deal of that burden usually falls on education, especially at the university level. But even politicians and bureaucrats cannot speak candidly of the prewar-versus-postwar mismatch or of the strange distortions of democracy that have resulted. How then can ordinary Japanese discuss whether the Emperor really is what the constitution says he is: a symbol of the people's sovereignty? And, if he is, why is the vast economic- and social-control bureaucracy that once ruled solely in his name still not assigned a public accountability *to anyone,* not even to the leaders elected by the people? Is national democracy or the current parliamentary system of representation really best for Japan? No one is allowed to seriously press for national debate, or for real answers. Hence is created the great intellectual vacuum at Todai and in the university system itself today—or rather, the vortex that swirls around them creating that vacuum.

The university contributes little that is public (other than the personal opinions of individual scholars who moonlight for the popular press) to the debate on where Japan is going, and where it should be going. The establishment does not and would not tolerate such an openly rebellious discourse on the many unresolved contradictions of the permanent capture of Japan's national agenda by the party-bureaucracy-industry establishment. Nor would the teachers want one—not, in any case, one that involved examining the positions of both themselves and the students, the members of the elite class that the whole system has functioned to elevate to the rarefied levels of Todai and the other Big Five schools. The students of course *are* the cadet elite of that triumvirate. The class system, plus devout personal dedication to the national myth of classlessness, has itself produced them, and the professors are its professional priesthood. An argument so candid as to expose any of these ideas, in this sanctuary of politically correct classlessness, is advanced only with a certain degree of real risk to everyone, because if pushed too far it just might end up invalidating the incipient right to rule of everyone here. Which is to say, invalidating everybody's meal ticket.

The pressures for change—and they are real—are likely to simply grow, whether or not toward explosion on the campuses, no one can say.

Why Todai Succeeds: Because It Must

Todai, then, is at the heart of the Japanese social system, not merely of its educational system. It informs virtually all of childhood and adolescent life with a common, universal set of values and imperatives. As early as age three children begin special instruction and tutoring to reach the best universities. In their preteens, those who strive (or who are pushed) toward the very top study fourteen hours a day, erasing virtually all social life outside the ambit of instruction and memorization, to reach for Todai and the other schools near its echelon. It is commonly accepted that one will not make it without, at the very least, a private room at home for study throughout childhood. "Pass with four, fail with five" is a common maxim among students: It refers to the number of hours one can afford to spare from study to sleep each night and still hope to pass the entrance exams.

There is today a great deal of quite public debate about this kind of pressure—one is tempted to call it institutionalized child abuse—on Japanese children. As noted, even middle-school students guaranteed by their scholastic records of entry into high school are under pressure to study for the mandatory and complicated entry exams thereto. Exams test their knowledge on such esoterica as the comparative rainfall rates in London, Stockholm, and Rome, and keep them awake nights studying the nature of physics as it applies to the distilling process.[21] Newspapers decry the abuses, the occasional suicides, the literally billions of dollars that are squeezed out of frantic parents by the massive cram-school and related publishing industries, which prey on their constant fears of failure for their children.

But the debate is a sham, a red herring, for two reasons. The first is that the Japanese educational system really serves the Establishment quite well. While commentators and journalists bewail the dropout rate that rises with "school refusals"—children apparently traumatized to the point they refuse to go to school—numerically, Japan's dropout rate from high school nationally is a mere 2.2 percent;[22] by comparison, the rate in many American states is close to 30 percent. Numerically at least, the system is nowhere near failure. One of the major reasons for the late 1960s campus riots in Japan was not Vietnam, but dissatisfaction of the students themselves at the quality of education they were receiving (or not receiving, to be accurate). As Japan's industries reached the takeoff stage, and baby-boomers reached college age, there was enormous demand for access to higher learning. In 1947 less than 6 percent of the eligible age-group went to college; by the late 1960s it was 35 percent. Private colleges and universities filled the gap, often with a notable deterioration of quality that came with abruptly admitting baby-boomers in multiples of up to twenty times (in one case, forty times) the number of students they had been licensed to receive by the Ministry of Education.[23]

The students may have been angered by standing-room-only classrooms, and "classes" for five hundred. But they were not really expected to learn much in college anyway—it was the entrance testing that was the point. And industry got its requisite level of tested recruits in the end. The majority of parents who wanted it did get their children into college, no matter what it cost. From the national standpoint, then, and at great strain, the system has so far supplied exactly what Japan believes it needs. So public criticism is diverted into endless debates of what is unjust, unethical, unreasonable, unfair. This media airing of "issues" is a well-known and harmless outlet in Japan for the pressures of public opinion. At least it helps ameliorate the hellish sense of failure in those homes where a student has been unable to pass the entrance exams.

There is a second reason, though, that these arguments will not go much of anywhere. What the Japanese are far less ready to admit is that the Todai system has a "back half" too—reaching out into the mature population, just as the front half reaches forward to the nation's children. Indeed it pushes the whole society of adults also onto tracks—the major elite, the minor elite, the white-collar and the blue-collar classes. In a lifetime employment system for elites, the school one graduates from determines one's whole career. *Gakubatsu,* or school factions, are very important to the advancement of ambitious bureaucratic and corporate elites, and to that of their sons, on whose behalf they will try as much possible to pry the university entry doors at least partway open.

Just as important are *gakubatsu* patterns working in the reverse to persuade scarce Big Five graduates into corporations that prize them as their own elite management recruits. For their part, young women from good families, or with ambitious mothers—or simply ambitious young women— are urged to set their romantic sights on graduates of Todai and the other top schools, as an even more important social guarantee than inherited wealth of a "good" marriage. Young college women themselves strive for employment in the major corporations and bureaucracies, just to have the opportunity to meet these prized candidates. Rates of employee intermarriage within a corporation can range above 50 percent (which may go a long way toward explaining the Japanese predilection for the term "our corporate family"; at the very least it enlivens their hallways with gossip).

In families of substance without a male heir, it is still common to legally "adopt" an adult son to inherit wealth, business interests, and political connections. A former Japanese prime minister, Eisaku Sato, has this background, and he was the natural brother of yet another prime minister: Nobusuke Kishi. Graduates of Todai and other prestigious universities are obviously preferred (both Sato and his brother were, by the way, Todai grads).

Todai Law graduates are known to favor the National Police establishment for careers. Such a mundane choice seems to make little sense for dedicated future elites—unless one considers that police bureaucrats are commonly given prestigious posts after their retirement, in prefectural government administrations, whence their influence and contacts extend even into Japan's lesser cities and towns. In many ways, then, social and professional, it is the graduates of Todai, and of the universities built closely around the Todai system, who run Japan.

At still a higher level, the homogeneity of the process that produces Japan's elites produces still more homogeneity. Japan may or may not be a democracy, but the elite values that prevail as common currency for entry into the elites are not those of democratic individualism, or pluralistic liberalism, but of the closest conformity. What guarantees preference in induction to conformists also ensures that *non*conformists and their ideas are kept out. This means that the values of the elite, unchanging as they are, tend to become those that rule the society, rather than the values of Japan's vibrant, increasingly heterodox society becoming those that influence its leaders. Thus, in a certain sense, it is the parents who are instructed (or at least manipulated), along with their children, through the Todai system.

This system of socialization as well as education, being so universally Japanese, reaches outward as well as inward. Japan's formal foreign policy is also based on its own "popular sentiments" of insularity, other-worldliness, elitism, and hypereconomic ethics: the very picture of an elite establishment contemplating its own navel. This is why it makes sense to virtually no one but the Japanese. "In international relations," writes Professor Ryuzo Sato of the Center for Japan–U.S. Business Studies at New York University, "Japan has long been a silent, faceless nation. Few Japanese are either willing or able to speak to the world."[24]

Notes

1. Seizaburo Sato, quoted in the *Financial Times*, "Row at Tokyo University Matches Oxbridge's Best," May 25, 1988.

2. "Educating the Establishment," *Business Tokyo* (October 1987).

3. "Todai Continues to Hold the Lion's Share," *Tokyo Business Today* (January 1987).

4. "New Presidential Crop Reflects Corporate Change," *Japan Economic Journal*, July 29, 1989.

5. "Oxbridge Feeling a Bit Pinched, but Will Muddle Through Somehow," *The Los Angeles Times,* reprinted in *The Japan Times,* April 11, 1987. (Since Britain's conversion of its Polytechnic schools into four-year university-degree-issuing institutes, this percentage has lowered considerably.)

6. "Japan's Private Colleges and Universities," private publication of the Japan Association of Private Colleges and Universities, 1987.

7. "Understanding Japan: Moral Education in Modern Japan" (International Society for Educational Information, Inc., 1989).

8. *Journal of Japanese Studies,* Society for Japanese Studies, book review of Peter N. Dale's *The Myth of Japanese Uniqueness* (winter 1989).

9. International Society for Educational Information, Inc., 1989.

10. Ibid.

11. Ibid.

12. Ibid.

13. "Report: Record Year for Colleges," *Daily Yomiuri,* April 8, 1989.

14. International Society for Educational Information, Inc., 1989.

15. "Exam Hell Linked to Depression," *Wall Street Journal,* December 26, 1991.

16. "Reform of Education System—Considering Alternatives to Pain," *Japan Times,* February 16, 1987.

17. Merry White, "The Japanese Educational Challenge: A Commitment to Children" (Tokyo: Kodansha International, 1987).

18. Thomas P. Rohlen, "Order in Japanese Society: Attachment, Authority, and Routine," *Journal of Japanese Studies,* Society for Japanese Studies (winter 1989).

19. "Tokyo University Students' Parents Are Richer," *Daily Yomiuri,* December 21, 1989.

20. "Higher Education Runs in Families," *Japan Times,* May 18, 1990.

21. "Hell Is for Children: High School Entrance Exam Questions That Stump the Brightest," *Daily Yomiuri,* October 1, 1989.

22. *Wall Street Journal,* January 15, 1992.

23. "Universities—Under Pressure to Change," *Japan Quarterly* (April–June 1987).

24. "Maturing from We-ism to Global You-ism," *Japan Quarterly* (July–September 1991).

2

First Principles: The Society

Chances to acquire cultural knowledge and skills should not depend upon one's class position, and so the school system, whether public or private, should be designed to even out class barriers.
— John Rawls, *A Theory of Justice* (1971)

In certain elementary schools in Japan, there are some athletic meets where the teachers train the students to cross the goal-line all together, rather than having one with more athletic ability come first. This is symbolic of the situation in which the whole community will survive.
— Professor Yoshiya Abe

Before we ask the Japanese university what it teaches its students about living in a democratic society, we first must ask whether Japan really is a democracy. The nation's educational system has accomplished Rawls's dictum quite ingeniously, its administrators will tell us, by eliminating class altogether. Indeed the country's great postwar social and economic successes are built, its popular mythologies affirm, on its tremendous success in embracing democracy to banish class from *all* of Japanese society: the equivalent of having everyone in the nation "cross the goal-line all together."

This is a truly enormous claim. Even if we accept the contention made by many peer-group advanced societies that they, too, have eliminated class, or at least its social effects on the distribution of opportunity and human rights, a full-scale accounting of the workings of every society making that claim is owed to all other societies who agree to deal with it equally on the strength of the claim, because the trust that subsequently is extended between them will be justified only if the claims are true. If they are not true, all other societies are left working with a set of false assumptions about the sociopolitical values of the claimant. In a world of interdependence and instant communication, that can create severe and even dangerous misunderstandings over real intentions. Precisely because "class" is such a semantically difficult concept to map within the realms of a specific culture, let alone on the bases of actual rights and opportunities, the claim may not really be valid: it may be nothing more than an assertion that the criteria of "equality" are met under the semantic terms of the *inquiring,* not the subject, society. (Many East Asian thinkers, for example, claim that their societies have adopted a "special" brand of Confucian democracy, whose own values legitimate a different approach to political fairness than do the standards of the West. Just what "exceptions" are Western societies willing to extend on account of this special claim?)

Yet in Japan's case the blanket claim to effective classlessness has been accepted at face value by a startling number of the advanced democracies, and particularly by Americans. This is partly because of Japan's electoral and parliamentary system, but partly also because the claim itself validates a widespread American belief: that democratic ideals, transplanted whole, *can* take beneficial root in alien soil—overwhelming even unhealthy native species of imperialism, and exotic ones like Confucianism, like some spiritual form of kudzu.

So it is important to re-examine Japan's claims to democratic conversion much more carefully. Why does it matter? It matters because Japan is no longer a student society, as it was in postwar days, and its underlying values and views are now important to the rest of us. Does a newly powerful, wealthy, and independent Japan amount now to a friend, an ally, or a rival? Do our civilizations share the same goals for the world's future? Do we all genuinely value highest the individual freedoms and responsibilities? Do we really want the same things for our children—or for the rest of the world's children?

Another reason it matters is that Japan is bound to begin transferring its values to us. The lowering of national boundaries in economics, trade, travel, and technology means, for example, that the Japanese lobby national and local governments for favorable treatment in America and in many other countries, employ and supervise hundreds of thousands of foreign nationals, influence capital distribution and investment policies in many lands, and insist everywhere on free trade and open markets for themselves. Masao Miyamoto, a psychiatrist and then a bureaucrat within the Ministry of Health and Welfare, expressed how this expansion of Japan has influenced us all with magnificent simplicity: "The Japanese, coming from the East, are trying to sell high quality products to the West. The Japanese ignore the rules and regulations of western society regarding working hours, and instead place all of their energy on producing goods. The only way for the West to compete with the Japanese is to extend their working hours. The result will either be a change in the fundamental values of the West, or, the western market will be inundated with Japanese goods and lose its competitiveness. It is therefore understandable that many western countries are angry at the Japanese."[1]

There's no need to look as far as Michael Crichton's novel of the '90s *Rising Sun* to imagine how the Japanese system of values can conflict with our own systems. Just watch the evening news reports on the competitive restructuring of Western corporations forced to keep pace with Japanese and now similar rivals elsewhere in Asia—often capitalized if not managed by the Japanese—and the resulting levels of American unemployment. Or, think what it would be like to be forced to work a twelve-hour day to keep up with the Japanese.

The Japanese cannot be blamed for working hard, of course; that apparently is just their way, and perhaps not so very different from something like the Protestant work ethic on steroids. Still, becoming a full member of the community of democratic nations is not a matter of just sociocultural style or of economics but of recognition of certain irreducible principles. One is that a society is bound, wherever possible, to accept the legitimacy of different schools of moral and political thought—even when they conflict with its national interests, and even when these conflicts loom within its own borders. Does Japan do so? It does not, instead constantly drawing a line between what is "legitimately" Japanese, *Nihonjin-teki,* and implying—if not saying—that all else is beyond the Japanese pale. The disingenuous Japanese explanation excusing this ethnically as well as culturally rooted discrimination—that "politics is separate from economics" in every sphere of life—is lame, disappointing, and ultimately impossible, inside or outside Japan.

And so we owe to the Japanese themselves the last major reason for critically analyzing Japan's claims to democracy. Some argue that, whatever the Japanese are or do, the vast majority of them agree with it—thus there must be a democracy at work here. Is that answer legitimate? How well do we understand and accept Japan's own political and moral reasoning, its own democratic definitions? And what right do we have, if we do not like the evidence, to criticize what we see? There is tricky footing here. In every society there is a gap between principle and practice—indeed, that is one reason universities exist: both to codify social and governmental theory and to serve as instruments of positive change in making the theoretical work in areas where it does not. To avoid violent, destructive change, liberal societies must possess such institutions, which operate on *principle.* Thus the validity of asking: what principles? While perhaps not qualifying these principles as "good" or "bad," before qualifying Japan as a democracy like our own, we must compare them to ours.

Universities have been of little help in so codifying and qualifying; indeed all by themselves, they have allowed Japan to create confusion about and within itself along these lines. As other nations have been drawn more and more into "framework" and "fairness" and "level playing field" arguments over the inner workings of their society, the Japanese have swung back and forth between proclaiming themselves legitimately, culturally "different" from the rest of the world *as a nation* and insisting that after all they are "a democratic, free-market economy" just like the rest of us. Can they be both?

All these questions can be explored under a single heading: the first principles of Japanese political and social thought.

Japan is certainly a democracy in form. Its national, prefectural, and local legislatures are elected through a system of universal suffrage enshrined in its constitution; it has a free and open system of parties and political affiliations that range from conservative to communist; its prime ministers and cabinets are chosen, like Britain's, from among the members of its lower House of Representatives—from among the common people, in whom sovereignty resides.

But a democracy is more than an electoral system. It is a national polity that reflects a philosophical contract among all the members of the society, and its irreducible foundations are the rights of the individual. This is where appearances confound not only outside observers but the Japanese as well. As a nationwide government poll recently showed, more than a quarter of Japanese adults surveyed do not believe that their nation guarantees personal freedoms and rights to its citizens.[2]

These respondents are on to something, for Japan's democracy is not built like America's, from the individual up. In fact it is a rented democracy, operating on a lease granted to a nation of impermanent tenants by a temporary landlord, Douglas MacArthur.

"The unfortunate truth," says Yoshiya Abe, director of the Institute of Japanese Culture and Classics at Kokugakuin University, Japan's premier institution for the study of native religious and ethical values, and something of an educational statesman with wide connections in academia, "is that democracy really was brought in by the authority of the Occupation forces. Can you say, then, that there is real freedom, when 'freedom' was actually introduced under some pressure? It was not real freedom; it was a survival technique. Democracy was adopted by the Japanese as a means of survival in an international struggle, in much the same way as modernization was adopted by the nation in Meiji days to survive.

"Democracy is not an end in Japan, then, but remains rather a means for individuals to survive within the structure. Otherwise, how could we account for the contradiction of so-called liberals coming back into power after the end of the war? These were the very people who were already in power before the war; they just shifted into this new power structure called 'democracy' simply by changing their convictions."[3]

He makes two good points: First, that even the most functional forms of democracy can be merely a coloration, and second, that among people anxious to survive, this separation between reality and representation might not be the most urgent worry. But we must turn to still more subtle claims, which have particularly captured the fancy of the current Western intellectual and economic establishments, that the successful creation of a "free-market" economy of consumers amounts, in effect, to the advance if not the achievement of political democracy. This thinking may owe most to the pernicious effects of the rise of Rational Choice theory among American political scientists, as Chalmers Johnson and E.B. Keehn point out with special reference to Japan: "These new theorists took their cue from economists in simplifying the motivations of political actors. Now behavior became a matter of how one calculated expected gains and losses. Voters selected candidates who could deliver the best deals, but they would not vote at all if they could not calculate a return. Legislators behaved in ways reckoned to promote their reelection. Bureaucrats followed rules because they feared the consequences of punishment if they went beyond the wishes of their political masters."[4]

Meanwhile, access to jobs, education, promotion, capital, profits, and most important, opportunity, leads ineluctably—runs a generation of thinking among liberal economists, developmentalists, foreign-policy specialists, and other promoters of "globalism"—to growing popular demand for voting freedoms and the enfranchisement of the masses, pressures that autocrats ultimately cannot resist.

Of course this is nonsense: Economy is the creation of politics, not the other way around. One look at prosperous, present-day Singapore (where hairstyles and everyday etiquette are regulated by the criminal code)—and not even to mention China—ought to warn such economic theorists that they are engaged in an intellectual conceit. After more than three decades of expanding industrialization, affluence, and middle-class growth, Japan today has neither free markets (as its international trade imbalances attest) nor equal social access to power and wealth—the rationing of which is the entire point of the national and higher educational systems.

In Japan or elsewhere it is not the level of affluence, industry, consumerism, or narrow dispersion rates of wealth that are the measures of democratic equality. It is human rights, invested in each person and inalienable from him or her—no matter by how large a majority or how urgent a political emergency—that make a democracy. What is true in democratic theory is the reverse: that equal political rights and equal liberties automatically entail equal economic rights, such as the right of all, and not just of some, to property and to job opportunity. This is because a nation's politics are (among other things) the essential system for deciding how to distribute its resources. Thus a true equality of all *political* rights ought logically, obviously, to guarantee equality of rights of opportunity within the *economy*.[5]

But of course this does not work in the opposite direction: No matter how "free" or efficient a nation's economic functions appear, if basic human rights and political equalities are not guaranteed then one or any number of power-holders in the country—an emperor or prime minister, administrators, politicians, elites or an army—can intervene at any time to alter both political *and* economic outcomes. And intervention in outcomes, both economic and political, is systemic within Japan. Those 30 million Japanese are on target indeed: There is no "proof" of democracy to be found at all in Hondas, Sonys, or five-dollar apples.

Class as Democracy

"The Japanese," wrote academician Ivan Hall, "for all their high-tech and their talk of 'globalization,' are still in the thrall of a resolutely defensive insularity, a racially based national consciousness and exclusivity."[6]

We have seen elsewhere how the insular character of Japanese cultural thought has been appropriated, laminated, and reinforced for the purposes of social control and nationalism by leadership elites. What we do not easily see are the ways this experience has shaped a Japanese world view; the ways in which democracy has been distorted and retrofitted to serve social principles that are inherently antidemocratic.

Here is where, and why, the Japanese accent falls so heavily not only on constitutionalism and electoral systems but on interpreting "free-market economic liberalism" as a proof of the existence of Japanese democracy. The exclusively economic goals of their national policy, carried on for nearly three generations without interruption, have allowed Japan's power elites to create and sustain the myth of a single, nationwide, economic middle class—and claim that this structure is itself in fact a democratic society. That is the reason Japan has seemed able to magically make class strife, and "class" itself, disappear: If everyone is in one class, then no one is in any class.

The substitution of pro-forma egalitarian values in the economy—mass membership in the middle class—for recognition of basic freedoms in the polity is a great sleight-of-hand that works well for Japan's elites. It high-jacks the appeal of democracy, to disguise authoritarianism operating through imposed consensus in the society and economy as democratic pro-cess. And if it blurs the distinctions of democratic equality for Japanese, how much more so for outsiders? Westerners who believe that all peoples instinctively value individual freedoms above everything see Japanese vot-ers going to the polls and Japanese consumers going to the markets, and mistake the trappings of democracy for its substance.

It is vital that this political mirage be made to suffice for reality. From the country schools where children are taught to cross the finish line to-gether, to the halls of Japan's biggest and best universities where students and their studies are tailored to the needs of the national economic system, this unchallenged theme runs like a thread through Japanese education: It is not individual distinction, or even individualism, that matters, but a form of controlled economic and personal competition, bounded on all sides by predetermined and approved forms of outcome, that will assure survival of the middle class and the nation. If there are any class distinctions (and, of course, in reality there are many), they cannot be acknowledged, because the divisive effects would corrode the "harmony" of the nation and the control that makes harmonious order possible.

We can see better here how the real ideal of an all-embracing economic middle class fits with the idea of a "special" mass democracy suitable to Japan. In a Western country like the United States, the government acts as an intermediary between the economy and society, periodically intervening to distribute by political methods the "winnings" of capitalism. In Japan, the government manages the economy itself—and so the economy becomes an extension of the government's very functions.

The legitimating conception for the Japanese of such a "democracy," the mechanism for harmony, is this: Everyone in that all-embracing middle class is guaranteed a place—guaranteed a social and economic welfare, that is—through his or her occupation of an approved socioeconomic niche. There is a place for everyone in the ideal Japan, in other words, and every-one is in his or her place. It is as if all Japanese had a job description, not a citizenship.

The substance of Japanese individual rights really amounts to a share in the society's political aims (which are mainly economic), and that share is only as good as one's willingness to honor the proprieties of each in-dividual's (including one's own) recognized social and professional stand-ing in the society—whether one is a company president, a farmer, or a grandmother. Therefore, the rights themselves are not inherent rights, but only political grants. And therefore they are not inalienable but informal; good only until some later set of elites, redefining the problems of national survival, writes a newer constitution.

"Survival is a kind of technology to us," as Professor Abe puts it. "In those elementary schools, for example, having all the children finish together is the understanding of 'democracy' by certain local teachers—and an adaptation of so-called liberal teachers to implement the idea of democracy within a very stringent equalization system." The education system itself is forced to follow this plan of equalizing of all young people, he says "as a basic principle of survival."

But to survive precisely what? Japan has lived for half a century with the ideal that only technology and economic strength count in defining the status and security of the nation in the world, and all polities must support the ends of building national economic power. This has come to color everything in Japanese life. The point of the race in Japanese schools or middle-class society is to triumph not as an individual, but as a group— over rejection, defeat, deprivation, even death. All these threats Japan has collectively seen hanging over its national head for more than a century, since the first Western Black Ships appeared off its shores. Japan insists that these same threats still hang over it today, so every serious economic competitor is seen as a national rival. Every effort should strengthen the group and the nation: Within each, competition and its outcomes are to be nonthreatening, predetermined, and infinitely managed, lest the creation of winners entail the creation of losers—a condition that no Japanese believes can be survived. It is the most important lesson these students will ever learn.

These managed outcomes are the foundation of Japan's understanding of its own democracy. Thus "linear competition is equality itself to the Japanese," as Abe puts it. "And I really do not think this is a kind of democracy operative in other democratic countries. This is another approach."

Believing in the moral particularisms of their society, the Japanese have neither reason nor opportunity to open it to others—nor even to compare it more than ephemerally to the functionings of other democratic societies— and so to subject it to the political tests of real individual freedom and initiative. The exclusionary, us-versus-them, nationalistic values that Hall describes, not liberal humanistic values, are the first principle underlying their society. That is why the Japanese system of egalitarianism is not a true social contract and why the average Japanese is so excessively hemmed in by decisions and constraints in everyday life that are imposed by others. (That inconsistency also is why Japanese visitors who live in the Western democracies are amazed to find them so astonishingly and refreshingly "free.")

The real question we are putting to Japan's democracy, then, is whether it can demonstrate that it really embraces equal rights, commonly recognized and unswervingly upheld by all the people and all the power-holders. If we read the Japanese constitution, where rights of speech, assembly, suffrage, equality before the law, and others are explicated, the answer seems plain. If we observe the practice of Japanese government, law, and courts, it seems equally plain.

But of course it really isn't that simple. Japan has a way of selectively upholding individual rights and of selectively abrogating them, which fits with the Japanese historical and modern experience and these customs of authority, power, and perceived "good" as the good of the group. As much can probably be said of any modern constitutional country, and indeed the political history of each is written largely in its struggles, large and small, between principle and power.

But the real proofs of the nature of Japanese democracy lie in the strength of the defenses its citizens can invoke to protect their rights—and in the common instruction they are given in school, in the family, and in society, as to the *moral* right each individual has to legally claim his or her constitutional rights.

The legal scholar Frank Upham, among other commentators on the subjective uses of legal rights and moral authority in Japan, puts the real case of rights versus authority in that nation unequivocally: "The common denominator in conflict and consensus, in litigation and denunciation, is the primacy of politics over law. And it is a politics of consultation and identification with the [government] bureaucrats; whether the vehicle is *shingikai* [discussion groups], denunciation, or litigation, effective avenues of social conflict, change and control eventually lead to the government."[7] That is, while the government does not abuse the law or the constitution, supersede its authority, or deny due process per se, it does insist that the values and goals of the government elites themselves take ultimate precedence over the directions of the law, whatever its concrete rulings may be.

The Japanese government stays in control, even in specific areas where the law finds against it, by "capturing" the larger process of conflict resolution: in other words, by making the government a part of the resolution to the problem, of which the government may even have been an original part. Solutions to such problems as the damage caused by industrial pollution or the appropriation of private land for public works have always been to create new agencies and forums for negotiation, consensus, and redress—

convened, managed, and legitimated by the government bureaucrats themselves. Since the government bureaucrats are the ones who set the policies for pollution control or land use, the fox is adjudicating penalties for infringement in the henhouse.

Nor is this dominance of politics over the law only a matter of philosophical discretion in the achievement of ends. Its inequitableness is real; it hurts people. In Japan's spectacular land-speculation "bubble" of the late 1980s, Hidetaka Moriya, a Tokyo lawyer who lives in the garden suburb of Den-en Chofu, saw his home explode in value from a hundred and seventy thousand dollars to over five million. Far from delighted in his fortune, he found himself fighting a one-man campaign to preserve his historic neighborhood from speculators and developers, and to secure fairer tax assessments for its homeowners, some of whom have been driven to suicide by multimillion-dollar inheritance levies. He has won some victories—but largely through his personal contacts and influence with politicians and government bureaucrats.

It is the ineffectiveness of Japan's public, democratic mechanisms at achieving fairness for all citizens in the face of the land value bubble that disturbs Moriya most. "In our society," he reflects in an interview in the aftermath, "we have become accustomed only to fighting our problems as individuals. It's as if they were mosquitoes: when they attack, each one of us simply reaches for mosquito nets or fly swatters. We never ask each other why there are mosquitoes in the first place, and then all go together to drain the swamps."

The inevitable way for a citizen to fight for his rights in Japan, lawyer Moriya is suggesting, is not to go to court but to petition politicians and bureaucrats individually: to make a special interest of oneself. This failure of the democratic system to offer viable alternatives to ordinary citizens helplessly caught in the mechanisms of frenzied financial speculations is not an accident. It is the product of intentional systems of social control that keeps constituents personally dependent on bureaucratic and political elites in Japan for their well-being at even the most elemental levels.

If Moriya's point is that the political system can be used by individuals only to achieve a dispensation rather than a rectification, then Upham's point is that Japan's version of democratic process is used by the political system to guide the majority not to equitable solutions but to acceptable "consensuses," supporting a goal determined in advance by elites. That this is in fact authoritarianism, not democracy, is proved not so much by the preselection of the goal as by the avoidance of the fact that the alternative— truly democratic solutions—are not necessarily agreeable outcomes to all participants. Individual rights, to be genuine, must in the end take precedence over the desires and sometimes even the legitimate interests of the majority.

But a dictated Japanese "consensus" supports no such priority of rights, whether constitutionally protected or not. Everything is fungible in the consensus process, and rights are traded away for other compensations or diluted to the point necessary to secure the satisfaction and endorsement of all parties. It matters not at all whether those protected by rights are ultimately willing as part of the consensus process to bargain them away for some compensation guaranteed by the state. An individual "right" whose endorsement is discretionary to the purposes of the state is no right at all. And if there are no rights, there is no democracy.

The proof of this reality explains to Westerners mystified by the lack of the Japanese consumer's power why so few improvements commensurate to the expansion of the nation's wealth have been made in the economic standing of the Japanese working family. However much it does so in principle, the Japanese style of government does not in practice recognize the rights of its citizens as inalienable. Thus, no consumer or other type of citizen interest group (such as those campaigning for the environment, against nuclear energy, for improvements in senior-citizen care policies, etc.) has any real opportunity *solely on the basis of its constitutionally guaranteed rights* to litigate effectively against the government or in turn any real power to legally protect the interests stemming from those rights. (In fact the government has boldly attempted the capture of such citizen movements itself. A 1992 news report gave accounts of efforts of grassroots organizations to band together specifically "in opposition to a bid by the Foreign Affairs and Home Affairs Ministries to have state and municipal associations in 45 prefectures and 11 Cabinet-ordained cities *bring all independent grass-roots organizations under their control* [emphasis mine]. Municipal associations had initially promised to provide funds to the organizations and let them make the decisions; funds now tend to be conditional."[8])

If a citizen brings suit against the government, it will be heard only if the government agrees that it should be. Between 1975 and 1990, according to the Osaka Bar Association, in a nation of 124 million, there were on average only 800 citizens' suits brought each year against government at any level, from national to local. In any year, an average of only 4 percent of the plaintiffs won.[9]

F "airness" of outcome is an understandable goal to many Americans, concerned as they are with the fairness of equal access to higher education in their own universities. But in Japan this "linear egalitarianism" of which Abe speaks, having different goals, works in a different way as it applies to real people in real schools. It is its own major flaw because it assures that "leadership" selection for an elite future is not really democratic at all. The system of school-entrance testing, to surmount ever-higher bars of admission to better and better schools, is in fact highly subjective, not objective. Because it seeks predetermined outcomes, it guarantees not more open access, but access increasingly restricted to those who hold establishment values.

Because both the testing system and the testing materials are provided by those already in the hierarchy, the tests assure that only people who conform to these principles of "linear equality" will themselves be admitted to leadership. It is a self-reinforcing class structure, in other words, access to which is based on criteria and authority of those in it, endlessly self-perpetuating the same standards.

The net effect is to block anyone with a new idea or a different background—most especially anyone with a rebellious form of genius, or who might have divergent, independent lines of thought. Thus democracy is vitiated at the very entry gates to the elite class. Energy and genius devoted to conformity is what is rewarded: What must be learned to enter the gates is chosen by those already setting the standards of what a leader is permitted, or trained, to be. Only those who answer to the national, introverted cultural values of the tests, within the tests, have a real avenue to elite status.

That is why so much of Japan seems to outsiders to be run from behind closed doors, by "good ol' boys" who seem able to move the goalposts with great facility whenever it benefits them. Everything is liquid; nothing is fixed. This explains why Western policymakers are so frustrated over changes Japan may or may not actually make—as opposed to ones it promises to make—in a post–cold war world.

Indeed if all this is true, it does pose troublesome prospects for all the exercises in "change"—internationalization, economic liberalization, democratic reinvigoration, administrative reform—Japan proclaims, and believes, that it is now undergoing. There is a real danger in this lack of fundamental democratic underpinning, especially potent in a society that thinks it *is* democratic. The Japanese subscribe to a popular convention that their society is adept at change. Old values have deep roots, they concede, and Japan may thus appear conservative to outsiders. But both the Meiji period and the Occupation prove nothing so irrefutably, Japanese commentators say, as that once the need for change is perceived, few societies can accomplish it as radically, rapidly, and even enthusiastically as Japan's.

In other words, they fail to see the incipient fallacy: that high rates of change in a society's basic fabric are the inverse of democratic functions. Democracy is a process of winnowing, of testing, the interests of various dramatically or mildly opposing groups. Achieving a quick consensus of conflicting interests for profound change toward a specified goal is the rationally opposite function of such a process: It superimposes order and decision-making on what is by nature a disorderly, intermediate process that has no preordained outcomes.

Japan's interest groups are, historically, just as sharply defined as America's. To achieve new and neat "solutions" between them quickly does not imply the messy, argumentative processes of democracy that produce change in America. It implies simply trampling certain groups to impose new policies autocratically because those groups have no right to dissent. Not only is it a proof of the weakness of democratic tradition in Japan's polity, but this "efficient change" model is indeed what disturbs Japan's neighbors and allies so. It implies a supraconstitutional, directorial agency within society; it is indeed a matter of men making deals behind closed doors, and not of democratic solution.

If this process has gained Japan spectacular successes in the past, it has also created for it profound problems. That the consensus system of political command through economic management has been vital to the success of the postwar Japanese elite leaders, and to all the successes of the society itself as well as the economy, is beyond doubt. But its merely disguising the placing of undemocratic, unchallengeable authority in the hands of elites is not the whole reason. Japan's triumph, though commonly guessed so, is not the employment of a great, technocratic management to harmonize all goals of the society. Rather, the triumph stems from persuading such large percentages of all sectors, at all age levels, of the society to *internalize* the values of the leadership elites, purely on the basis of the latter's informal moral authority. That success is the reason, of course, that Japan seems to the world so politically intractable as a society. Japan does not really think of itself as part of the world at all; thus it is little concerned with whether it truly is or is not a democracy.

Westerners, descendants of a Judaeo-Christian history that makes every individual answerable to a transcendent moral order, and all heirs to a textual, literalist political tradition that says all laws must be spelled out plainly, search for the locus of social responsibility within the Japanese individual and hope to reason from there where his society will go. The locus is not within the individual, and the rules are not written down. So the search will be fruitless.

Meanwhile, the democratic world confronts troubling new questions about the impact of ethnic nationalism in places like the former Yugoslavia, the former Soviet republics, and the Middle East. This it does without ever realizing that what Japan is, in reality, far from a democracy, is a huge, ethnically paranoid, nationalist power proceeding inexorably along a course aimed at global self-aggrandizement.

Notes

1. Masao Miyamoto, "Japan: A Bureaucrat's Paradise, But Where Is Democracy?" private paper, 1993, p. 14.

2. Prime Minister's Office, "Public Opinion Survey on Society and State," April 1991, p. 1.

3. Interview with the author, October 1992.

4. Chalmers Johnson and E.B. Keehn, "A Disaster in the Making: Rational Choice in Asian Studies," in *The National Interest* (summer 1994).

5. See John Rawls, *A Theory of Justice* (Cambridge, MA: Belknap Press of Harvard University Press, 1971), for a fuller discussion of the logical interplay of principles of rights.

6. Ivan P. Hall, "Samurai Legacies, American Illusions," in *The National Interest* (summer 1992).

7. Frank K. Upham, *Law and Social Change in Postwar Japan* (Cambridge, MA: Harvard University Press, 1987), p. 218. I am indebted to this fine study for a better appreciation of how "the bureaucracy does retain a surprising degree of control over the pace and course, if not the substance, of social change in Japan, [with] one of its major instruments for such control . . . the manipulation of the legal framework within which social change and its harbinger, social conflict, occur" (p. 17).

8. "Grass-roots Groups Set Up Network," *Asahi Evening News,* November 24, 1992. Emphasis added.

9. "Lawyers: Government Refuses to Disclose Information," *Asahi Evening News,* March 11, 1993.

3

First Principles: The Individual

In Shintoism, we worship our ancestors as gods. As a result, everyone becomes a god upon his death. And at the pinnacle of these gods stands the Emperor of Japan.
—Rep. Seisuke Okuno, national cabinet minister, quoted in "Recognizing the Religion–Politics Problem," *Mainichi Daily News,* June 14, 1988

Otherness is a challenge that has always been met through the self-defensive activity of interpretation. The typical response to otherness—or foreignness—is to defuse it through explaining it in some fashion.
—William E. Paden, *Religious Worlds,* 1988

The Japanese do not seem to think very much.

Hospitable as they may be when meeting foreigners, enthusiastic as they are for new information, and prodigious as is their attention to detail, somehow the silences that fall when talk turns to ideas, values, and events in the larger world often grow embarrassing. Perhaps, you will surmise, it is just language shyness, or polite deference, or unwillingness to offend with a controverting opinion. Or, might it just be those fabled introversions of Japanese culture?

Often it may be all of them. But, in the end, one too often gets the surprising impression that a Japanese friend, acquaintance, or informant simply has no opinions on such things, that he or she in fact thinks, or cares, little at all about questions that go beyond daily life, or, even more unexpected, is distressed at having such topics introduced.

Of course the Japanese elites have opinions. And, even for a foreigner, when a relationship grows comfortable enough to think of a Japanese as a friend, you may actually begin to hear them. But the truth is that a good deal of the thinking of most Japanese on larger matters is actually done for them. They do not find it necessary to spend much time on it themselves. And what opinions they do hold, on life, religion, politics, class, and the human condition are, often as not, prepackaged for them by designated thinkers: those whom the Japanese meet throughout their lives, or whose opinions they hear via the media, or whose writings they read, who hold the social sanctions to decide what is correct interpretation in their world. This is not by accident of culture or through Confucian traditions or a result of intellectual indifference. It is by political design.

To understand what the Japanese university teaches the nation's young elites about that most important element of education, thinking for themselves, we have to give some consideration to whom it is teaching. What are the "raw materials," of ideas, principles, and traditions, that make up the incoming student body, and its *Weltanschauung?*

The trouble with Americans," remarks an acquaintance who has had vastly frustrating experience at the nexuses of trade, business, and economic negotiations between Japanese and U.S. diplomats, "is that they can't resist looking for some Grand Unification Theory, on how all of Japan 'works.' They think if they can only figure out the one big secret, they'll become successful in dealing with *all* their Japanese problems."

Grandiose theorizings are no substitute for the hard information—all too often, the kind Americans have neglected to gather—on what power games and pragmatism are at work when Japanese negotiate. And, whether in official or simply social dialogue, Japanese certainly do take offense at being lumped into a condescendingly simplistic "they" in Westerners' preferred preconceptions.

But the reason foreigners almost always end up fumbling with ascriptive generalities in trying to analyze the individual Japanese they deal with is because often they are simply forced to. The Japanese frequently seem to prefer to present themselves, formally, to outsiders in no other way. They have indeed been raised, largely through the educational system, to a habit of thought that assumes that the coloration of a mass identity in formal life is in fact exactly what makes them Japanese. (It also, by the way, makes it very convenient for presenting a united bargaining front in negotiations.)

To understand the way the Japanese elite sees him- or herself in society —the human values held in respect to self and others—is the point of this chapter. It starts by tackling the proposition that the average Japanese individual assumes that he or she is foremost not so much an individual as a member of an organization. It might be a family, or perhaps a part of a company or a school or a government agency. But the group, it is a commonplace to observe, makes the person.

When a top executive of a major corporation, an individual well-known throughout society, is invited to speak publicly he will step to the podium, after a long and fulsome introduction, to inform the audience first-off "I am

Suzuki, of X Corporation." Of course no one could be in doubt whether it is indeed Suzuki. The executive is merely making an expected social obeisance, the point of which is to acknowledge that the very legitimacy of his appearing before them derives not from himself as an individual, or even from his rank, but from his organization.

Foreigners are often told how group-centric the identities of Japanese people are. It is hard for them, however, to grasp how important this is to the individual's whole sense of himself, how it invests his "being Japanese" with an extra dimension of social awareness—and how much it automatically ingrains a nationalist purpose into his life.

Here is where the university, and the whole educational system that fans out beneath it, play a pivotal and highly mendacious role. They introduce the individual to the group, carefully socialize him to it, and then convince him that subordination to group values is his own natural inclination. It is a way of controlling the values of each individual by brutally forcing his or her own cooperation in internalizing them.

If not with Japan's group-oriented society, the reader will certainly be familiar by now with its middle-class economic manifestation, the lifetime employment system. In elite echelons, it functions something like a military career: Young men enter the managerial academies—the four-year colleges of the universities—by dint of enormous rote work of memorization to pass the entrance exams. There, even before they graduate, they are recruited by enterprises and initiated into what will be the lifelong brotherhoods of their career collectivities.

There are special organizational codes of ethics and conduct to which most of them are initiated—sometimes through arduous Zen or even actual military training. And then will follow a period of rather monastic living in company dormitories, as the recruits acclimate themselves to a regimen of on-the-job training with workdays lasting twelve or more hours. Together with induction, sealed in the alcoholic rituals of after-hours drinking parties, into the corporate fraternities in which their whole professional lives will be bound up, this is the gateway to the world of the elites. They have labored long—many since the ages of three or four—to pass through it.

The correlate, of course, of the individual's guarantee of lifetime security is his commitment to lifelong service. Just as if he were actually in the military, the elite cadet can only contemplate leaving his corps with the knowledge that he will find no home of comparable prestige or security in any other service—for no other elite Japanese corporations will hire him. This means he must bear up, no matter what, under the strain of a hated boss or a miserable assignment, whether his station be in Tokyo or Guayaquil.

Often enough, if he has no luck on his own in the difficult search for a suitable bride, his supervisors or colleagues will introduce him to marriage prospects as well. Often enough, when he finally has a family of his own, his mortgage payments will be subsidized by his employer. Often enough, in his free time he will play softball in the company's league, or even take his family on holiday to the company's mountain lodge. Often enough, at special times he will attend services or festivals at the company's Shinto shrine. And often enough—when the time comes—he will even be entombed at the company's graveyard at a Buddhist temple.

Seen through a macro lens that focuses much more broadly than simply on "the job," the resulting potential for intellectual indifference to the world beyond the lifetime employment system is obvious. At its fullest extension "the frightening thing about (the) absolutes" of Japan's business system, as a senior journalist with the *Nihon Keizai Shimbun*[1]—Japan's *Wall Street Journal*—recognized, "is that they sooner or later rob people of the ability to think. When forced to make a [business] decision, one ends up deciding on the basis of what others are doing and naturally does the same thing. If there's only a single correct answer, then all one has to do is memorize it." In a system where all things are given—for life—there is little reason to question anything.

Of course the "Organization Man" is no stranger in any industrialized society. Success of individuals in a large, bureaucratic organization often persuades them to identify with its institutional values. And in truth the full-blown bureaucratic system of lifetime employment embraces less than 50 percent of the national work force—even when women, who make up nearly half that force, are not included in the accounting. But, especially in an employment economy that offers very few alternatives, Japanese are simply compelled to socialize themselves to the "group harmony," of ideals as well as goals. The alternative is ostracism.

Yet can it really be that these ethics of the Japanese group are potent enough to supplant personal values? Do teachers, employers, supervisors, fathers, and coaches really tell people what to think?

In a word, the answer is often yes. But there is a larger context, that of the society itself, in which it truly does not matter what the individual thinks: it matters only how he or she acts.

In any civilization as old and ethnically uniform as Japan's there are certainly homogeneities, both the genuine and the merely polite. But there should also be, in a society that so values learning, a tradition of intellectual autonomy. Indeed it is part of the university's mission to teach and to support the right to this autonomy. And in a society both as self-disciplined and as knowledge-oriented as Japan's, there should be some transcendent human values, such as those that issue from family, religion, or even community groups, to which each individual ought to answer, above the logic of job or even country.

Unfortunately these have been largely vitiated in elitist Japan. Families have become, for reasons noted elsewhere, adjunct to the economic purposes of their breadwinners—small groups attached, as it were, to the company itself. Social power, and its concomitant ethical authority, within the family are not unimportant. But they relate mostly to the mother–child relationship rather than to the now-symbolic uses of patriarchy. And of course the mother, in socializing the child, is almost institutionally linked with the school, in theory and in practice, rather than with any independent culture of her own kinship.

The intellectual community demands a much more careful analysis. Because, in addition to the "intellectual cartels," to use Chalmers Johnson's term, of accepted academic orthodoxy that are residual within the universities, there are many other influences on the thinking of the Japanese elite: the media, the arts, foreign social and cultural ideas, nonmainstream political parties, the vast array of freelance commentators known generically as "critics," and so on. Most Japanese are exposed to these regularly. What the academies have propagated of course tends to honor the received wisdom of the generations of elites they themselves have produced. What ideas are generated in the larger world of popular and intellectual thought—and how they are received—is much harder to characterize.

Here if anywhere is where the closest thing to a free competition of ideas exists in Japan. Its very prolixity—in some cases one is tempted to say frivolity—however, set against the orderly spheres of thought devolving from the Japanese academy and those sectors who are part of the establishment with it, such as government and the mainstream media, militates against a great deal of it being taken very seriously by the individual. Some of it is sincere and thoughtful, but much of this material has the flavor of the trendy and fashionable about it: Remember, another thing the Japanese are told is that they are inherently highly adept at selecting the "useful" from among the new and foreign, while constantly preserving the essential purity of Japanese culture. And unfortunately, its topical focus is highly subject to manipulation by interest groups within the Japanese establishment. The Americans, who both run a $60 billion trade deficit with Japan and often find themselves publicly accused through the megaphone of the media of using "unfair trade practices" against the same country, can testify to that.

Religion, as a stimulus to thought about transcendent values, is another and obviously more complex matter, to which we return below. For now, it can only be said that as a moral force in the society at large it too has been largely diluted.

Yet to understand why the Japanese individual so often seems to outsiders so indifferent to larger questions—a propensity that many Japanese refer to in cultural shorthand as a preference for "action over words" (or put less idealistically, "Just do it; don't think about it")—and what place individual choice finds in Japan, we will have to look beneath the "group-oriented" exegesis that flourishes in all discussion of Japanese culture, to the individual human standing at its foundation. And here we make an interesting discovery. Japanese as individuals have not been so much homogenized by their society as the opposite: They have been atomized.

What has happened to Japan since the apocalyptic end of World War II is this. Layer by layer, over generations, the inheritance of traditions, mores, and communal ethical values dating back centuries have been peeled away from the urban Japanese, until the individual has been left spiritually naked to the moral influence of those who hold the kind of direct, pragmatic power described above over him. Changes in the family alluded to elsewhere have had much to do with it. But it has been accomplished mainly in the process of his passing through the vortex of the modern, nationalist educational system.

Japan before its modernization in the late nineteenth century was essentially a feudal society. Grand patterns of liege and lord, domainal government, and a homogeneous and unchallengeable ruling military class—the age of the *shogun*—are famous even abroad. Their validity as an explanation of how rigidly all Japanese society was governed is generally acknowledged.

But formal postulations seldom align with reality in anything as complex as a whole society. In fact there were many systems of government, or at least many sources of moral authority, in everyday life in the Edo period: family heads, and the headmen of villages above them, for example. And there were many informal moderators of the "absolute" values imposed by feudal rule: Artists and poets, local teachers and landlords, priests and brewers of sake and soy sauce (who were influential through their wealth) all moderated the tenor of local life. Many temples operated schools, and literacy was surprisingly widespread. The brokers and merchant families, such as the Mitsui, who on a larger scale made Japan run economically, even created their own household codes of strict ethical accountability, exercised rigorously within their walls although not recognized outside them. The pattern of moral loyalty to a corporation—the company as "family"—has it roots here.

Then came Japan's historic awakening, the formal cornerstone of which was the Meiji Restoration that began in 1868. As seen above, one of the most seminal things the new Meiji rulers, preoccupied with ensuring loyalty to themselves, did was to institute a new, nationwide educational system that made all teachers and administrators answerable directly to Tokyo. And they wedded this educational structure to the new socioeconomy by making it to a large degree meritocratic.

While this opened varying prospects of fortune and career to members of almost all classes of the old society, it also had the effect of placing every student in the new educational system on a track of competition with all of his contemporaries. In other words, the Meiji leaders made schooling virtually the single gateway for all commoners to the power hierarchies of government, industry, academia, and the military. In doing so, they undercut the traditional moral authorities that had grown up in all the previous years in all layers of the old society, and now forced each would-be elite to compete to climb a single ladder of a new, centralized authority to success. The rungs of this ladder were the progressive levels of examinations.

This system itself was in reality not absolutely monolithic. New elites, allied through families to the various clans and later to the leading personalities that headed the Meiji government, always enjoyed informal precedence in the power and access order. But below the aristocratic level, very few students from any part of society who wished to succeed by winning career opportunities in the country's dynamic modernization and industrialization found any intellectual validities that related to this goal *outside the school system*. In essence, all students became part of a huge bureaucracy called the educational system. And all internalized its values, which were intensively political as well as educational.

This struggle to advance up the national ladder, pitting each student against all other students, created the vortex that pulled in all the most promising and ambitious young people and atomized them into lone individuals whose ultimate motivations were simply to reach the top.[2] Of course not every young Japanese was ambitious; nor did most get very far up the educational ladder. Indeed the highest levels of the Meiji educational system, especially the elite universities, contained few farmers' sons and more than its share of scions of the country's wealthier and more influential families. Shigeru Nakayama points out that as late as 1890, almost 70 percent of the faculty at the Imperial University, the forebear of Todai, were themselves from the *samurai* class.[3]

But the moral authority of the educational system to dictate as "politically correct" the nationalist polity of the oligarchs in Tokyo was irrefutably enshrined. (It was this authority of politics over knowledge, and over pedagogy itself, that later led teachers to abet such corruptions of the school system as the direct assignment of imperial military officers to high schools, and the introduction of state Shinto and Emperor worship directly to the campuses.) Like their descendants in today's corporations, students could differ openly from the values this "establishment" taught only at the implied risk of ending their career aspirations.

The Meiji evolution was naturally not an overnight phenomenon. It lasted nearly half a century, and the accompanying penetration of a national educational system into all levels of society was fraught with many setbacks, slowdowns, and adjustments. Most of its students left at the completion of the compulsory course and were reabsorbed in essentially rural communities where family values persisted. It remained for them to be socialized to the new nationalisms later, in the Imperial Army, or perhaps for their grandsons, through the more recent atomizations of urbanization and the emergence of the lifetime employment system after the war.

But the Meiji period was heady days, full of fundamental transformations of the country and yeasty with the promise of new opportunities to make one's place in the changing world. "Boys, Be Ambitious" is a famous admonition inscribed in those days at the gateway to a Japanese college. The inscription is still there today.

No matter at what university each student ended his climb up the elite ladder, he left it not only outfitted with a modern education, but imbued with an ethic of personal purpose, to make himself useful to whichever of the institutions of government, industry, commerce, academe, or the military that he found a career with—and through them, of course, to Japan's national purposes. Thus while young Japanese elites were being cut off from their traditional roots, atomized through ruthless individual competition and transposed to the expanding industrial and commercial venues of the cities, they were at the same time being drawn into the group-value orientations of the modern, secular economy and society.

In assigning character-formation powers to Japan's modern educational system, however, we should be careful not to impute too much. It is not this system that turned out, fully formed, the reticent, group-oriented, intellectually diffident young Japanese elite of today. What emerges is not an indoctrinated automaton, but merely a *malleable* person: one capable of adapting to the ethos, customs, and usages of whatever group he or she attaches to.

While defenders of the prewar and postwar systems would call it all "flexibility," this ethical malleability is something different. It leads to an easy manipulation of the individual and of the whole society. The past can, in and out of school, be mythicized to sanctify pragmatic national purposes or absolve critical national responsibilities. This, in our own era, is how so much of the history of the Pacific War has been expurgated in contemporary Japanese thought. A great deal of what the Japanese tell themselves is venerable tradition, meanwhile, is in reality no more than a few generations old. The lifetime employment system itself does not predate the postwar period. The interpretation of phenomena such as family suicide as being profoundly "Japanistic," on statistical evidence, goes back no further than the modern era itself.[4] The ancient, authoritarian system of the *ie* (household) was extended from *samurai* households to apply to commoners only with the advent of the Meiji period.

Myths that range from mundanities—that Japanese are uniquely adept at nonverbal communication—to misrepresentations—that the Japanese were victims, not perpetrators, in the Pacific War—to the ludicrous—that Japanese have longer intestines, or divide their brain-hemispheric functions differently from or are more spiritually attuned to nature than other societies —have a provenance often no older than the persons speaking them. Parts of the recently presented "ancient" rituals of marriage ceremonial observed by the imperial household actually go back less than a century.[5]

If many Japanese elites are aware of these deliberate or partial fabrications, it does not seem vital to openly refute them. How much more stubborn, then, are the national myths that present no pragmatic facades that can be challenged, but are ingrained as basic values through socialization in the schools: that the Japanese are "harmonious," that they dislike Western logic, that they are by nature all thrifty, industrious, intuitive, and so on?

The character of much education, not only in universities but in the entire national school system, has had a dampening effect on the very nature of Japanese self-awareness. The "knowledge" dispensed is not open to a process of intellectual investigation by students. It is a store of information resources, to be absorbed in the largest volumes possible by the individual for regurgitation in the examinations. It is not education at all, but training. This process of learning itself is a socialization: To succeed in life one does not need to think so much as merely to know. The memory is the highest organ of intelligence.

With its priority of dispensing information, and intermediating the constant competition between students racing to absorb it, the education system almost completely fails to imbue students with a sense of the integrity of the individual intellect. In a sense the race to "catch up" to other countries, through producing more graduates at every level ready to serve the national struggle to "modernize," still goes on. Thinking about the things one learns is not prized; only knowing them is necessary.

If the intellectual process of questioning—thinking—is not validated as an important goal of education, then its products of ideas, insights, and pursuit of the rational truth are not values of the society. Ideas and truths sometimes have a way of contravening official wisdom, or at least its purposes. That is not useful to those who administer the education system, or those who employ its graduates.

The result is that the individual in Japan is discouraged—prohibited, actually—from forming any transcendental values, individually arrived at. There is a need for an official wisdom, even an official mysticism, and besides these there needs to be, for Japanese national purposes, nothing. The Japanese conceptualization of life, embracing job, family, ethics, reward and punishment, and all social contracts, is held to be complete enough for everyone, needing no ramification or intellectual examination. Its obvious historical success invalidates the very authenticity of critical re-evaluation.

And in the process of internalizing it, through the ever-deepening ingestion-and-examination system of knowledge management, Japan's most successful students actually become its greatest exponents.

We may now perceive one possible answer to the question set out above: What and how do the Japanese think about broader questions of society and civilization? There is no need to think about them. Independent intellectual inquiry is certainly not actively discouraged; the Japanese are voracious readers of their own and the world's most seminal thinkers. Examining the reports of colloquies and interviews of the leading experts, at home and abroad, on the "problems" of Japan domestically and overseas is a favorite pastime.

It is just that critical, individual judgment of "the big questions" is little promoted, and is not considered useful beyond the level of rhetorical exercise. At best it can be only theoretical exegesis, or an amusement—and perhaps even a dysfunctional one. No matter what the *individual* thinks, it doesn't matter.

It is because the average individual feels allegiance to few transcendent values—principles or ideas that are more compelling to the person than those of any group he or she may belong to—that all ethics become relative to the life situation one finds oneself in. And in Japan, one almost always finds one's life situation in a group. Thus, the group's values should be handily adopted as one's own.

This is not to say that young Japanese elites (and especially women) find all their employers' values, customs, and cultures immediately agreeable. They occasionally find them onerous. It is just that they, from their junior station, have little choice but to accept them. And no compelling reasons for believing they can do anything to change them. For aspiring elites, that's just the way it is.

One of the consequences of possessing no transcendent values is that the individual finds himself with little conscientious ground for demanding change, or even for objection, even when he recognizes injustice. It is precisely the quasi-sacrosanct, even fanatical, nature of the loyalty that Japanese groups can "legitimately" demand of their followers that led to participation in the grotesque abominations seen in the Aum Shin-Rikyo sect, a "religion" most famous for its leaders' being placed on trial for the Tokyo subway gassings. An individual ensnared even in this moral jungle has no ethos and little sociocultural foundation for objecting even to murder, on personal grounds.

Of course individual Japanese do complain, and do take institutional redress against grievance, when injustice grows intolerable personally. But that does not have the same meaning as holding society up to judgment by one's own ethical lights.

"The logic of modern civic society," observes Todai sociologist Munesuke Mita, "dismantles the straitened villages and families, dissolves their communities, and chooses its own victims. 'It is the parents who are bad.' 'It is the sons who are bad.' 'It is the neighbors who are bad.' "[6] But never is the *society,* the all-encompassing Japanese group, bad. Crimes, misdeeds, inequities, mistakes, and failures, where they become public, are assigned always as the fault of individuals or discrete groups. Until very recently, few Japanese were heard publicly blaming or even questioning the society itself. That has not been allowed because it is not valid. No one's ethical credentials are recognized above those of the established order.

In this context, we can also perceive a possible cause for the failure of democratic institutions that can intermediate between people and state in Japan to develop independently. If the people can be convinced that their moral and ethical values and the state's are also essentially correlate, then what really is the *need* for any intermediary institution, separate from both?

We need not descend to cultural mysticisms to see how the guarantees to the elites of the lifetime employment system, on the one hand, and its demands, on the other (coupled with the impressive reassurances of Japan's economic successes), impel Japanese elites to adopt the ethic of the organization in general and the group in particular. There is one more ramification, however, to the failure of transcendental values to develop in Japan, that binds Japanese individuals tightly within their primary groups.

The vitiation of independent, value-imparting intermediary institutions such as religions, political parties, service groups, youth groups, the nation in a patriotic sense, and so forth, in the lives of most Japanese elites means something more than that all ethical orientations become situated within the primary group. It means that human relations themselves become politicized.

This should not be surprising. Not only do loyalties run strong between individuals in any society with few other claims on ethical allegiance, but these personal loyalties by default become the *only* channel for personal affiliations. If there is no other authority to which the group member can appeal in the daily conduct of affairs for sanction, recognition, validation, award, and approval but the leaders in his or her group, the member will naturally become so dependent upon those leaders as to identify his or her own personal interests with theirs. This is precisely how vertical human alliances, some of them lasting a lifetime, are formed in Japan.

The professor that helped to guide one through college and into a corporation is one's *sensei* (teacher) for life. He is owed obligations and loyalties not only for that reason but because the *sensei* himself has networks of his own allegiances that can prove useful in the later climb up the organizational ladder. The supervisor at work who oversees one's performance ratings, promotions, and assignments can virtually wreck a subordinate's career if animosities or even open differences of opinion are carelessly allowed to develop, because the subordinate cannot change jobs to escape. Conversely, a supervisor who thinks well of his team member can arrange for advantageous introductions, juicy work assignments, transfer at the proper time to an important company section, and even help in locating a suitable marriage partner.

Senior classmates from college days can, with cultivation, help open important doors to customers, partners, influential friends, or employers later in life. Teachers of hobby crafts can arrange for one's works to be entered in important, socially prominent amateur contests and for introductions to equally socially prominent people. Something will need to be given in return, certainly, but that is nothing more than the social currency of this enormously political and largely informal network of human affiliations.

This is the basis for *senpai–kohai* (senior–junior) relationships that are acknowledged and relied upon sometimes for life. This is the basis for "getting along" in spheres important or ancillary to one's career or family life or financial prosperity. This is what very many Japanese rely upon in place of independent, only nominally democratic institutions, which have no such power or influence to help them in a secular world.

But it is also highly subjectivizing in terms of focusing an individual's ethical priorities and choices. The personal tastes, preferences, beliefs, and even fillips of a junior elite's seniors tend to become guiding standards for his or her own behavior in such an intimate and subjectively particularized association. These artificial affinities are what lead in turn to the primacy of *jinmyaku* (human relationships) in the settling of promising, delicate, or difficult issues of relations beyond one's own realm of *senpai* and *kohai*.

And *jinmyaku* can largely vitiate the guarantees of objectivism and justice that institutions and hierarchies would otherwise supply in matters of conflict, competition, or aggrandizement.

This is also dangerous because it has a way of sealing the individual's loyalties beforehand to commitments whose ethical implications have no way of being obvious in advance, as well as of making it extremely difficult for the individual to demur when the commitments and personal debts come due, even when objection seems called for. It creates personal obligations that can "situationalize" ethics and destroy objectivity, even more strongly than can the primary loyalties and impulsions within the Japanese group.

It strengthens still more the tendencies that the educational inheritance truly implants before all others in the young Japanese elite: to think, in all matters of importance or future consequence, about getting ahead by linking himself to whatever ethos, whatever leader, will give him a leg up.

We have come full circle, from the individual to the group and back to the individual. This is all circumscribed purely by self-interest, which beneath layers and layers of cultural semantics remains the defining Japanese elite value.

What was sketched here is the classical model of the secular, mobile society that results from radical modernization, when old values, as well as old hierarchies, are rooted out abruptly to effect the kind of radical transformation needed to "save" the country. One is tempted to compare the Japanese experience from the Meiji Restoration to the present with the early Marxist successes of the Soviet leaders, who were also concerned with building an elite "new man" through the pragmatisms of the scientific method. Here too, intermediary institutions and their values, such as the church and the landlords, were eliminated, creating a vortex in which elites were socialized toward a national purpose.

But the differences are crucial. Where the Marxists attempted to create a new orthodoxy of the scientific man, the Japanese succeeded in capturing a much older and native institution—Confucianism—and adapting it to fit their own hierarchy of national authority. The Meiji bureaucrats vested themselves not only with secular authority in their modernization, but with the same moral authority that the leaders of the feudal state had claimed. They accomplished this by acting in the name of the unchallengeable authority of the imperial throne, the Restoration having served to "return" the Emperor to his rightful place of preeminent authority. This was the reason that state Shinto, in its ideological extremes from the 1920s onward, could be used to elevate the Emperor both to "father" of the nation and to an approximation of a mystical god himself, to which all Japanese owed a spiritual allegiance.

The effect of the Meiji Restoration then was the opposite of rationalist. The *shoguns* from whom the Meiji oligarchs inherited the Japanese social order had long since vitiated, or absorbed, the ethical integrity of Japan's religions, Shinto and Buddhism, and these faiths merely continued in their own service to the administrators. To this day the Japanese ecclesiastical faiths have not really transcended the secular political powers of the elites in moral authority, and there is a very good reason why (aside from that provided by the war, whose outcome immediately betrayed all those Japanese taught to accept as a sacred article of state that the Emperor was, or even could be, a "god").

The Meiji leaders captured not only the authority but the enforced ethical orthodoxy of the feudal period. And they kept it, within the confines of the national education system, under rigid political control. This meant that the Japanese could be taught as truths about themselves anything the Meiji autocrats felt would serve their own purposes. When the initial successes of the Meiji modernization began to wear off, losing their gloss of universal progress and their image of ever-growing materialistic success (and their implied promise of an endless supply of elite careers), this power was used to transform the way Japanese thought about themselves. The opposite of the scientific man, the Japanese were told that they were "uniquely Japanese" in ways that transcended all other patterns of civilization and social organization, all other cultural bonds among societies, on earth. The Japanese were different; the Japanese were indeed unique.

A growing body of spurious exegesis has, to this day, invested with great earnestness the spread of this conviction; a body of interpretations of Japanese experience that "prove" Japan is a special society in the world. Peter Dale has called this phenomenon, generally known as *Nihonjinron* or studies of Japaneseness, an "ideology of culture."[7] Karel Van Wolferen is more unambiguous, naming the body of neo-orthodoxies that Japanese intellectuals have consciously and mendaciously woven through this theme "what the Japanese believe that they believe" about themselves.[8] And it is not only the Japanese; many Western students of Japan have in their turn fallen under the influence of *Nihonjinron* interpretations of what otherwise seems mystifying about the Japanese structure of political control over the society. They too have bought the "uniqueness" theory.

Nihonjinron is not an ideology of mere national pride; not something similar to the Americans conceptualizing themselves as "creative" or "individualistic," nor something comparable to the axiomatic assertion that all cultures are unique. *Nihonjinron*'s tenets insist they are all-embracing in describing the Japanese character; and still more silly, that they apply only ethnically. In its more extreme manifestations, such as the fascist propaganda generated in wartime that Japanese have "longer intestines," better suited to the digestion of cereals than other peoples, have been laughed off with some general embarrassment. Yet not long ago, a Japanese cabinet officer addressing an audience of American officials and members of Congress repeated it as an argument for why imports of beef to Japan should not be liberalized. All sorts of nonsense have grown from *Nihonjinron*'s claim that Japanese have a special perspective on culture; a few years ago, a respected Japanese thinker could suggest in a mainstream newspaper that he discerned that the spread of homosexuality was at least in part the result of capitalism, which of course came from the West.[9]

It is hard to tell how seriously individual Japanese elites take these asseverations. Yet facets of *Nihonjinron*'s permeation into the general ethos can be seen everywhere. In one randomly picked-up issue of the *Japan Times,* for example, one could read the following op-ed "explanation" of the Japanese character through the importance of nonverbal intuition in Japanese social settings: "Effective communication among the Japanese entails reading nonverbal as well as verbal signs." As this is true in varying degrees in all societies, and Japan is relatively homogeneous compared to, say, America, the premise is so far not unrealistic.

But exegesis proceeds: "When we [Japanese] are able to get our message across without having to open our mouths, we are usually quite pleased that telepathic understanding has been achieved. . . . Such perceptive people tend to be successful no matter what they do. If they go into business they will have many clients. If they hope to get married they will have many proposals. If they work as a shop attendant they will ring up a high volume of sales. It appears that in Japanese society, people that are quick to catch on to the unspoken messages—reading between the line in written texts and appreciating the significance of the 'white space' in ink paintings—are valued quite highly."[10]

Not only have we gone in a single bound from the mundane to the near-mystical, but we have hammered home a lesson here: Those Japanese who do not accept all this as a specifically "valued" Japanese propensity are in danger of winding up in second—or worse—place in life. It is not the value of the statement as truth or hyperbole that attracts our attention here: It is the coercive force implied in the proposition, stated as an innately Japanese value, to which the Japanese person is being involuntarily subjected. The resultant corollary of this kind of "popular" *Nihonjinron* that *we* should accept: The Japanese not only believe, but had *better* believe, that they must be adept at a special quality of "telepathic understanding" because there might be consequences to disbelief.

This is what both Dale and Van Wolferen refer to. Japanese uniqueness is not mere semantic or intellectual playing (it is far too prevalent in society for that), but in certain ways a political ideology pursued by the state and reinforced by academia, either through promulgation of culturalist "interpretations" or through refraining from criticizing them as invalid. To this day, one can meet students and professors alike who aver that Japan is, far from being the world's Number Two economic power and the equivalent of two Germanies, with its enormous military establishment and the largest foreign-aid program of any nation, still only a small, weak, unaffluent nation that must struggle "to survive," too often beset by an American ally that bullies it over fictitious trade complaints. This is precisely a *Nihonjinron*-sculpted view of reality. The essential Japanese response to the differentness of "the Other" has been not to defuse it, but instead to define the properties of *Japaneseness* as a condition exquisitely, quintessentially different from the rest of humanity.

"The Japanese don't have much religion," an editor in a prestigious Tokyo publishing house once told me, "because being Japanese itself is a full-time religion." This is a much-remarked comparison of the ethical force of *Nihonjinron* ideals to those of a religious faith. Religion (aside from a few modern, proselytizing sects, the equivalent of America's more aggressive evangelicals) has been so tightly infused with or supplanted by the ethics of the state that, not only has it little moral force left in the realm of transcendental ideas and values, but the ideology of culture can be said to have superseded it altogether.

And *Nihonjinron* has its own authentic impact on individual behavior. The Japanese agree to be "harmonious"—to repress the personal impulses of dissent that are natural to all humans—Van Wolferen has pointed out elsewhere, because they are taught that not being harmonious is un-Japanese and, worse, will lead to genuine retribution. If at any rate such retribution is real, it does no one any good to dispute the basic contention. Better to accept that "harmony," "consensus," and all the other trappings that serve to eliminate human disagreement and bind group members to mandated plans of action is the uniquely inherited—one might almost say genetic—Japanese way, and better to adhere to it.

At the very least, anyone who has "gone along" in harmony with the program cannot be singled out in blame if it fails.

If transcendent values, the integrity of the intellect, and even the ability of the individual to question what he is told are his "unique" endowments for affinity with the goals of the power structure are all repudiated, then what can be left that is human in response but emotion? No wonder, as the critic Ian Buruma puts it, "Perhaps more than most people, the Japanese, on the whole, are ruled by their emotions."[11] A psychologist of my acquaintance, with a clinical practice of twenty years in Tokyo, goes much further: "The 'Italians of the Orient' are what I call the Japanese."

This is more than a matter of evidence or proposition in the arts and literature, in which the Japanese do indeed express and indulge in a broad scale of grand, romantic, and sympathetic—not to say Gothic, in some instances—passions. This is really to state the logical reduction of what we have said above. When a society is intellectually blocked and dialogically muted, there is nothing left through which to express oneself as an individual but raw emotions.

That is why the underlying currency of social exchanges taking place in Japanese groups—so many of them, in a setting where people cannot express themselves candidly, so necessarily subtle as to seem "telepathic"— cannot be anything but emotional. When real problems, from those of daily communication to those of the human condition, intrude in such a way that even the self-abnegation of the "harmony" ethic fails, then feelings simply boil over. This can be a dangerous condition for most Japanese because there are not many ways in his or her practical experience to vent the pressure acceptably, or to contain the damage.

Indeed a great deal of romantic literature and theater in Japan is almost hortatory in this regard, pointing out that the person who allows selfish passion to outrun loyalty and obligation can only be doomed to a tragic end. A great deal of modern fiction expresses both the pain of the individual's self-repression and often the tragic consequences of his or her failure to *gaman* (endure) under that pain: Loss of a love, loss of a family, loss of a career, loss of a life are the prices commonly paid.

Emotions are the part of human character that are never fully under external control. They are therefore the part that the social-control elites work and worry hardest over containing. That containment makes the emotions of the Japanese all the more poignant when they do explode beyond the narrow channels of self-expression they are allowed—the drinking camaraderie among men; the close physical and psychic contact between mother and child—into full-blown crisis.

Notes

1. "Japanese Must Make Choices Following Collapse of 'Absolutes,' " *Nikkei Weekly,* September 20, 1993.

2. For an insightful study of the effects of both Westernization and Meiji meritocratic social policy on these generations of the nation's youth, see Earl H. Kinmonth, *The Self-Made Man in Meiji Japanese Thought: From Samurai to Salary Man* (Berkeley: University of California Press, 1981).

3. Shigeru Nakayama, *Academic and Scientific Traditions in China, Japan and the West* (Tokyo: University of Tokyo Press, 1984), p. 166.

4. Munesuke Mita, *Social Psychology of Modern Japan* (London: Kegan Paul International, 1992), p. 327.

5. "Imperial Wedding Ceremony Shrouded in Deep Mystery, Steeped in Tradition," *Japan Times,* June 8, 1993.

6. Mita, *Social Psychology of Modern Japan.*

7. Peter N. Dale, *The Myth of Japanese Uniqueness* (New York: St. Martin's Press, 1986), p. 14.

8. Karel Van Wolferen, *The Enigma of Japanese Power* (New York: Alfred A. Knopf, 1989). I am indebted for much of this analysis of Japanese ethical and socio-political dynamics to the author's perceptive and multilayered study.

9. "Coming Collapse of Capitalism," *Daily Yomiuri,* January 14, 1992.

10. "Artists of Communication Can Fill in the Blanks," *Japan Times,* December 24, 1993.

11. Ian Buruma, *A Japanese Mirror* (London: Jonathan Cape, 1984), p. 142.

4

The Ivory Basement

Learning which cannot tear itself loose from literary exegesis and enlighten men on ethics and other practical matters is as good as no learning at all.
—Arinori Mori, founder of the modern University of Tokyo, in *Gakumon no Taihon* (Cardinal Principles of Learning), 1854

It has already been 40 years since the end of the Occupation. And still we cannot teach ourselves history.
—Professor Akimasa Mitsuta, former official, Ministry of Education

On one thing nearly all can agree: Higher education in Japan today is in crisis. There are those who might applaud such a fact; who indeed believe that part of the mission of the university is to *be* in crisis: to constantly inject the ferment of new ideas into society, to retry old dogma, to prod the young to challenge the old. Crisis might be the university's most important product, really, or at least its most invigorating.

Others more reflective, watching the storm waves of change and trial batter the nation and its leadership, are inclined to measure the university's failings by the yardstick laid out for educators of the 1990s by historian Eric Hobsbawm: "Myth and invention are essential to the politics of identity by which groups of people today, defining themselves by ethnicity, religion or the past or present borders of states, try to find some certainty in an uncertain and shaking world by saying, 'We are different from and better than the Others.' They are our concern in the universities because the people who formulate these myths and inventions are educated people: schoolteachers lay and clerical, professors, . . . journalists, TV and radio producers. Today most of them will have gone to some university."[1] And tomorrow these products of the university's wisdom—or its myths and inventions—will lead Japan.

But few in any case are encouraged by what has happened to Japan's colleges and universities or heartened by the possibilities that lie ahead. The system of higher education is going increasingly awry. It is producing graduates for the wrong future, taught by professors who are largely indifferent, and it is failing in providing society with the enlightenment, knowledge, and energy it will need to meet internal and external hazards that loom.

Though Japan's higher education, driven by its elite universities, has contributed to the modern metamorphosis of the nation into the world's Number Two economic power, it is no longer disputable that the system has fallen seriously behind America's, and Europe's as well. The deficiencies on Japanese campuses and in faculty circles not only threaten to leave the country with a leadership incapable of meeting the global challenges that are already appearing, but they may well be irreparable.

"If Japan cannot and does not correct the flaws in its system of higher education promptly," one university president has written, "Japan's present-day miracle may well turn out to be short-lived."[2]

Right-wing hard-liners assault a state-run college campus with loud-speaker trucks blasting propaganda; threatening phone calls and poison-pen letters are flowing into the school's administrative offices. The university has provoked this attack by inserting a question into its annual entrance examinations for high-school graduates, asking them to analyze the responsibility of the late Emperor Hirohito for the war. The Education Ministry (more formally, the Ministry of Education, Science, and Culture—but universally known as *Monbusho,* which translates as simply The Ministry of Education or The Education Ministry) officially frowns; the school takes its cue and resolves the controversy by apologizing.

At the University of Tokyo, a graduate student is pleasantly surprised, if mystified, to find himself at term's end awarded a course grade of A—from a professor whose classes he skipped entirely. But perhaps it's not so startling, he reflects, when he recalls another professor who himself showed up for only one of his lectures in an entire term.

A visiting foreign research student, in his first day at the famed law faculty of the same campus, receives a warm hello from a Japanese colleague who has been asked to introduce the guest around the department. His host "was really a nice guy, very helpful, and I thought we hit it off." Then suddenly came the cold shoulder. "The very next day when I saw him in class, he ignored me: said absolutely nothing. Just gave me a blank, 'what are you doing here?' look that left me frankly confused. And it was like that for months."

Each of these vignettes is a kernel of the truth of the three debilitating illnesses of the higher education system in Japan today. They tell us not only why the universities and colleges are in trouble as institutions of teaching and learning, but why they are not contributing to the solutions Japan needs, to turn itself around and face the future.

- Universities and colleges largely discourage young Japanese from questioning the shortcomings of their own society. Nor, amazingly, do they challenge students to plan their own professional goals, or even to form and stand up for ideals of their own.
- Very little teaching, and very little study, goes on at almost all under-graduate liberal-arts campuses. Graduate programs in all disciplines, meanwhile, range from seriously impaired to nonexistent. And far too many schools do not care.
- The outside world beyond Japan remains a sealed-off, foreign domain from which useful, practical knowledge is extracted for application, but from which humanitarian values, philosophical principles, and even scholars themselves are frequently rejected, or at best only tolerated.

No system or institution that calls itself a university can fulfill more than a small part of its obligations in an academic landscape like this.

There are many reasons for these failures, but by far the most important is that Japan's university system began life as a creature of the state. The first university was Todai itself, founded in 1886, some eighteen years after the Meiji Restoration. But "the history of Tokyo Imperial University," writes former journalist, educator, and Education Minister Michio Nagai, "can be retraced through a whole series of earlier institutions, the first of which were founded in the Tokugawa [shogunal] Period. Its earliest begin-nings lie in the *Temmon-kata* [Astronomy Office], a *Bakufu* [shogunal gov-ernment] research institute for Dutch studies established in 1684 under the rule of the fifth *shogun*, Tsunayoshi."[3] The forerunner of the university, then, began as a government office for the import and study of "barbarian" knowledge; almost as if it were a foreign-intelligence agency. Though many reincarnations were traversed to reach the form of a modern, Western-style institute at Todai two centuries later, this imprint of official mission—learning things foreign, and learning from them—remains with the school and with the entire higher educational system to this day.

The reason is obvious enough. Meiji Japan, engulfed in the period of late colonialism in Asia, was a modern nation born scared—imbued first with the sense of crisis connected to its own survival, and later with the national purpose of employing modern knowledge as a tool for empire-building and colonial adventure of its own. "The early Imperial Universities devoted considerable attention to basic research after the pattern of higher education in the West," as Nagai puts it, "but they were not 'halls of learning' where truth was pursued for its own sake. At key points, the nature and purpose of research was prescribed by the state." Indeed, the very Imperial University Ordinance that created Todai itself as the country's first school of higher learning charged it with the task to "inquire into the mysteries of learning in accordance with the needs of the state."

The significance of this charge was not so much that the research accent fell on the state's pragmatic needs, which after all was quite natural, as that the whole institution was swept up in the state's scramble to "catch up" with the West: It was politicized by nationalism from the start. Todai was invested as a place where scholars would review as much as possible of all that passed in the West in governance, diplomacy, technology and science, agriculture and the arts of war, and economic and financial management. And then distill those learnings and advise the young Meiji leaders on just which ones would be useful to adopt for Japan's own modernization.

Any history of Japan recounts the speedy, energetic, and enormously successful adaptation of this wisdom of the West and testifies to, as scholar Ivan Hall, who is a long-time member of Japan's academic community and who has taught political science at some of Japan's most prestigious universities, put it in a conversation with the author, "one of the strengths of Japan: that it was not afraid to go out and 'pick the brains,' so to speak, of the rest of the world" to make those adaptations. (Before the formal proclamation of Tokyo Imperial University gave the institution its name, for example, the number of foreigners who actually held teaching posts in this, the nation's only school of higher learning, ranged to as high as two-thirds of the faculty.)

Indeed, the advisory role that native Imperial University teachers (the foreigners were gotten rid of as soon as possible) played in the government itself was probably at least as important as their roles as scholars. The purpose of Todai's *Hogaku-bu* (Law School) itself, points out scholar Byron Marshall, "was never meant merely to be the narrow study of jurisprudence for prospective lawyers"—a fact to be kept in mind when considering the omnipresence in Japan's government and economic power structure of Todai's *Hogaku-bu* grads today. "Rather, the study of law entailed the broadest study of comparative government, economic systems and social thought—what might somewhat anachronistically be termed the policy sciences or public administration."[4] Todai Law was from the start really a school of government and an academy of elites.

So from the very beginning Japan's first university was meant not merely to turn out scholars, or even professionals, but also men who would advise or *become* the government themselves. Its professors were (and are) civil servants. Indeed so powerful, and so prestigious was faculty appointment to Todai that, as early as the beginnings of the 1890s, just fourteen years after Todai's official founding, Marshall notes that a full "fifteen current or former Todai faculty members were named imperial appointees to the first House of Peers"; this was among the greatest honors the throne could bestow on commoners. Body and soul, the Tokyo Imperial University was an institute founded on service to the state: to legitimate it, to perpetuate it, and to strengthen it. Despite the changes in outward form of Japan's government and state apparatus, it still is.

The foundation of an entire new community of national and private schools, in fact, including those that would later become famous in their own right (Kyoto Imperial University [1897], Keio Gijuku, Hitotsubashi, Waseda), took place very much in the shadow of this precedent. Generations of ambitious young students looked to these schools as well, to find the same kind of propulsion to preeminence in the new nation through education and its validation of both credentials and of ambitions.

This volatile mixture of intents and ethics has led to the Japanese university's present spiritual illness. Far from being an ivory tower, it has pursued engagement with so many of the minute, nationalist purposes of the administrative elites, and become so intricately involved in the mundane purposes of its society's "personnel processing," that it is no longer really certain of what a university is supposed to be. And it has in the process sold so much of its soul to nationalism that the one thing it really was founded to accomplish—drawing and applying lessons from abroad—has become a talent now lost to the university. It cannot now even reform itself.

It would be, however, unjust and inaccurate to imply that all of Japanese higher education is simply formal and informal servitor to the state: While it may be true of national universities, nearly three-quarters of all Japan's universities and more than 80 percent of junior colleges are private. Nor would it be fair to imply that they are intellectually Philistine throughout: In the same work quoted above, Marshall points out that even the early Meiji state, preoccupied as it was with building a modern military and industry, devoted major parts of its education budget "to long-term investment in Western humanities, social sciences and theoretical natural sciences." Or, that scholarship is uniformly substandard: "Most of the highest-level technical research journals in Japan are abstracted in the international scholarly indexes, and very often the journals themselves are entirely in English," notes Dr. William Wetherall, a scholar resident in Japan whose work connects him to two government ministries, of the intellectual product of some of Japan's better universities and institutes. "These annual citations show just how influential certain work has been in the scientific world, where many Japanese have established reputations and their papers are held in regard," Wetherall told the author in an interview. (Not all of these scientists work within the university, however.)

Rather, it has been the concept that government should be the *controlling entity* in higher education—to this day, even private colleges must seek the accreditations and the direct permissions of the national government to so much as expand their campus by a single building or open a new faculty department—that has damaged it so badly. The public perception, not far removed from the reality, that government controls all these campuses and ratifies not only the academic but the social choices they make has crippled the world of higher education in three ways:

• It has inflicted the lifetime employment system on faculties, especially those of national universities, guaranteeing that mediocrity will become the professional standard of almost every one of them. Further, because of the history of the government's strong efforts to control campuses directly through budgeting stringencies, administrative guidance, and the disbursal of subsidies, it has raised the issue of "academic freedom" to an emotional pitch that clouds the substance of many critical issues and hides the incompetence or irresponsibility of many marginal teachers.

• It has subordinated the undergraduate education of the college and university to the process of public education. In effect, it ensures that the majority of students who arrive for their freshmen year on campuses not only here but all across the nation will come unprepared for college life. They will bring with them only long strings of useless entrance-exam results from rote-memorization contests over state-dictated curricula, little understanding of what a college-level discipline entails or promises, and no more deeply rooted goals for the four or two years ahead than to "get a good job." Once there, they will find teachers and a school administration largely indifferent not only to their academic choices but to their progress.

• It has allowed higher scholarship in the universities—the research mission —to languish, leaving huge gaps in the pure-sciences capabilities of the nation, and perhaps even imperiling a generation's worth of the social, policy, and internationalist change that Japan will need to find its new place peacefully in the world.

There is a fourth damage, beyond the campus, that this obsession with the national control of education has inflicted on the society. In the half-century since the end of the war, the primary and secondary educational, as well as the higher-education, systems' national purpose has been to turn out suitable candidates in sufficient quantities for every level of employment in the effort to rebuild, expand, and guide the economy. Because of this, and because Japan's social economy sanctified college entry alone—not real scholarship or creativity once there—as the worthiest moral purpose for Japanese youth, it came to be expected by employers that universities and colleges would produce humanities and social-sciences graduates who actually have few practical skills in the white-collar professions. In fact, as we shall see, this actually *suited* the corporations that hired them: organizations that wanted smart, proven team players rather than complex thinkers or independent individualists. With these employers' consent, a system grew up by which colleges and universities graduated whole classes of unfinished "generalists" from the sciences, humanities, and social sciences. Essentially business recruits, in other words, proved more capable at doing fast "takes" on material than at mastering a professional interest, and people who had showed mainly in their college years they could *nakayoshi*—make friends and get on well with others.

The employers recruiting them preferred to supply the finishing education —the true professional training—on-the-job, within the continuum of the lifetime employment system and among the people and the organizational units that would be "home" to the recruit for his whole career. This railroadlike connection, from entrance exam straight through college and into the lifelong job, helped as much as government control to damage the vitality of higher education in Japan.

With students arriving at college from high school with the equivalency almost of a bachelor of arts degree, achieved by their long hours in grade school, high school, and cram school preparing for entrance exams, and with very little demand from private enterprise for master's or doctoral graduates at the other end, the state found it could largely ignore what actually happened on the campuses. And, at the same time, it could get away with underfunding the campus's research mission, for which it had made itself largely responsible. Research in general (including for the most part developmental and applied) has passed largely into the hands of private enterprise, which after all was the best at turning it into real goods and competitive products—the end-targets of the superindustrialization of the nation and economy. And Japanese academic scholarship began to contract to a secondary stature, from which some academics fear it may recover only with the greatest difficulty. As recently as the fall of 1995, in fact, there were press reports that the Science Council of Japan was complaining loudly that the Japanese government still funds basic and "strategic" research at less than half the levels of the U.S. and French governments, when measured as percentages of gross national product.

The cost of this negation of the academic responsibilities of Japanese higher education has been great. Japan's expenditure on R&D in total, which rose by 50 percent in the five years from 1986 to 1991 alone, is producing an incommensurate return on investment: More than a third of the world's scientific and technical literature in 1991 was produced by Americans; only 8.5 percent by Japanese.[5] Not only that, but Japan is losing its brighter young stars of research to the frustrations and inefficiencies of the crippled, ossified graduate school structure. "The U.S. lures intellectuals from across the world and Europe's greatness hasn't yet diminished," in the words of Katsuhito Iwai, a highly regarded economic theorist who is a Todai graduate and professor, but who earned his own Ph.D. at MIT. "But the current Japanese system, on the other hand, is hampering a generation of creative talents."[6]

The resultant truth is that what the universities are engaged in most heavily today is nothing but the preservation of Japan's national labor economy as its "culture."

The Faculty

I first met Professor Kazutaka Kunimoto several hundred miles off the California coast, on an airliner returning him to Tokyo for the fall semester. He had spent a large part of the summer doing research on the economy of Mexico and the expected impact on it of the North American Free Trade Agreement, which is a subject very close to the interests of Japan's government bureaucrats and industrial captains alike. He had had a wonderful time, had learned much that was insightful—and had paid the expenses for the entire expedition out of his own pocket. He had no idea whether the material he had gathered would ever form part of his lectures to the graduates or undergraduates of his university, Meiji Gakuin Daigaku, but he had no regrets. "Meiji Gakuin is not a research school. It's an education school."

Going abroad for research at his own expense allowed him to slip the bonds of teaching for awhile to expand his own intellectual horizons. "There are some faculty members who do their own research with pocket money, and I am one. It's easier for me to go my own way on vacation time than to apply for a grant. I'll be going again on winter vacation. But every fifteen or twenty years, I *can* get a sabbatical," he laughed.[7]

Kunimoto's is a private school, and not only grant money but simple time for research is tight. "Even if I were to get a Fulbright research grant next year, I have to teach here. It's very difficult to get permission for that much leave time, because then some other teacher must compensate for my absence by handling my class load." With his own fund resources to finance his off-duty studies, Professor Kunimoto has little complaint—and he is officially free to travel anywhere in Japan for conferences and other short-term research work, even during class terms. But his situation illustrates just one of the strictures binding the world of the Japanese college faculty.

There are many other restrictions in the rigidly hierarchicalized academic world, cutting more deeply into the body of academia than many outsiders realize. The most damaging of these is the *koza,* or chair system of faculty organization. In the first years of Meiji, Japan's infant higher-education structure drew eclectically on the examples of many American and European university organizational schemes. But in 1893, seven years after the formal constitution of the University of Tokyo itself, German science and its global prestige were on the rise. And so the Imperial University system, anxious to absorb and harness only the world's best models, was invested with the German faculty organizational blueprint, the chair system. Among the former eight Imperial Universities where the chair system was emplaced,[8] it remains to this day.

Later national universities, and most of Japan's 384 private universities, use a course system rather than the chair in their faculties and departments, but the chair system has been pernicious in its effect on recruiting in the most prestigious of the nation's schools. It calls for a single, senior scholar to hold the post of full professor in each chair (there are several hundred at Todai), and each in effect is a small department, with one associate professor, and one or two research assistants, attached. Of course, there are many other appointed lecturers and visiting scholars at a school of Todai's size. But the major problem is that the chair is a system for, in Ivan Hall's words, "instruction in a given subject *up through* the doctoral level"[9] (emphasis added). In other words, each associate professor and research assistant is bound permanently to the full professor in the chair and can qualify to become full professor himself only with the permission of that professor.

What this amounts to in practice is a kind of academic primogeniture, with full professors of the nation's best schools grooming and promoting their own underlings to eventually replace them. This system is stultifying, and often damaging to the quality of faculty, because there is very little career transfer of teachers among universities and because professors at the national universities, as civil servants, occupy their chairs as lifetime employees. Their subordinates must wait for up to decades for the opportunity to succeed them—and those decades are often spent in intellectual sycophancy to the professor seated so comfortably in the chair above. Few professors want aggressive, creative young scholars as associates, who might show them up. "Usually professors would prefer less smart *deshi* [associates and research assistants]" is the wry comment of President Shigeo Minabe of the public University of Nagasaki at Sasebo. "In this way the professors can lead easy lives, without being criticized."[10]

Though the chair system formally commands only eight of the nation's top universities, the general underdevelopment of the graduate schools system throughout the universities has meant another misfortune for aspiring young academics: Grad schools are considered largely to be responsible for producing only more teachers, not advanced-level professionals. And for that reason they have been left under the jurisdiction of the main university faculties; there is in most cases no separate faculty for graduate school. Thus, most students have to look forward, no matter where they pursue graduate studies, to the same kind of stand-in-line subordination to whatever professors happen to have authority over their academic progress. As teaching-job placements after winning a degree are virtually the monopoly of the senior professors at most schools, who not only choose new junior colleagues from among the applicants to their own departments, but whose recommendations are needed no matter which school their own new graduates apply to for employment, few students dare to do anything but follow the exact directions—and intellectual predilections—of their professors.

"Existing universities tend to reproduce their faculty members" as a result, writes Minabe. This explains the large number of Todai professors who are also Todai alumni. And in many instances, it is common knowledge that "less brilliant graduates have been recruited by their own professors. The quality of the schools declines [so that] older professors can lead easy academic lives."

"Every student who reaches the level of graduate school," adds Wetherall, "must be aware of the politics within that faculty or school. The rules of the game sort of dictate that you are fairly low-key in your approach to what you're doing. Your rewards are from the professors. So there's a lot of self-selection going on, so that you end up with disproportionately fewer people who are really creative left over in the university." He means that the next generation of faculty will in all likelihood be composed of graduates whose principle demonstrated skill will be not having "shown up" or even disagreed with their teachers. "It's a self-selected group. They know what they're getting into." Those really bright students who do not want to play this game simply leave college and enter the world of work.

Even for students who do not replace their professors, but who are recommended by them to other schools, primary skills will not lie in educational trail-blazing. "In a notorious case at Keio University that I know of," says Professor Erich Berendt, who has been teaching at Chiba National

University for twenty years, "a core-curriculum English-language professor was a specialist in Chaucer: Middle English. So what he did was read Middle-English poetry to these kids in class. So you know what this does: They certainly don't learn much English."[11]

What, then, of the last traditional bulwark against this kind of professional malpractice: peer review? Professor Akimasa Mitsuta of Obirin University, a retired administrator from the Ministry of Education, Science, and Culture and former vice-president of the Japan Foundation, who has taught at university overseas, scoffs openly at the effectiveness of such review in a lifetime employment system, where professors all know they are highly likely to spend their entire careers with the same colleagues, in the same departments. "The *kyoju-kai* [faculty meeting] is the place where they meet to choose their peers, choose their supporters—for instance, faculty newcomers. So they are not the persons to evaluate each other. Because there cannot be [mutual] evaluation among a group of people who should live together for thirty or forty years. It comes through the lifetime employment system. It is particularly so in our national universities because the status of professors is protected by law—they are civil servants."[12]

"Today," says Professor Yoshiya Abe, a ranking professor of cultural studies at Kokukgakuin Daigaku and an experienced educational administrator who set up Japan's national University of the Air, "I know, out of slightly over 125,000 persons who are on the tenured track of faculties of universities in this country, those who are academically capable—that is, defined by the fact that in the past five years they have published either a book or more than one article in refereed international journals—[amount to] only about a quarter of the total."[13]

One great reason, though it goes largely unremarked, why this power to paralyze faculty renewal asserts itself again and again lies beyond the realm of factional politics or bureaucratic self-aggrandizement of those professors who hold "the ring." It is, perversely, a way of asserting scholastic freedom. When the Occupation realigned Japan's educational system after the war, great stress was laid upon academic freedom in the universities and colleges. This was held to be the most important tool of all for accomplishing what the American reformers thought was the most important job of higher education: reforming the Japanese into individualists and democrats. The liberal course of studies was prescribed as the priority for universities, to the detriment even of academic research. And the teachers were eventually secured in two more-or-less absolute "scholastic liberties": the freedom to teach whatever they wanted, and the freedom to select whomever they wanted to fill the vacancies on their faculties. (This last prerogative is formally subordinate to approval by the Education Ministry in the case of national schools, but in practice whatever the faculties decide is rubber-stamped.) What more, an observer might ask, could any professor ask of his job—aside from the practical assurance of lifelong employment security, which is also guaranteed?

But there was more to the Occupation structure than that. The reforms also removed from the national universities the power to handle their own budgetary affairs and gave it to the Education Ministry. The American reformers did not see that, as former Education Minister Nagai points out, "making decisions regarding the allotment and use of this enormous budget is tantamount to determining the basic direction of university education and research." Meetings of the faculties can discuss and advise on the question of the budget with an eye to its impact on the scholarly course the university steers, but in the end "they do not participate at all in determining the total budget allotments.

"Under present conditions," as Nagai sums up, "it is virtually impossible for [national] universities to develop five- or ten-year plans based on firm financial calculations." The university *community,* in other words, is not master of its own fate. This means virtually all funding for research, and certainly for any expansion in the national system, comes directly at the pleasure of the government. In the private universities, even when funding does not come from government subsidy, government *permission* for expansion or major change is requisite. As a 1992 issue of the respected *Nature* magazine put it, "every academic employee's pay-cheque [in the national system] is written by Monbusho (the Education Ministry), not by the university. That practice symbolizes not just the dependence of the national universities on Monbusho, but their national obligations."[14]

This, and other powers Monbusho exercises over the private universities as well, have naturally triggered deep rancor within the schools toward government controls and made it all the more certain that the faculties will jealously guard the three prerogatives left to them—freedom of curriculum, of choice of their own research topics, and of recruitment—against any reform proposed, much less imposed, by the government. "As I got more and more involved in administrative work and university committees," says a young professor in the Todai undergraduate school who took up his post not long ago after earning a doctorate in the United States, "I began to realize how Monbusho controls *everything,* except for curriculum. I resent it. And many of my colleagues do as well."[15]

The result is a legacy of bad will that leaves an atmosphere of suspicion around every reform the ministry suggests—and a countervailing, egoistical stubbornness among the senior academics to protect their prerogatives above all. As a result, little change ever sinks through to the foundations of the school, the departments.

The career immobility within the Japanese academic world—the essentially frozen nature of the faculty's universe—is the final great weight compressing its intellectual horizons. Even in private schools, with no connection to the civil service, professors tend to stay their entire careers. At a junior-senior campus of seven thousand students, Meiji Gakuin Daigaku, Professor Kunimoto says he sees no more than one of his colleagues in every three or four years resign to join another university. Normally only younger scholars who have taken their degrees from the prestige universities, and who may "park" themselves in a teaching job at a lower-ranked school while waiting for a vacancy to open up at their alma maters, will look forward to the job mobility that can recall them to the bosoms of their original faculties. "Nepotism is the recruiting system of the professors," admits Abe. "It's a pity, but indeed, somebody who retires will designate his disciple, who is inferior in caliber. This is a practical rule."

Another, equally important hope for faculty rejuvenation and revivification in this era of Japan's proclaimed "internationalization," the hiring of foreign professors at Japanese universities, also seems to have stalled. In 1982 laws were passed allowing national universities to hire full-time foreign scholars, acknowledging them as government employees but only on fixed-term, renewable-contract bases (though these were purportedly renewable indefinitely, to retirement age). Ten years later, according to a report published in the Asahi Evening News, only 201 full-time non-Japanese teaching staff members were numbered among the 37,000 professors, associate professors, and lecturers in the national system—representing just 0.5 percent of the total.[16] Forty-five national universities and research institutes had no foreigners at all as full-time staff; they had only a smattering of non-Japanese lecturers working on one-year contracts signed with the individual schools. In the 384 private universities, meanwhile, the record was not much better: 1,780 of the 67,000 teachers, or about 2.7 percent, were not Japanese nationals. (By comparison, there are about 7,000 Japanese teachers now employed in the American higher education system, according to one source.)

The Japanese university is simply not a competitive world marketplace of ideas. To meet the stated goals of "internationalization," universities such as Todai (where only thirteen non-Japanese professors were on staff as of 1992) have taken on, instead of foreign scholars, Japanese academics who have completed at least some of their graduate work overseas. "They are more outspoken. They are more straightforward. They have overseas contacts, and they do not care about their domestic status" is the evaluation of one Education Ministry veteran of these convenient "returnees." Are they not at least a small breath of fresh air in Todai's stuffy corridors? Yes, he admits—and for that very reason they are not being allowed by their colleagues into the mainstreams of their own faculties.

In formal academic structures both on-campus and off-campus, the aversion to "outsiders," especially non-Japanese, continues to hold sway. Even at the higher pinnacles of research: "From the point of view of whether this place is closed to foreigners," summarized one Rochester University scholar attached temporarily to a Japanese research project a few years ago at the National Laboratory for High Energy Physics, "this place is closed to foreigners."[17]

"The truth is," acknowledged Takamitsu Sawa, a Kyoto University economics professor in a newspaper column in the late 1980s, "unlike other enterprises, Japanese higher learning remains a world untouched by change and where the need for competition is largely ignored. To this day, the Japanese management principle of 'harmony above all else' rules supreme in these citadels. Their rigid recruitment and promotion policies reflect as much."[18]

The Students

"In Japan," opined Henry Rosovsky, former dean of the Faculty of Arts and Sciences at Harvard University not long ago, "even in the most prestigious institutions, students in the humanities and social sciences can and often do treat college as a three-year vacation; tennis appears to be the favorite 'major.' "[19]

That certainly is the appearance. Undergrad students cut classes with abandon; drop courses at a whim; and spend far more time in club and social activities and even in part-time jobs than in study—even in the best schools; even at Todai. Everyone acknowledges it; everyone disparages it. "The implication" of a set of comparative studies of higher education conducted by Martin Bronfenbrenner, bluntly affirms the Japanese university president who cited them, "is that the average Japanese student does not learn anything in the time period he spends in college or in graduate school."[20]

And almost every outsider is mystified by it. How could Japanese students, these small *samurai* of their nation's march to economic and productive preeminence, be allowed—or even allow themselves—to waste what are likely the four most seminal years in all their formal educational lives?

Former Education Minister Michio Nagai sees the same phenomenon from a different perspective. "Under circumstances in which the life of research is so circumscribed, the tendency toward low-quality general education and lackluster lectures becomes difficult to avoid. The result is a loss of vitality in the lives of students as well as teachers, and a rise in the numbers of students who absent themselves from classes. *The intellect is not developed in Japanese universities, it is worn down*" (emphasis added).[21] The answer, then, is that these are not at all the most seminal years of formal education for most Japanese.

The national educational system has already put these students through their most important training. They come to campus with the formal intent to expand their knowledge of the world (an intent expressed rather more by the university than by the student), but the twelve years of elementary, middle, and senior high school have already injected into them a world view and an intellectual arsenal sufficient to the accomplishments society expects of them: join a work group, learn its tasks and mores, and above all other purposes sacrifice yourself to its success.

It is a willful deception that the Japanese higher education system imparts, as was intended by its reform under the U.S. Occupation, a "liberal arts" grounding, a classical humanist finish to the emerging adult, or a loyalty to pluralist democratic values among its students. While some students may gain some appreciation for some of those values, it would in the general sense be impossible for universities to do that because the rigors and the limited skeins of academic disciplines that are pounded into these very students in the process of their trying to survive the ever-winnowing examinations on the way to college permits them little or no attention to other subjects of either academic or social interest.

As such subjects would be meaningless for students struggling to get into college—they are not on the tests, and thus no time could be spared for them—they remain largely foreign and insignificant on the college and university campuses. Subjects such as the study of Descartes, Hume, and Hegel, appreciation of Western opera, and the doctrinal roots of the religions of South Asia are indeed taught here. But virtually none of the students will have a background of exposure to or interest in either them, or the larger universes of political values or aesthetics they have helped form. And so they will have little meaning. Less conventional, still more experimental disciplines such as the emergent ecological sciences and studies of political ethnicism are even less familiar, and thus colleges do not invest their precious funds in developing departments and faculty: Part-time lecturers can treat them if necessary, moving along with the trends and fads of the day in "survey" fashion.

All these students will have considered themselves to have already passed the most pressing "final." That is, their mere acceptance into college guarantees, in the tradition of at least two living generations, access to good or at the very least acceptable white-collar employment. They know that their corporate recruiters will pay little attention at the end of four years to grade-point averages because the recruiters will know that academic standards have so differentiated, if not collapsed, from college to college, faculty to faculty and teacher to teacher as to be almost meaningless: Grade inflation is the normal condition. I have met at least one professor who claims the university he taught at made it plain that he was not too fail *any* student, no matter how bad the academic performance. Students (excepting those in the sciences and technologies, which are examined more closely) do not have to study more than a bare modicum to complete their degrees.

Because these same students know they will be hired, but not by whom, and because they have never been faced with any choices except which schools to try to gain entrance to, very few will come to the campus with any chosen profession in mind, or even with any specific desires about what to do with their lives. They will all be simply preparing, they know, for the "generalist" job-entry track, in which their employers will decide with what skills they will earn their livings. Facing no graduate schools, there is no particular incentive to master anything—and thus no professional codes of ethics to imbibe along the way, either.

Japan, far from being a nation of political activism, presents students who have been largely out of touch with the analytical meanings of current events during their high school years with no ethical dilemmas. AIDS, the environment, homelessness, the aging of the population, the spread of nuclear weapons, the future of Japan on the world stage: None of these are their problems. A very large number, in fact, would likely be unaware even that their nation faces important choices in the world. Realistically, why would such students have to compete academically for *anything*?

And if they have little interest in real work in their courses, why should their teachers hold either the students, or they themselves, to tough academic standards? In introductory and lecture courses that range from hundreds up to a thousand students per class, what intellectual captivation, other than personal curiosity, could bind them to the disciplinary rigors of scholasticism?

Of course, it is grossly unfair to brand all students, all schools, and all their teachers under such a clumsy rubric. The fact is that since the postwar period, the Ministry of Education has set the standards for coursework to be completed in the progress toward a bachelor's degree. In line with the classical liberal-arts system created under Occupation authority, 48 of the 124 credits required for graduation fell into the murky world of "general education": the core curriculum, offered in the first two years on campus. Opposite this general, or *kyoyo,* curriculum is the *senmon,* or specialist, courses that the students are eligible to take in the final two years.

While general education has deteriorated through a sort of curricular aimlessness into the large, survey courses and modern-language requirements that everyone is anxious to miss, it is most often in *senmon* where any real work is done. And it should be noted that it is done, by students and teachers alike, in some cases. Erich Berendt, the professor at Chiba National University, gives seminars and small classes in linguistics in which his students—writing their papers in English—turn in work "better in many cases than an American master's degree candidate."[22] Steve Creighton, an economics Ph.D. candidate at Todai with a background in engineering, says that engineer undergrads at his school are by their second year of college "doing stuff in the lab that you'd expect of doctoral students in the United States."[23] Dr. Ivan Hall is amazed at the amount of study some students will invest—strictly on their own time—in *kenkyu-kai* (research clubs), teaching themselves subjects they are personally interested in and giving, in campus festivals, display-presentations of their results that literally fill the walls of classrooms. These are not the easy, save-the-rainforest types of topics, but reach into such delicate subjects as the future of the imperial system, says Hall.[24] In some Todai Law School seminars, students and teachers alike pursue levels of true scholastic excellence and open exchanges of opinion.

Japanese students do know how to study; professors do know how to both do research and teach. It is just that they are seldom given a reason to do so by their schools.

In fact the faith, or lack of it, that teachers have in their charges may be more the reason students do so little with their college time than the inclinations of the students themselves. One professor at a private university, after explaining that his school admits freshmen who are "not good students— not bad ones, but just not very good ones" and laments that they do not study enough, qualifies the majority of these same students as those who "will never be leaders. Just very good staff. We don't train them to be leaders, but we give them training that will prepare them to become good staff." This assumption of the fate of the students being settled by their having won admission to an elite or to only a non-elite school is damning, because among the latter it destroys feelings of responsibility for the society —among those, that is, who are given to know they will never be in positions to lead it anyway. If, in any school, Japanese professors don't *demand* the best their students can give, how can these students be asked to *give* their best—enough to prepare themselves to become "leaders"? The elite-led, socioeconomic regimentation of the entire society permeates even the philosophies of university campuses. These are not individualists with independent human values, or liberal humanists, who are being turned out: They are parts of a machine, and they know it. Alienation affects many of them. As some teachers drone repetitiously from lecture notes drawn up years before, or read verbatim from textbooks, frustrated new students disappear from campuses for days, even weeks. It strikes even the upperclassmen—Berendt tells of students in each semester, "at least one or two kids out of every class, who are going into psychiatric help. I'm not talking about little emotional things, just drifting off; these kids are going into care, really shattered."

And now looms what could be the meanest fate of all for them: Increasingly these liberal-arts and social sciences students are being turned into parts that may simply no longer be needed. As industries feel the rising pressures of the collapse of Japan's economic bubble and face the facts that the heady days of Japan's closed economy, self-ratcheting growth, and open mercantilism are ending, the day of the generalist may well be too. Corporations have cut back on their hiring: Japan's major corporations were planning drastic recruiting reductions of over 15 percent for males, just under 28 percent for females, for the 1995 fiscal year alone.[25] And when they do hire, they are beginning to show awareness of the need not for generalists but for specialists, prepared to face a new future of new demands in communities where Japan and its corporations will be held accountable for more than merchandising.

The costs to a family of raising and sending a child all the way through school from first grade to a four-year college degree, reported one published study, total nearly $200,000—or up to half a million dollars, in the case of a medical student going all the way to a license via private schools.[26] The average outlay for a college student living away from home comes to more than $20,000 a year; and some parents with offspring in prestige private universities are paying 35 percent or more of their annual incomes to see a single son or daughter through college.

Even now, "it doesn't pay off," in the words of Dr. Masao Miyamoto, a psychiatrist who was formerly an official in the Ministry of Health and Welfare and who finished his own professional training in America. "Not in terms of the quality of life it gives you in the future."[27] The average lifetime total-income expectation of a university graduate in Japan, a country where average home prices now routinely exceed a half-million dollars, is less than two million dollars. The government itself, in a recent White Paper on Science and Technology[28] surveying the loss of young people's interest in research careers, was forced to admit that even "typical occupations in the fields of science and technology are widely perceived to receive inadequate financial benefits to compensate for their hardship required to reach such positions." Even for the kind of jobs that *will* demand candidates in the future, in other words, Japanese students in general have no interest because there is nothing they offer to repay the work required to get them.

Worse than that, the downsizing of the corporation—and still worse, the gradual dismantlement of the lifetime employment and seniority career systems—may be coming to Japan. The social contract could well be breaking. The increased value of the yen puts all of the world's resource markets —labor (both skilled and unskilled), raw materials, land, energy, transportation —on bargain sale to Japanese, who are responding with a mass transposition of manufacturing capital—of manufacturing and even management jobs—to Asia and the West. Major Japanese corporations are already eliminating white-collar job slots for recruits by the thousands, and calculations that contemplate possible shortages of jobs in the millions by the end of this decade, if premature, are already beginning to circulate. The idea that just getting into college is all one needs for affluence, social rank, and security that lasts a lifetime may already be dying.

Involuntary job mobility is undoubtedly headed toward an upswing. The corporations are clamoring for more specialists of the kind that only legitimate graduate schools doing real research can turn out. For the young man with the meaningless four-year degree in economics, or the young woman with the B.A. in English literature, there may no longer be available the automatic place for which the universities are still busily preparing them.

"I suspect," wrote economist Robert Heilbroner of the present-day workings and woes of the American economy, "that we will not discover the way out of the present impasse until we find an economics that projects a moral vision along with a technical diagnosis comparable in its power to that of the [Keynesian] General Theory in the mid-1930s."[29] A paraphrase could well apply to Japanese academe: No solution to what colleges should prepare their students for will be found until there emerges a valid concept of *citizenship* in society, positing a morality that transcends the all-powerful vision of Japan as simply an economy converting human beings into "personnel resources."

The Curriculum

"It is said by some," recently wrote Dr. Junichi Nishizawa, president of Tohoku National University and one of Japan's most respected scientists, "that the [scientific] theories emerging from Japan are not necessarily original. Many of them are said to be improved and expanded versions of those published abroad. This is not in the direction of real internationalization."[30]

Nor is it, however understated, in the direction of true scholarship. A recent report of the Japan Economic Institute, titled "Japan as Number Three," makes the rather alarming case that the country's failure to invest sufficiently or intelligently in basic scientific research—the conduct of which is one of the primary functions of graduate schools—may begin before long to seriously cripple the nation all by itself. Pointing out that Japan has long since caught up with the rest of the world, that the rest of the world is now in fact in the process of catching up with Japan's innovations, such as its state-of-the-art quality and cost-control manufacturing systems, the report notes that there is a danger to Japan of falling returns on capital invested simply in more manufacturing capacity. "Accumulating evidence suggests that science and research are key activities that keep the returns to investment from falling to zero. Although the case is by no means fully proved, studies of the American economy show that private R&D has a dollar-for-dollar impact on productivity that is several times greater than corporate investment in plant and equipment. Even more important, *the returns to basic research are several times higher than to applied research*" (emphasis added), the forte of the Japanese economy.

"A little over fourteen percent of American R&D is classified as basic research compared with slightly under thirteen percent in Japan. Although these shares are quite similar, the Japanese definition includes much more applied work than is allowed by the American definition." While the easy flows of cash prevalent in the years of Japan's bubble economy in the late 1980s encouraged companies to sink R&D funding into projects with low projected capital returns, they are now paying a higher price for having ignored the imperatives to produce more real science, the report implies. "The evidence clearly suggests that the Japanese economy may be suffering [relatively speaking] from weakness in research and science. . . . Stated government policy has placed budgetary priority on these areas for several years, but Tokyo and the relevant institutional structures appear to be making little overall progress." This, among many others, has been one of the reasons that "the average productivity of Japan's market economy [excluding government and health outlays] is 60 percent of the American level; [while] manufacturing performs at the 80 percent level."[31]

Without the engines to produce more and better-quality raw science and technological innovation that truly heighten productivity, in other words—the major product of a first-class graduate-school community—Japan's dysfunctional higher-education system may even contribute to, in the report's words, "the failure to promote a more open, competitive, and productive Japan, [which] most likely would have equally profound political effects, as

Japan could slip to number three economic power (behind the United States and the People's Republic of China) . . . or even lower."

But Japan's graduate-school system is in a downward spiral, and though the Ministry of Education, by all reports, is hard at work trying to reverse that spiral, no one is certain it can be reversed. The share of Japanese researchers working in universities, as opposed to research institutions and corporations, has actually fallen by 5 percent over the past decade. "The survival of Japan's graduate school system in the next century is in jeopardy" is the way a Tokyo journalist began his report on the situation. "Thus so is the nation's leading edge in high technology." The proportion, he explained, of graduate students in universities is 4.8 percent in Japan, compared with 33.5 percent in Britain, 20.7 percent in France and 15.6 percent in the United States.[32]

Even allowing for different national ratios of student populations, and different systems of graduate studies, only 8 Japanese out of every 10,000 have graduate-school experience, compared to 71 in the United States. Some of the reasons are already plain.

• The "official" accent in higher education since the Occupation reforms has been on democratic reform and imbuing a humanistic liberal tradition, rather than on professional instruction. As we have seen, this purpose has long since largely degenerated (with some exceptions, such as medicine) into a system of mass production of nonspecialized, but simply university-"credentialed," pools of general careerists quite happy to allow a future employer to select and provide training for whatever professional specialties the enterprise may require.

• The ossified faculty structures have actually discouraged any but, for the most part, those students intent on themselves becoming academics from hanging on for higher degrees. Coupled with this is the fact that precipitous drop in the number of eighteen-year-old aspirants for college entrance (the total of Japanese eighteen-year-olds will fall by a quarter between 1992 and 2000) means that the demand outlook for future college teachers is clouded at best. Many private colleges are in fact simply facing eventual closure.

• The nation's businesses and industries, accepting the basic situation, have grown to prefer recruiting only four-year graduates; meaning those who stay on in school with professional hopes face uncertain futures.

• The government has left graduate studies largely underfunded, believing that the most important research work would be done in corporations. From 1983 to 1991, the annual government budget increases to schools for science and research have averaged only 5 percent a year. Private schools, for the most part more attuned to humanities and social sciences in their curricula, have large funding problems of their own in trying to finance modern research laboratories, first-class libraries, and so on.

Now, the results are showing: Applications for graduate school spaces in the sciences and engineering are falling at both national and private universities. Interest in science and technology among young people is likewise declining sharply. And not only are "many of the brilliant and brightest students going to companies instead of staying in the postgraduate levels," in the words of Professor Susumu Yamakage of Todai,[33] but a lot are heading to America and elsewhere for their advanced degrees. Japan still has about as many engineers as does the entire United States, with only half America's population. But no one is sure how many are really producing advanced science, of the kind that could be extracted and referenced in international journals, and how many are simply striving to produce better toasters and TVs for their manufacturer-employers. The odds are that the overwhelming majority are in the latter category.

All of this, especially in the sciences, has a progressively synergistic effect on the overall weakness of the nation's basic-research posture. Understanding why this is so requires that we consider just how pure science really works. It does not work, regrettably for Japan, in a series of strategic programs supervised by team managers to achieve clear-cut goals targeted by groups. Science, rather, goes on through an unending assortment of experiments, carried on both in large scale and small, across a vast global community. No one knows what the results of these experiments will be. The majority in fact are failures. But equally, no one knows what other, perhaps unforeseen, wisdom is gleaned, and how these unending, often dead-end explorations will inspire some researcher somewhere, young or old, to try something completely new (or very similar) that someday leads to a groundbreaking success. Basic research, then, is a pyramid structure in any society, with the thousands of experiments and activities going on resting on a foundation not only of money and equipment, but on large numbers of research assistants to drive the work forward—precisely the kind of staff produced by graduate schools. The broader and stronger the research efforts, the more graduate schools and graduates needed to assure adequate pools of competent scientists.

This can be achieved, of course, only if graduate schools have significant economic support, both from government and industry, to finance real, ambitious science within the schools themselves, and, even more important, if young researchers are permitted the freedom by older professors to branch out and pursue their own creative projects, of the kind where true discovery and insight surfaces. For these are the real places where break-throughs are made.

Without the resources and the atmosphere of freedom—both largely lacking in Japanese graduate schools—a "critical mass" of competent sup-port workers, *and* a number of proven innovators and successful scientific pathbreakers to act as leaders, will not be produced. This in turn means that few truly important projects and programs, capable of attracting a similar, international core of high-caliber scientific innovators interested in doing new work (and, not incidentally, in advancing their own careers) in partnership, will be generated. Also, if the civil-service wage structure of Japanese national academia pays these foreign scientists so little as not to attract them in the material sense either, then there is nothing with which to lure a first-class group of international talents to work together. Science today may be large-scale, requiring equipment and resources in the hun-dreds of millions of dollars, or it may be small-scale, requiring little more than access to a good research library. But in either venue, science has advanced so far today that most progress now can come only internation-ally, and if science cannot be internationalized in Japan, it cannot achieve much success.

As a result, Nobel laureates and other recognized giants of research are neither produced in Japan, nor attracted to work there. This means that younger, aspiring scientists who might be lured from abroad, as well as those produced in Japan, can get no opportunity to work with or learn from them. In fact, the truly good scientific candidates Japan is able to produce will all want to go overseas, to work in such company. That is precisely what two of Japan's Nobel laureates in science, Susumu Tonegawa and Leo Esaki, had to do to win their prizes.

One way of putting Japan's dilemma might be to say that bureaucrats interfere with—because at the institutional level the bureaucrats ultimately budget so much of—the direction, extent, and goals of pure science. Dr. Masao Miyamoto of the Ministry of Health and Welfare puts it into context succinctly. "Japanese governmental research is divided into two categories. One category is where funding is given to qualified scientists by the Minis-try of Education or the Science and Technology Agency with no strings attached. The second category, which you will find in the Ministry of Health and Welfare, the Ministry of International Trade and Industry, and the Ministry of Agriculture, Forestry, and Fisheries is where a certain goal is set by the bureaucrats and then scientists are chosen who will be able to reach this goal. In this research category the scientists cannot change the goal that has already been set.

"This second category is perhaps a clue as to why the Japanese have become a major economic power in the world. . . . This approach can be extremely effective, particularly when you view Japan as a huge corporation which has the aim of expanding its influence and power. [But] the drawback of this system is that it does not permit the fostering of independent scientific projects, nor does it encourage scientists to develop their own creativity, since major funds will only be invested in those projects designed by the bureaucrats, based on group consensus."

There certainly are, then, "strings attached" in the former category as well as the second: the obvious underfunding of general science in the graduate schools, as priorities go to national purposes, is one of the strings; the national focus of resources outside the schools on science projects that deliver strategic economic goals for the power elites is a second. And the resultant failure to foster a Japanese scientific *community,* anchored in the values of independence and genuine creativity, with its own leadership and its own diplomacy of international intercourse and cooperation, is a third.

On the business side of research, meanwhile, the celebrated R&D outlays the corporations make also hinder the formation of a true scientific community, because almost all their research is based on the development of competitive products. Scientists they employ necessarily do much of their work in isolation from their colleagues at other companies, with whom they dare not share their commercially valuable findings. This is true of corporations all over the world. But in Japan, where universities might serve as a neutral meeting ground to discuss pure research (not a very great deal of which goes on in Japanese corporations anyway), or might profit by contracting to conduct some of that research for corporations, the perennial underfunding and understaffing makes them a very unattractive resource for industries interested only in the cutting edge and in getting to market quickest with the product.

A still more disturbing fact about Japan's scientific dilemma is that using science merely as a competitive commercial weapon actually increases the danger that the whole national economic strategy itself will founder. Money taken from pure research and spent for development, just to hasten products into the marketplace, is money in a sense stolen from the future, as seen in the study mentioned above. A developmental R&D philosophy, accenting production of salable products to earn foreign capital, may be an economically excellent one for a developing nation, but is ultimately impoverishing for an advanced nation. It means that, in a sense, all of Japan's achievement as a productivity-based socioeconomy is now riding on a failing system of diminishing returns on R&D investment on the old paradigm that worked so well *in the past.*

The result is what Dr. Junichi Nishizawa, of Tohoku University, alluded to: that Japan is forever forced to import real research achievements produced elsewhere and modify them for application at home. This obviously leads to tensions, not only political but among researchers themselves. "Remember, JETRO [Japan External Trade Organization] holds a meeting every six months here on the West Coast for every Japanese scholar working in California," relates Professor Chalmers Johnson, the American scholar who is president of the Japan Policy Research Institute and author of the major policy history study *MITI and the Japanese Miracle* (1982), "to learn from them what's going on at Stanford, what's going on at San José State, what's going on at Berkeley. I've known of many people who have gone to these meetings, some deeply irritated by it on grounds it is presumed that just because you're a Japanese citizen, if you're going to study in America it is your obligation to go to the government and tell them what you're up to."[34]

But Japanese education now has so badly lagged in fundamental research and needs such huge investments and such enormous reforms (reforms that demand removing not only the political ossifications of lifetime-employee university faculties and the policy dictates of national bureaucrats, but reorienting many universities away from the undergraduate teaching mission toward the independent research mission) to catch up that many fear it will never happen. Of course Japanese researchers will continue to turn out outstanding results in some sectors of the sciences and will also continue to do brilliant work in research settings abroad. But a broad and balanced national research base that can expand to meet challenges in any direction may never be erected.

It is not only in the sciences that the underdeveloped state of research on Japan's campuses may be ultimately endangering the society. Far worse damage may lie in the cultural and national chauvinism that the university's intellectual weaknesses fail to erase from the assumptions of Japan's young adult elites. As much faith as the society puts in them, the universities are not preparing Japanese leadership elites to guide their country through its impending emergence into the "real world."

Where is that real world? Deutsche Bank economist Kenneth Courtis sketches its boundaries when he points to the significance of the new trend toward regional economic integration now under way in Asia. Japan (until 1995, when the yen experienced upward and downward swings), has been in the early 1990s earning capital surpluses at roughly twice the rate of the 1980s—if continued at that rate, he estimates, the country could accrue more than a trillion dollars in surplus by 2000. Tens of billions of dollars per year of that surplus are flowing into direct investments in Asia, which itself will represent a quarter of the world's economy by decade's end. Not just Japan, but other nations in Asia as well are strengthening the resultant transborder economic networks along the western Pacific rim with capital investments of their own in each other's territories.

"The increasing integration of the region," concludes Courtis, "is set to give to Asia's new economic weight a force, coherence and structure that will change and profoundly influence not only the global balance of economic power but also the international balance of political power."[35]

He is saying, in other words, that a new, vast theater of Asian political and economic interaction is being built. And it will need directors—directors capable not only of publicly, willingly assuming the mantle of leadership but of guiding and influencing events and building open markets in a way that will keep positive, progressive growth on track, and danger from the inevitable conflicts and crises under control. As Asia's richest, most internationally active nation, Japan simply must contribute to meeting this demand for leadership. And as Shoichiro Toyoda, the then-chairman of Keidanren, pointed out in his inaugural address to the foreign press, "nations also expect Japan to speak up for Asian interests in dealings with North America and Europe."

Japan, whose only real diplomatic philosophy has for half a century been focused almost wholly on maintaining a workable balance with its global sponsor, America, has few leaders and even fewer national credentials qualifying it to assume that leadership. It is just not ready, and it is not getting ready. In view of its ever-present trade troubles with America, it will soon not even be able to fulfill Toyoda's proposed, ultimately self-serving role as a "spokesman" to the West. As both its interests and its vulnerabilities now spread exponentially throughout Asia, and as a huge historical liability of its unresolved attitude toward its responsibilities for and growing from the Pacific War continues to color its relations with such important neighbors as the two Koreas and China, Japan is facing a crucial change in political epochs. Typically, it is either revolutions or universities that prepare new leadership generations to guide nations through such monumental changes of course. Japan, for all its changes, has not had anything approaching a legitimate "revolution" since the days of Meiji. So almost all demand for the fresh thinking about the future now falls upon the shoulders of its universities and finds them unprepared.

Graduate schools in the humanities and social sciences, repressed by their weak professoriates into neurasthenic centers of circumscribed book learning and arenas of ferocious careerism, have developed no globally or regionally outstanding centers for applied international research into the social sciences, area policy studies, diplomacy and international relations, communications, or developmental and economic environmental studies. There is a strong, almost frantic, effort now under way at the Ministry of Education to push universities to foster such graduate studies, and the biggest schools, such as Todai, find themselves struggling to respond. But what one member of the ministry's *daigaku shingikai* (university council) involved in this effort calls the "parochial system" of the present Japanese faculty chair is an enormous roadblock; so much so that, he admitted in a 1995 interview, that "Japanese universities are facing a very serious revolution" of their own.

Indeed the ministry is not blind to this, and would like to see a revolution on the campuses of the national universities, or at least on some of them. But, ironically, the controls that have been so finely divided, apportioned, and monopolized over half a century prevent real revolution from arising at the only source it legitimately can: the school itself. Universities are trapped in their own systems of lifetime employment and the jealously guarded prerogatives of internal curriculum and recruitment selection.

Thus even their best students go on graduating in the blithe beliefs that "Japan is a small country, with not much wealth or influence in the world" and that the warp and woof of larger events in that world are largely beyond its control or concern. Elites educated to this unreal polity cannot introduce new thinking or new convictions in the ministries or even in the corporations they are meant to command; elites so clothed in this national insularity are about to lead their country down the road to collisions for which it is wholly unprepared. Only that handful, from academia, government, or industry, who have been or are subsequently sent to take advanced degrees abroad will find the necessary balance of perceptions to understand Japan's real position in the world.

But it is precisely because they have those different perceptions that, on their return, they are largely ignored by their seniors and peers alike, when they try to promote change from below. This explains the continuing fear of the outside, engendered by generation after generation of graduates from the same neighborhoods of ignorance.

The Ivory Tower?

To say that the Japanese university is disconnected from its responsibilities —of research, of fostering individual creativity, of preparing realistically the next generation of leaders of the society—is another way of saying that it has become an extreme, almost grotesque form of an ivory tower: cut off not only from everyday reality but from its own raison d'être. It speaks only to itself.

One man who would not disagree with this characterization of the Japanese ivory tower is Akimasa Mitsuta, a retired bureau chief of the Education Ministry and a former vice-president of the Japan Foundation who has been invited to teach at the University of California at San Diego. "Not only universities are ivory towers in this society," he explains. "Each organization, each government ministry, each unit of Japanese society is an ivory tower. They do not have a connection with the outside world in the true sense, as in the United States. It comes with the lifetime employment system: The focus of each such employee is not on the outside of his organization but on the inside. Each organization is its own terminus; the most important thing is how to develop good relations with bosses and subordinates within. So it is the institutional character—but not only of the university—to be self-centered. It is just particularly so in our national universities, because the status of the professors are protected by law."[36]

Mitsuta has had his own run-ins with the ivory towers of the national universities in his career and faced his own frustrations in trying to get them to change. But his point—the similarity of dynamics between the university and the mainstream Japanese organization in business and government—is not about stubbornness or even pride. It is about power. Japanese compete individually for advancement and influence, for power, within an arena composed of the organization itself, not by what they accomplish in the outside, or even in the professional, world.

That these are the survival imperatives of the university professor makes academic independence, achievement, and discovery in too many cases a secondary consideration to the jockeying for better position. This in turn has made it easy for the elite power establishments outside the campus to "capture" the prestige of the university for their own narrow purposes, by capturing the ambitions of the professors themselves.

Aside from the teaching itself, there are only three acceptable "outlets" for the professional research activities of the Japanese academic. One, of course, is publication in books or learned journals. These range from respected reviews in their fields to simple, intradepartmental bulletins for which much of the submissions are puerile and of low quality. In these fora, academics naturally speak only to other academics.

A second outlet is the production of commentary for, or the appearance in, the mass media. Op-ed pieces, columns, and essays produced by academics appear regularly in newspapers and weekly and monthly journals that range from the popular to the intellectual. Commentary from professors on the topics addressed by everything from documentaries to daily news lends credence and gloss, as they do in the West, to the magazines', newspapers', television or radio stations' reportorial efforts, if not always to their depth or accuracy.

These forays into the public world are seldom expositions of scholarship or the platforms for expressions of truly revolutionary ideas. "I think [their effect is] mainly in creating a mood" is the way a senior scholar and specialist in international relations puts it. "The trouble with these people who do write what we'd call op-ed pieces [is that] they tend to write them on a regular basis for a particular paper, where the paper has a certain line, [or] the group they are writing with has a certain line, and they themselves become so committed to their own line they just find it hard to change." The intellectual factionalism of the faculty, in other words, tends to be what is communicated to the world outside. "There isn't much hard criticism. Or, it's criticism of the things that particular paper likes to criticize. It's not really a dialogue. A strong point of the American system, for example, is that you have real ideas in opposition, and they clash, yet people still remain civil to each other. That's still got a long way to go [here]."[37]

But the longest distance to go to find a place to be heard (discounting Japan's think tanks, the most prestigious of which are allied to corporate families and tend to do research that benefits only their commercial interests) is to the place many academics only dream about reaching: to the government's 220 advisory councils, the *shingikai* and discussion groups that are set up ostensibly to help the ministerial bureaucrats sound out and form policy ideas. Japan has no Henry Kissingers, no Robert Reiches, or even any Laura Tysons: The academic's career is tied for life to the university, and the bureaucrat's to the power of his agency. No one is invited to cross the lines except for practical purposes of liaison, known as secondment, or under the very controlled conditions of the *shingikai,* or in some ad-hoc formats that serve powerful politicians quietly and informally in much the same way as brain trusts.

The *shingikai* is meant to be the Japanese equivalent to the congressional hearing, but with major structural differences that make them utterly unequivalent. All participants in these groups—which are formed around specific policy issues because the bureaucrats, not the Japanese political parties and parliamentarians, form Japanese policy—are invited personally. The body includes the bureaucrats themselves, who form the discussion council's secretariat; a smattering of experts from the corporate and connected local-government worlds, some representatives of public interest groups, a few members of the "public" (often journalists), and one or more university academics. The meetings are not hearings; they are closed to the public. They are almost always heavily orchestrated by the ministerial bureaucrats, who dispense all data and official proposals to the group members as basis for the discussion and determine the agenda and meeting times of the council. And they are the only places (with the exception of the ad hoc circles that gather informally—and that rise and fall—around some politicians at the latters' behest, and in which people from outside as well as inside the academy lend their brainpower at the price of politically committing themselves to one political-party faction or another) where university academics can garner the prestige of "advising" the government—a faint echo of Meiji days, when Imperial University professors would hurriedly leave their class lectures to attend and advise cabinet meetings on some emergency or other.

Of course these *shingikai* appointments—some temporary, some quasipermanent—are enormously coveted at the top schools because of the prestige and aura of influence they confer. Whether they actually *do* confer any influence depends on the council in question. Some are merely shadow groups, set up largely to give an imprimatur of public respectability to a program the bureaucrats have decided upon anyway. Some are of long standing, and there is a real chance that their professorial members—if they do not cross ideological lances too often with the bureaucratic hosts—can stay as members long enough to acquire genuine expertise and some measure of influence, even of authority. This is the pinnacle for a politically minded Japanese academic.

Such men still fail to see, however, that their status is not their own, since it did not rise from their own intellectual independence. It is conferred by and can be withdrawn at the pleasure of the bureaucrats whom they are essentially summoned to serve. These *shingikai* are not really places to debate ideas, unless they are ideas congenial to the purposes of the ministries. A bureaucrat who has attended many of these meetings describes the relationship this way: "A government official will not come right out and say, 'If you don't go along with the government, you will no longer be a member of this council,' but his softer words carry much the same message. The Japanese sense of shame, or face, particularly when they are removed from a position before the end of its tenure, is psychologically the same as the removal of decoration from an army officer's uniform. More importantly, removal from one's position in the advisory council will also mean a loss of income. This is particularly persuasive in the case of university professors. While the advisory council position brings only nominal income, because of its prestige, the members receive numerous offers of research from private industry."[38] Through the artificially created status of these *shingikai* members, the prestige—and the power—of the ivory tower is captured and pressed into nationalist service of the ruling elites whom the universities themselves originally bred.

Whether or not the power of the bureaucracy to manipulate these intellectuals is resented—either by the latter, or more likely by those who have so far failed to earn an invitation to the councils—does not seem an important point to the outside world. It merely assumes that the process of reaching a "consensus" is taking place within the closed council chambers and that what emerges in the form of ministerial policy, to be duly passed by the national Diet into law, is what is best for the nation. "People do not challenge the system. The inability to criticize and challenge is directly connected to the Ministry of Education's policies, which encourage uniformity."[39]

Over lunch with a young Ministry of Education bureaucrat, himself a University of Tokyo graduate, for example, I heard expressed his purely personal view of Japanese education in general: that it has benefited from the centralized control the ministry holds over the nation's entire primary and secondary school system. While central, national control has its faults, he admitted, it does serve as an essential safeguard against usurpation and manipulation of the schools and their curriculum by politicians. Under national control, that is, education at least remains "politically" pure. (This is the kind of logic, I felt, that would probably also be used to justify the ultimate power that bureaucrats constantly hold over professors in the *shingikai*: a *moral* justification based on their elite status.)

Doubtless the view is a cautionary reference to prewar days, when bureaucrats and military officers (and not "politicians") dominated educational philosophy. But two major and dangerous sophistries are buried deeply within it. The first is the automatic assumption that the bureaucrats holding this power themselves have no "politics," no wish to indoctrinate, of their own to inflict on the educational system (and this is said in a nation of schoolrooms where the causes and events of the last world war are purposely obscured almost to the point of myth). The second is the glossing over of the implicit struggle for power that goes on constantly between administrators and party politicians and the *inherent distrust among bureaucrats of the democratic process itself.* Not merely a distrust of national politicians, with all their ineptitudes, crudeness, special interests, and outright corruption—but of the vital, constitutionally based processes that should produce community school boards, and community authority over selection of education superintendents, curriculum, and textbooks for its children, but which, thanks to the bureaucrats, do not.

Moreover, taking a step further to higher education, this attitude—that the external world of "politics" itself doesn't belong in education—is killing Japan's universities. To function as a nexus of debate and the development of political and philosophical thought, the academy must experience intellectual contention, argument, threats to entrenched positions, almost turmoil. This means turmoil of thought and contention of ideas, rather than of factions. The tremendous intellectual orthodoxy that has imposed itself over Japan's colleges and universities, the warm feeling expressed through the term *ware-ware* (what we as Japanese instinctively hold in common), have cut off escape from the land of conformity to the wild territories of possibility, along all the intellectual horizons that lie just off Japan's dialogical shores.

The careful preservation of order of this kind, an *essentially* political order, keeps the ablest thinkers of the academy largely in thrall to, rather than in participation with, national purpose, and maintains power in the hands of the administrators.

B ut Japan, by almost anyone's definition, is a successful society. Does not the achievement of fewer drugs, fewer guns, fewer crimes, earn the Japanese educational system, however regimented, a dispensation from existentialist criticisms of foreigners? Certainly students in Japan, as they do anywhere, will learn as much from the real life they lead outside the classroom as they do from texts and lectures. What, really, are the sins of the formal Japanese system of production of elites?

Dr. William Wetherall, a graduate of Berkeley and a two-decade-long resident of Japan whose research specializes in social issues like ethnicity, aging, and suicide, recounts a Japanese television program he watched one day in Tokyo not long ago. "There was this woman, a sort of celebrity type with a certain command of English, who went off on horseback with a Nez Percé American Indian chief through parts of Idaho and Montana, for a documentary on the centennial of the state of Montana. This was part of the buildup for the year of the world's indigenous people. So out there at the sweat lodges, looking at some of their rituals, she says, 'You want to preserve your culture, of course,' And he said, 'Yes, it's hard to do in a white man's world." And she said, 'Well, we Japanese understand that, too!'

"And that goes down *so well* here," says Wetherall, "without any sense that there's complete dishonesty: as if she and the Indian chief had the same problem. There is a strong element of historical paranoia, of self-pity in Japan. And the arrogance that, if we Japanese could only be understood, the world would be at peace and people would recognize our superiority. And the belief, as if in magic, that if only we could be in control of the information that is disseminated about ourselves, that the others would *ipso facto* understand us. And the form of understanding would be acceptance."

What the tale of the Japanese maid and the Indian chief illustrates,

Wetherall is saying, is the way "there is implanted [through schools as well as through media] this idea of Japan *itself* being a culture. That, to me, is a destructive notion. It's perhaps a natural thing to do, unless it's tempered by the idea that *all* cultures are social systems, and yet nevertheless remain collections of diverse individuals. Unless you get the full message, you're easily led to this one-culture, one-language, one-race sort of mentality."

As a college student in Japan, he says, "In almost everything that you're going to read, especially if you're coming up in the humanities, there's no way that you can avoid having been thoroughly indoctrinated with culturalists, with culturally deterministic viewpoints." And that's one of the saddest failings of Japanese higher education. It does nothing to *dispel* these interpretations, which ultimately leave Japanese elites isolated not only from the world but from honest self-understanding.

It is at work in far more than popular television. Wetherall recounts an example of its influence even among Japanese scholars and specialists discussing, say, mother-and-child suicide cases. Among themselves, he says, such specialists would discuss "real" problems that lead to such tragedies: problems in the marriage, in the child's personality, financial difficulties, or the types of motivations that might lead to such an ending anywhere. "But as soon as someone like myself enters the discussion, there's a sudden felt need to shift into a cultural explanation. And so Japanese mothers kill their children out of love for them, as a conditioned reflex, so as not to leave the children behind to suffer from the stigma, or to burden someone else, etc. They're [then] saying that we have to talk about Japan as something which has a [special] boundary. And if there's any attempt by me to say 'Let's stop spinning these cultural defense theories; let's actually look at cases and see if there's any evidence of this,' you don't get a lot of enthusiasm. Because this would destroy something which is vital to these researchers, and to a lot of monthly-magazine intellectuals too. They need to believe there is something different. It's almost a point of pride."[40]

Certainly, cultural chauvinism is not taught in any Japanese university. Rather, it is learned—at schools and from the social atmosphere—by students who have reached university, and it is reinforced there by the absence of an active effort to reverse it: to acknowledge it as a phenomenon or as a problem and to discuss it. As Hobsbawm implied in the quotation given at the start of this chapter, cultural, ethnic, and national chauvinisms are much in the news these days worldwide, and certainly America and the most advanced nations of Europe have their own cultural chauvinisms as well. But the Japan-as-a-culture syndrome—when viewed in Japan's setting of the social imperative of group values—has an additional ramification and a darker result. The ramification is that the rest of the world, all of it and not just certain disagreeable nations, is not just different but to some degree a competitive threat to Japan and therefore an intrinsic danger. "You can't stress that enough, when you dig under the surface" is the way Professor Ivan Hall has expressed it to me. "It's so *ingrained,* this seeing the outside world as a threat."

This leads in turn to the most unhealthy result: the belief that Japan should be, must be, kept *socially closed* to outsiders. Foreigners are by definition outsiders, thus none could ever fit into a Japanese group not specifically designed for the purpose of dealing with them. Universities in Japan are not designed to deal with foreigners, so very few of them teach there despite strong "encouragements" from the Ministry of Education to admit more foreign faculty, and despite the presence today of some 54,000 foreign students in Japanese schools and educational establishments.

This culture-as-value-system is perhaps the most damning evidence of all of the unshakable closure of the mind of the Japanese elite. I discussed this brand of intellectual malaise in an interview with former Monbusho official Akimasa Mitsuta, who was himself born on Taiwan and is a graduate of Todai. Japan in 1945, he says, "was a society bitter, bitterly defeated. But it has already been forty years after the end of the Occupation. And we still cannot teach history. The first thing we should do is maybe recover the pride, to get away from the Occupation's teaching that what we did was all wrong." This assessment, startling at first, actually makes sense: What responsibility can Japan begin to accept as an Asian nation if it cannot openly debate the totality of impact on its neighbors of its modern imperial era, going back from the postwar period through the war to the Meiji Restoration? "This takes a long time, a very long time. It's a renaissance. After the majority of Japanese start to feel really depressed, and do not know who they are and want to know who they are, the renaissance would be to start reading history again, by their own initiative."

Within the universities, he believes, little will change until the status quo is broken: until more professors become comfortable with the idea of going abroad not only to learn but to teach. "In a sense, Japan hasn't really finished graduating from the Meiji Restoration. It is still in the process of learning from the Western world." The renaissance on campus must reach back to the history before the war, to discover the passions, energy, and turmoil of Japan's modernization. "We have to go back again to the Meiji Restoration. Because that generation which dealt with revolution had already been educated, or educated themselves, with traditional [Japanese] ethics. They went to Europe to learn something useful, to strengthen their *own* philosophies. But now, after two or three generations have passed, the basic endowment disappears, because these traditions themselves have disappeared." The ethics native to the great civilization of Japan, two thousand years old, are the only legitimate point from which to reckon how far and in which direction Japan has come since modernization, and where it should go from here, he feels. Too many Todai professors today "only read books, but never talk about the real world. Only part of learning is left; only the repeating of knowledge, of what Keynes said, what Nietsche said, what Kant said; everybody knows all that well enough. But all of these cannot help you to build Japanese society."

But I ask, what about the way the system produces its leaders today? Do these modern Japanese students really learn to think about questions of right and wrong and ethics for themselves, for their society? "People who are in responsible positions, who know, are very worried about that."

"Do you mean," I press him, "worried that no one *is* thinking about them?"

"Yes. If you talk with, say, former vice-ministers in private occasions, we always share the same kinds of feelings."

"The feeling of dismay—that no one is talking at all about certain kinds of values?"

"Yes."[41]

From all this follows the failure of both gods and humans in the Japanese university.

What this all means is that the ultimate tragedy of the university is that it cannot reform itself—or it can only, as Mitsuta suggests, be reformed with the passage of a "very long time," time that Japan might not have. A constant game goes on between government and school now. It is a game in which the Ministry of Education, anxious not to upset the vast population of parents and students who have invested so much in the system on faith, by imposing the sweeping changes it really wants to make, delicately tries to be seen as maintaining the status quo—while actually trying to entice the schools to make voluntary changes on their own. "Sometimes higher-ranking officers at Monbusho, they are very progressive in reforming," says a member of the ministry's *daigaku shingikai* who is deeply concerned with graduate-school modernization. "But sometimes the university professors are much more conservative. On the other hand, the government system itself has not changed. This is the very peculiar Japanese system."

Peculiar, confusing, misleading, and, in a sense, dishonest. Everyone who is part of this dialogue on the universities and what is wrong with them is quick to claim that the locus of power—that is, responsibility for the problems—lies with someone else. It is said that teachers stubbornly refuse to change; it is said that university professors will not use the power they hold to encourage, or to force, change. It is said that the various government ministries cannot agree on what kind of graduate "product" they want the campuses to produce. It is said that Monbusho plays a duplicitous game, openly encouraging universities to experiment, yet holding always in reserve the whip hand that can derail any "disagreeable" experiments, and careers along with them, with the stroke of a pen on a budget sheet.

In the meantime, the university stands progressively less prepared for four great challenges that are about to engulf it, along with the rest of Japan's "economic society."

• As we have seen above, the research capabilities of the campus, in an age when progress not only in science but many disciplines, and their impact on the welfare of the national economy, is accelerating constantly, have fallen desperately behind and may not be able to catch up. Japan's intellectual community, because of this, trends toward greater isolation, and not internationalization as the government proclaims.

• The country's university, college, and junior-college community faces the imminent threat of financial disaster. The number of applicants to tertiary education, that is those in the eighteen-year-old cohort of the Japanese population, will fall by one-quarter between the early 1990s and the end of the decade. Private colleges, already strapped financially, face closure in large numbers if some new system, admitting more of the general population to higher learning, cannot quickly be devised. But the Ministry of Education seems to show no inclination to disassemble the entrance-exam barriers, which of course would be the same as dismantling its own controls over not only the curriculum but the very character of the primary- and secondary-school systems that are the gateway to higher education. To de-accentuate the examinations would directly dilute Monbusho's control over the nation's youth.

• The university system never asks the student what he or she wants to *be*. With some exceptions, Japan's humanities and social-sciences curricula, coupled with the whole system of selection of students by the Procrustean winnowing machinery of the examination system, put no real emphasis on the nurturing of professional aspirations of entering freshmen. The liberal-arts and even the business-school campuses remain geared to producing the essential generalist who will eventually be shaped professionally by an employer—not the young man or woman who has a dream to become a historian, a lawyer, a criminologist, an international trade specialist, or a social worker. Yet because Japan's lifetime employment system is under the greatest threat now since the rise of the postwar economy that produced it, graduates will have to develop both independent skills that can be sold in many places on the labor market and a new attitude to life-long education and self-retraining. But once this reorientation takes place, to a system that puts students on personal tracks of their own to desired careers, the emphasis on group harmony as an overriding "skill" will begin to dissipate. More ominous for Japanese society is that the general self-conception young Japanese have of being members of an essentially "classless" society will begin to evaporate. Individual, professional merit, and the differentiated rewards depending upon it and upon choice of a career itself, will dissolve the harmonious assumption of social equality as young people begin their life's work in the social economy. No one can tell what impact this will have on the social stability of Japan's elites.

• Last, Japan's higher education philosophy will have to adapt itself to the ineluctable implications of real internationalization: that more and more immigrants, whether economic, cultural, or refugee, will eventually have to be accommodated in colleges and universities on the same terms as Japanese. With the birthrate falling, government forecasts show Japan's labor force shrinking by as much as 10 percent within the next twenty-five years.[42] Not only to meet political and social demands from its Asian neighbors, but to keep the nation's socioeconomic "bicycle" moving forward by a growth rate of at least 3 percent with the injection of young, low-cost labor into the jobs no young Japanese want to accept, Japan inevitably will have to receive large amounts of foreign in-migration. Many of these immigrants will seek naturalization, or at least the same social and economic privileges as Japanese while living in this society. That will include full access to the educational ladder that leads to the professions beyond. The challenge was described with deserved poignancy by the noted writer and member of the Art Academy Ryotaro Shiba, as follows, "As the century wanes, doors will open in Japan. . . foreign laborers will be entering Japan in enormous numbers, just as surely as the sun rises. When we awaken one day, surrounded by foreigners, will we continue to insist on our 'Japaneseness'? Will we still try to draw emotional sustenance from myths of our *samurai* spirit, or derive our individual identities from our collective primordial past? Can we?"[43] Universities and colleges will have to respond to Shiba's challenge in a way more profound than the mere acceptance of exchange or research students. It will be their obligation to share the work of socializing immigrants, perhaps large numbers of them, to equip them to live and work in Japan for a long time, and even to enter the ranks of Japan's elites. It will be their responsibility to begin admitting and training immigrant teachers for Japanese campuses in their own graduate schools— and then employing them and integrating them into their own faculties.

Virtually no one has faced the full implications of this looming inevitability.

The university in Japan, then, is only in small part, and only in Japanese character, an ivory tower. Rather, as it is founded on a mission to supply the social economy with the requisite number of trained workers, and not on a mission to propagate debate over whether Japan should be this kind of society, or some other kind, in the first place, it has in the intellectual sense relegated itself to the position of an ivory basement: a kind of stockroom, from which should issue whatever the elite leadership structure of the nation needs, when it needs it, in terms of both manpower and intellectual product. It is a tower only in the sense that the faculties who command within it hold themselves as aloof as they can from political accountability on a personal basis, and often, unfortunately, on a professional basis.

Notes

1. "The New Threat to History," *The New York Review of Books,* reprint of a lecture given by Eric Hobsbawm, December 16, 1993.
2. "On Japanese Higher Education: In Commemoration of Professor Takashi Tsuruda," a paper given by Shigeo Minabe, 1994, p. 6.
3. Michio Nagai, *Higher Education in Japan: Its Take-off and Crash* (Tokyo: University of Tokyo Press, 1971), p. 22.
4. Byron K. Marshall, *Academic Freedom and the Japanese Imperial University, 1868–1939* (Berkeley: University of California Press, 1992), p. 31.
5. "Japan as Number Three: Long Term Productivity and Growth Problems in the Economy," Japan Economic Institute Report No. 17A, April 29, 1994.
6. "Unorthodox Economist Takes Multidisciplinary Approach," *Nikkei Weekly,* March 7, 1994.
7. Interview with the author, December 1993.
8. Ivan P. Hall, "Organizational Paralysis: The Case of Todai," in *Modern Japanese Organization and Decision-Making,* ed. Ezra F. Vogel (Berkeley: University of California Press, 1975), p. 311.
9. Ibid.
10. Interview with the author, April 1994.
11. Interview with the author, December 1992.
12. Interview with the author, April 1994.
13. Interview with the author, October 1992.
14. "Japan: Time for Change" *Nature,* October 15, 1992.
15. Interview with the author, February 1993.
16. "Second-class Citizens in the Academic World," *Asahi Evening News,* May 26, 1993.
17. "Foreign Researchers in Japan," *Japan Times,* April 13, 1988.
18. "Management in Higher Ed," *Japan Times,* April 18, 1988.
19. Henry Rosovsky, *The University: An Owner's Manual* (New York: W.W. Norton, 1990), p. 34.
20. Minabe, "On Japanese Higher Education."
21. Nagai, *Higher Education in Japan.*

22. Interview with the author, December 1992.

23. Interview with the author, August 1992.

24. Interview with the author, April 1994.

25. "Recruiting to Fall 17% at Major Firms: Survey," *Japan Times*, June 28, 1994.

26. "Will Parents' Investment in Higher Education Pay?" *Mainichi Daily News*, attributed to *Gendai* magazine, April 2, 1988.

27. Interview with the author, April 1994.

28. *White Paper on Science and Technology—The Relationship between Young People and Science and Technology—(summary)*, Science and Technology Agency, Prime Minister's Office, Japan, December 1993.

29. "Acts of an Apostle," a review of *John Maynard Keynes, Vol. II: The Economist as Saviour 1920–1937*, by Robert Heilbroner, *New York Review of Books*, March 3, 1994.

30. "To True Internationalization," *Japan Times*, March 29, 1994.

31. JEI Report No. 17A.

32. "Grad School Ranks Thin, Costs Surge," *Japan Times*, January 3, 1992.

33. Interview with the author, February 8, 1993.

34. Interview with the author, March 1994.

35. "Japan's Tilt to Asia Gaining Momentum," *Nikkei Weekly*, March 28, 1994.

36. Interview with the author, April 1994.

37. Interview with the author, April 27, 1994.

38. Masao Miyamoto, "Japanese Bureaucracy: The Major Structural Trade Impediment in Japan," speech delivered to the Netherlands Chamber of Commerce in Japan, September 16, 1993.

39. Masao Miyamoto, "Ethics of 'Yes' and 'No': Discrepancies in Japan-U.S. Communications," speech delivered to the America-Japan Society in Tokyo, March 28, 1994.

40. Interview with the author, April 1994.

41. Interview with the author, April 22, 1994.

42. "Sharp Fall in Workforce Predicted," *Japan Times*, June 29, 1994.

43. " 'We Japanese' Need a Change of Heart," *Asahi Evening News*, May 25, 1991.

5

A Tale of Two Citizens

An institution is the lengthened shadow of one man.

—Emerson

The goal of our educational administration is . . . purely and simply the service of the state. In the case of the Imperial University [Todai], for instance, the question may arise as to whether learning is to be pursued for its own sake or for the sake of the state. It is the state which must come first and receive top priority.
—Arinori Mori, founder of Hitotsubashi University, and Japan's first minister of education

The government is encouraging education, discussing new laws showing better methods in commerce. Thus they admonish the people sometimes, demonstrate new methods at times, and try many other ways, but even to this day, little improvement is evident; the government is still the same autocratic government, the people are the same spiritless idiots. Sometimes improvements are seen, but in comparison to the amount of labor and money invested, the results are very disappointing indeed.
—Yukichi Fukuzawa, founder of Keio University, and Japan's first modern educator

For Kenji Yumoto, nothing at all seemed difficult about the pathway to college. When he was in fifth grade, his father, a university-trained research pharmacist with a Ph.D. from Todai, was assigned by his employer, a Japanese pharmaceuticals giant, to its defense team arguing a court case brought by a patient over liability for alleged product defects in one of its medicines. Kenji was too young to go to court with his father. But he found himself with a burning curiosity fueled by his dad's dinner-table accounts of each day's judicial developments, and he began surreptitiously following the case in the newspapers.

Eventually Kenji began to experience his own pangs of guilt, though, as he realized that he was fantasizing about *himself* as the leading attorney, a full-fledged lawyer, in that same courtroom—but representing the plaintiffs! "I had always had this image of the law as a rigid, precise thing. But as I followed my father's case I learned that, OK, facts are really pretty hard things to find—especially when the judge himself doesn't know anything about medicine or chemistry. You have to prove everything to him. If I were a lawyer then, I would have represented the plaintiff because I just knew I could find something to help prove they were right—to help them win!"

At a time when other ten-year-olds were seeking to perfect a slider that would help the perennially popular Yomiuri Giants to win the pennant some day, or practicing the perfect karate blow to help the Tokyo Police capture a nasty gangland murderer some day, Kenji Yumoto was already planning how to get into Todai Law School, to help folks win in court some day.

And Kenji (a name I have given him in place of his real one) made that plan come true: Three years ago he completed his bachelor of laws degree at Todai with a 3.7 grade point average, entered graduate school, shortly thereafter interrupted it to accept a one-year scholarship to the University of Chicago law school, returned to Todai to finish his Japanese master's degree, and the following year was to take the New York State bar exam. He no longer, however, had the hope of helping plaintiffs or serving justice in a Japanese courtroom, but instead held the ardent wish to become an investment banker for Lehman Brothers. Times change.

This chapter is the story of time and change for two college graduates— Kenji from Todai Law and Osamu Taniguchi (again, a *nom d'école*) from Keio University's Shonan campus at Fujisawa, who are two very bright, very ambitious young Japanese products of schools located at opposite ends of the very short spectrum of Japanese national and private prestige universities.[1] What both schools seek to instill—the one, a sense of service to the state, and the other, a sense of responsibility to better the self and the society through education—are as opposite as one can find in the operating philosophies of Japanese higher education.

A description of these two students and their school careers will show how they both ended up, for all the philosophizing over the intents and outcomes of Japanese education, in largely the same place, once it was all over. In the process, we can see what is wrong with university education at both ends of that spectrum.

The Imperial University, as Todai was first known, was assembled from a jumble of predecessor schools operated first by the Tokugawa shogunate and later by their Meiji oligarchic successors, as institutes for the collection and study of the Western learning that Japan was increasingly determined to master to save itself from dominance by the colonial-industrial powers. With a faculty staffed heavily at first by contracted, foreign professors, it had actually gone, piecemeal, quite a way toward building a respectable higher-educational foundation when Arinori Mori became Japan's first education minister in the Hirobumi Ito cabinet of 1882.

Mori was one of the those protean Meiji reformers—ex-*samurai,* part Confucian traditionalist, and part enthusiastic modernizer—who peopled the constantly jammed ranks of government in the early days of the reforms. He had spent time on a Christian commune in America, been an ambassador to two European countries, contributed to the foundation both of constitutionalism and learned societies in Tokyo, and profoundly shaken and shaped Japan's national educational system, all by the time of his assassination at the age of forty-one in 1889. In the words of his biographer, Ivan Hall, "No other education minister in modern Japan comes anywhere near Mori in the extent of his personal imprint upon the entire school system."[2]

The reason is that Mori bound together the many tenuous threads of both educational structure and philosophy that had grown from Japanese tradition or been transplanted there from the West into a single cord, leading straight to the Imperial University—and not only to Todai, the first *daigaku,* but eventually to other imperial schools of higher learning that were to follow. He first made of education a stairway, with Todai at the top and all the steps that led to it, from primary through secondary educational structures, which not only trained the society's human resources at every level of the climb but also sorted out potential elites from the young and channeled them toward national leadership roles.

Briefly, in Mori's day a system had been created of eight years of compulsory public education; a great deal of contention followed about how teaching and learning should proceed from that base. Once installed as education minister, Mori consolidated two separate systems of competitive-entry "middle schools" atop all these grade schools. One of the middle schools, lasting five years, he intended to produce graduates in arts and sciences who would serve society "neither at the upper nor the lower ranks."[3] The second, lasting only three years, was the golden gateway through which potential elites were projected on to higher education—in the Imperial University. Mori dismissed the foreign deans of the imperial colleges and replaced them with Japanese scholars. Following from his nationalist vision, he also wanted to replace the traditional Japanese, Confucian classical view of elite education as a literary exploration of the venerable texts, with pragmatic instruction in practical subjects including law and the humanities that would lead straight to jobs in the establishment. Graduates of the Imperial University Law Faculty could enter elite-track, civil-service careers in Tokyo without even having to take qualifying exams; such was the esteem in which Mori intended the university's educational "product" to be held.

The nature of elementary, secondary, and higher education has changed somewhat in form but little in substance since Mori's day: The university, of course, is still the gateway to elite status, which in Japan is to say, to power.

Thus Kenji Yumoto, in a rather unawares fashion, was following in a very hallowed tradition when he decided at age ten "to prepare myself to go to a private junior and senior high school"—the better to have a real chance at entering Todai Law.

This came, Kenji recalls, as quite a surprise to his parents, who were a squarely middle-class couple living in a rented apartment in Saitama prefecture, an hour's train ride from Tokyo. "My parents never wanted me to go to cram school, or any of that other stuff that my friends were being pushed into to get ready for all the entrance exams to good middle schools. It was something *I* wanted. So I had to talk them into sending me to a *juku* (cram school), so that I could pass the entrance tests to the junior high I had already picked out." Yumoto's mother, who had grown up in a wealthy family before the war and had bad memories of being forced to study flower-arranging, *koto* (Japanese harp)-playing and the other "feminine arts," did not want her own children oppressed in their childhood years by the Great College Race. But she and her husband both had grown nervous over the amount of violence—between students, and by teachers against students—already evident in the public schools all around them, Kenji recalls. And their son, with no advice from them, had already set his heart on getting into Kaisei High School in Tokyo, a joint junior–senior high school that is known through the land for placing anywhere from two-fifths to fully half of each year's graduating class of 400 into Todai. So they consented to let him go to cram school, to prepare for the entrance exams. Kenji Yumoto, it seems, was acting a bit like a lawyer already.

Kenji succeeded in entering Kaisei and spent a blissful three years there not studying very much, but having a good time with sports and other campus activities—assured by his mere presence at Kaisei of a very good shot at being accepted at Todai. "We had great campus athletic events at our school," he recalls fondly. "Full of really good fights. Not anything like *kendo* or *judo,* but our own special games, where we'd divide up into teams and try to capture each other's goals." Apparently the fear of public-school violence was cheerfully overcome, because, says Yumoto, these fraternal contests themselves could often produce as many as six or seven game-interrupting injuries per day. "I was in charge of organizing the meet one year," he says proudly, "and I used to have to call the ambulance, oh, sometimes ten times a day, it seemed like. We had a neighborhood hospital, operated by an alumnus, who gave us a discount on our medical bills." Kenji says his grades were nothing special. But it seems he was certainly learning organizational talents that would serve any young attorney well.

Finally, though, a more serious future loomed. A year before high-school graduation and the Todai entrance exams, Kenji recalls he was bluntly told by his home-room teacher that he did not have the grades to make it: In fact, he ranked in the bottom quarter of his class.

"So, that's when I began to study. At that time I was president of the organizing committee for the athletic events, I was chairman of the school festival, I was in the musical band group, and I was also a member of the school swim team. And off and on, I had been playing drums in a rock-and-roll band. It all went out the window—it had to.

"I had just one year to prepare for the tests, and I went after every exam subject all at once. I bought some texts and reference books, and then study, study, study! I had friends who were already at the university, and they could tell me which types of books would be most helpful to use. For that full year, I put in seventeen hours a day getting ready. No TV, no holidays, no nothing. I was back in cram school at nights. But I was getting results: my school grades were climbing, and I was doing better and better at the mock-entrance exams the *juku* gave us." Yumoto, scared at first, considered trying for a lower-ranked university instead—but then he made up his mind that it would indeed have to be Todai. By the time his final high-school semester ended, his grades placed him in the top fifteen of his class of 400, he says, and, he claims, he was regularly placing in the top 10 and 20 percent on a nationwide scale, on the battery of mock entrance tests that his *juku* was giving.

"Actually, people don't understand what the tests to get into Todai are like. There's no multiple-choice, no fill-in-the-blanks, not even any dates or places to remember. To get into the University of Tokyo you don't actually have to memorize anything—all you have to do is write logical essays. For Waseda, or Keio, you have to memorize things. That's why I didn't even try those schools. In the Todai exam, they just give you blank sheets of paper, and essay questions. That's all. You write a title, and you compose. In the subject of world history, for example, all you have to know is the kind of waves of nationalism, or of capitalism or whatever, or how the world has changed most dramatically. You don't have to know what year anything happened. History had just four or five questions. Japanese language and classics, just seven. The math wasn't easy, but there were only four questions to answer in two hours: I just had to think flexibly, that's all.

All I did to prepare was to stretch what I had been learning in high school."

It took a more than a month for the entrance-exam results to come back. The cold March morning he went down to see the postings on the signboard at the campus—a very old tradition at Todai—and saw his name, he felt some relief, but mostly a kind of curious letdown. He had passed, thus joining more than 150 of his classmates from Kaisei, in grasping the shiniest of the brass rings Japan has to offer an eighteen-year-old. Just like that.

I t is a safe prediction," wrote management theorist Peter Drucker not long ago[4] "that in the next fifty years schools and universities will change more and more drastically than they have since they assumed their present form more than 300 years ago when they reorganized themselves around the printed book. What will force these changes is, in part, new technology, such as computers, videos and telecasts via satellite; in part the demands of a knowledge-based society in which organized learning must become a lifelong process for knowledge workers; and in part new theory about how human beings learn."

It was new theories of learning—that students and teachers were coequal in the educational process, mutually enlightening each other as they discussed ideas and facts around a table of level social and functional stature—that stimulated Yukichi Fukuzawa, a contemporary and sometime colleague of Arinori Mori in the reform process, to found a school of his own in 1890: what would become Japan's first and most prestigious private university, Keio Gijutsu, later Keio Daigaku. In this same spirit but also in the vision of modern seers like Drucker, his school, Keio, has spun off a new campus, Keio Daigaku Shonan campus at Fujisawa, where three thousand students use computers, e-mail, the Internet, and software resources of every description to earn degrees in two of the frontier disciplines of Japan's current "reforms," Policy Management and Environmental Information. It is a refreshing atmosphere, this modern, parklike compound of new concrete buildings set amid the rolling hills and green trees of the countryside southwest of Tokyo—even if the warm breezes wafting across it each summer do fill with the ruminant air of the neighboring dairy-cow industry.

Fukuzawa, who was every bit as influential intellectually in the early days of the Meiji reforms as Mori, but chose all his life to remain outside government service, considered himself an "enlightener." He traveled twice to the United States and once to Europe between 1860 and 1862, and became famous after he published his reflections on the meaning of Western progress for the changes his countrymen would have to face in such seminal volumes as *Things Western* (1866, with a staggering quarter-million copies sold), an *Encouragement of Learning* (1874), and his scholarly *Outline of Civilization* (1875), which summarized his conceptions of Japanese civilization and its future tasks. Indeed "his interest covered the whole range of civilization," as one editor of an anthology of his work puts it, "and as his life's work he chose to introduce the entire civilization of the modern age to the Japanese people—and that in great haste."[5]

Fukuzawa lived the public life of an intellectual with not a moment to waste. It is therefore something of an irony that his own legacy, Keio Daigaku, instead of recasting itself institutionally to meet Drucker's dictum, has chosen instead to build its own "next generation" school separately, in a distant suburb. This decision makes the Shonan campus appear something of a tentative experiment—a research center to explore the promise of tomorrow and whether Japanese higher education really can do something internally to reform itself, as the whole nation once did.

O samu Taniguchi was one of the those young, "different" Japanese who gambled that it could. His parents lived an international life, his father a corporate manager for a Japanese electronics firm who spent time working in and, eventually, heading subsidiaries in Europe and the United States. Osamu spent ten years studying in Japanese and foreign schools in America, in West Germany, and in England. He never had plans to go to college when the time came. "For me, Japanese college seemed like some sort of moratorium between childhood and career life, where students never really study and where things like playing tennis and belonging to clubs are the most important achievements; that's why I felt it was useless." He thus suffered something of a surprise when he discovered that his parents did have such plans for him. "We talked about it a lot. I really tried to convince them I didn't want to go. But in the end what they told me came down to an old Japanese proverb: 'It's the weak dog that always barks loudest.' I guess I finally understood they would be very disappointed if I didn't go."

But still he asked himself: "What did I want to be? When I was old enough to go, I still hadn't arrived at any answer to that. I found myself thinking that what I really wanted to do was change college itself: make the study real, make the work mean something. Finally a friend of mine, a professor at Sophia University, said 'If you want to change the Japanese educational system, you have to be there, and you have to finish with it yourself—and then you can start making a difference.' I guess that's when I changed my mind."

About what? "About making the effort to get in, and deciding to go through with it after all. It was very hard. I had to study outside in cram schools, for the entrance exam, for two full years after I came back to Japan. But I put up with it because I really became enthusiastic about wanting to change college itself."

Change college itself? "I hated college students at first, because they don't even know the meaning of why they are in college. If I didn't know what I wanted to be, none of them did either. That's why now, after I've graduated, I'm going to graduate school. I want to change the system, change the curriculum, change the way the professors think. And I myself plan to start bringing some of that change about. I'm going to start as a teaching assistant right here next April, and I'm going to push on for my graduate degree in psychology. It will take three years, including some interning in a hospital. But for my field, intercultural communications, psychology is perfect—it crosses so many areas. My idea is to unite all the fields taught here at Shonan together: policy studies, modern economics, environmentalism, to answer the international Japanese questions of the day. All students should learn something about each of these fields.

"There's all these frictions in intercultural communications, like between Americans and Japanese over trade. And you can't solve them just by talking about one area, like economics—you have to consider the problems universally: cultural contact, individual contact, language barriers. . . ."

But to do that means crossing all the internal boundaries of the faculty world: departments, bureaus, specializations. Can you really find professors who will agree with you?

Taniguchi laughs. "I hope so. At least I'm prepared for the fight. No matter how hard it becomes to face them. After all, I got in here in the first place to do just that, didn't I?"

The University of Tokyo, an educational Disneyland with 22,300 students studying everything from the English language to the ranching of open-ocean species of fish to the likelihood of volcanic eruptions close to Tokyo, has for Japan the kind of physical appearance that itself would seem to justify the phrase "alma mater." Its senior and graduate studies campus, located not far from the Imperial Palace, is full of tree-lined lanes fronting on row upon row of neo-Gothic buildings that put one in mind of the venerability of Cambridge; cluttered behind them, in back alleys and tiny quads, are jumbles of everything from high-rise office stories to moldering brick facades. But what is ancient is not visible here: The Gothic facade was erected in the mid-1920s, to replace the devastation left by the Great Kanto Earthquake. The general library was built with the support of the Rockefeller Foundation of the United States. And in the basements and back rooms of the science laboratories, too much of the infrastructure is crumbling, with researchers packed into spaces so tiny that they have to stoop over to avoid hitting their heads on low-slung beams; ventilation so bad that they have to open windows in all kinds of weather to let out the odors from the restroom plumbing down the hall. It is the grounds, rather, from which Todai grows that hold its native tradition: the fifty-six hectares of an old Edo estate of a feudal *daimyo,* allotted to the school for its home, still with its famous *Akamon,* or Red Gate, to remind those entering here of the national soil from which the national university system springs.

It is an ambitious place: With sixty-four institutes, hospitals, agricultural stations, computer centers, and museums, it absorbs two billion dollars a year of the national budget, a figure equal to more than half the government's total subsidy for all 357 private universities in the country, where 80 percent of all college students actually matriculate.[6] Yet for all the quiet tumult that these students, activities, and their four thousand educators generate, it would be very easy to miss the four quiet buildings just inside the main gate that produce every generation of the leadership of Japan, the law school wherein Kenji Yumoto realized his life's ambition.

Actually, for his first two years Yumoto was not even here. Todai divides its campuses into two: The famous Hongo campus is for junior and senior undergraduates and for graduate and institute study; Kenji spent his first two years with all the other freshmen and sophomores at the school's Komaba campus, near Shibuya and across town—and light years away from anything resembling a first-class university.

Komaba is where the "core" courses are taught—or perhaps it would be more accurate to say are offered. Few students pay much attention to instruction in these enormous sections, where five or six hundred lower-classmen and -women are pressed together in halls for survey and other introductory courses that have to be given by loudspeaker. Teachers often do not pay much attention either: Cancellations are frequent because professors know that not many of the students will be conscientious anyway.

"Most of the students didn't study at all for the first two years. They just took the exams that were necessary to pass the courses, based on the same lecture notes that everybody else had. We all distributed the notes among ourselves, and no term or class papers were required, so we just showed up for the exams—as long as you had the notes, it was pretty easy to get through." Yumoto says there wasn't much cheating—but not much was needed, with the omnipresent notes available to everyone, and professors themselves extremely reluctant to fail anyone.

Instead, Komaba had more activities. Yumoto joined the sailing club, which had him going out to the marina at Hayama at least twice a week (though mostly on weekends), and an international student organization for business management, which took up at least two of his nights on campus each week. "I don't say I got bad grades—I mean I studied a lot more than many of the other students. But I didn't care about the grades at all. All we had to do was to pass those exams—I was also busy tutoring cram-school students for pocket money, and I put a lot of time into that international student organization. I became one of the directors of its Japanese national committee. It was a lot of work by itself, but the contacts were very good. I felt sorry for the engineering and science students, who were at the opposite end of the spectrum at Komaba. They knew they would have to take competitive qualifying exams for the junior year in the technical faculty they wanted to enter, so they had to study pretty hard. With them, the grades meant everything. To us—well, I didn't care."

But all good things must come to an end, and so did the skylarking of the Komaba campus. Yumoto moved on for his third year to Hongo and the specialty he sought, law. He started taking a courseload of a mere seventeen hours a week, reading "code, code, code." Lectures were the thing here, too, for the 670 law undergrads who often filled lecture halls at the rate of 300 or 400 students per class. The workload was not demanding—"I think less than half the students attended their lecture classes on any given day, and that's the only reason those who *were* there could find a seat!"—but there were annual exams to prepare for, and in each semester there was a seminar course of up to fifteen students whose workload was fairly intense. "You had to do a paper for each, and that meant a good month of evenings spent in the library."

The relatively easy pace allowed Yumoto to keep up his sailing, and join another global group, the Japan America Student Conference, for which he helped raise, he says, $380,000 in donations to stage a grand international conference convocation in Tokyo. Social life had been filled with parties during the first two years at Komaba, but he discovered a strange discontinuity when he reached Hongo: the school was really more like a commuter campus than an Ivy League university.

"Unlike American schools, we have a really hard time making a campus life here. You have to make appointments to be with your friends, and then even if you meet them on the campus, there's nothing other than the activities of the student clubs themselves to do here. So that's why we all go outside, out on the town to eat and drink, to shop, to earn pocket money, to live. The economy of student life at Todai is based completely outside the campus. To meet girls, the boys sometimes go to clubs, or to parties, or to the 'meat-market' bars, the singles joints—all kinds of things. Since only a few percent of the students here are women, it seldom happens that we date Todai co-eds. I heard, before I got into Todai, that women were always trying to meet Todai men. But once I got in, I found it's the opposite. As long as you're still in school, most of the girls assume that you're some kind of a grind—a nerd, even. It's definitely not a good pickup line in a bar to say, 'I'm going to Todai.' In fact, none of us wants to disclose it, because the women will turn off right away.

"But I'm so pissed off to have found out that once you've graduated, then it's all completely different: you become a target. Some of the women, then, are *only* interested in Todai graduates: they're headhunting for husbands who've already found jobs. It seems we make the ideal mates for ambitious women.

"Nobody marries in college, and I'd say less than two—no, less than one—percent of students are living together off-campus with a member of the opposite sex. It probably has more to do with the financial situation we're in than anything else."

Despite such social letdowns and the complete absence of anything like a frat life, Yumoto managed to stay busy during his two years at Hongo—so much so that he found himself being squeezed into another dilemma as graduation drew nearer and nearer. "I had three things to worry about. One was this big conference I was putting together, which really involved me in meeting a lot of people, arranging for speakers, reading up on wide ranges of subject matter, and that sort of thing. Of course," he says with a disarming smile, "I couldn't just let them all down by writing it off. It was my job to see the thing through to a success—which it eventually was. The second thing was keeping my grades up while all this was going on. And the third thing was *shushoku*" (a word that gives every grad stomach butterflies): job hunting. "Of 670 law graduates each year, about a quarter go into the elite government jobs. And another quarter go to the Legal Training Institute (which leads either to the bar or to a judgeship). A small number go to graduate school." And the rest go out looking for the best jobs." This search begins with the April before graduation—almost a full year before completion of the BA degree—when students become consumed with interviews, résumés, contacts, and introductions from their professors. Of course, finding elite-track employment of some type is never a real worry for Todai Law grads. But it is, in a way, one more distraction from the education that law students are supposed to be getting at Hongo. No professor will interfere with a student's job search on the complaint of missed classes—this is a lifetime decision for the young people because they will stay with whichever employer chooses them, for their entire career. No one wants to derail them.

But Yumoto "couldn't do all three in the same year—I just couldn't. So I devised a strategy: what time I didn't spend on the conference, I spent studying. While my friends were preparing for civil service exams or running all over to interviews, I pumped up my graduating grade level to almost 3.7. That assured me I could get into Graduate Law School here, which deferred the need to search for a job for a year or two."

Yumoto's strategy worked perfectly. He was accepted at grad school. The next year, he won a year's scholarship to the University of Chicago graduate law school. And then he was back and savoring his last year at Todai grad school—and preparing to move on to New York.

And how does he now assess his educational experience at the nation's Number One university? "You know, I was never really 100 percent content with the education I got at Todai. For about 60 percent of what I needed, it was fine. I missed studying in the Komaba years, though I suppose that was mostly my fault: My commuter train took me home right through the heart of one of Tokyo's best amusement districts, and the temptations were just too much. And as I said, nobody else was studying either.

"But I missed the contact with professors at Hongo as well. For an undergraduate, they were very difficult to talk to. If I had had more access then, more time for counseling from them, I think I could have prepared myself and benefited much more from my studies—even though my grades were good anyway.

"In fact, I have been thinking for a long time to rebuild the society, or rebuild the system, from the inside. I found out it was not really a good system. I mean from elementary school, I was not really unhappy, but I had dissatisfactions. At that time I told myself, well, OK, someday I'm going to be working for the Ministry of Education or something, and then I'm going to change it. But I saw so many friends who entered that same ministry with the same ambition to change society—and it's just too hard for them to maintain that ambition, *because* they are insiders! And their desire for change becomes totally incompatible with the desires of the Ministry of Education, sooner or later.

"I still have hopes to change things; even as an American investment banker I think I can find some way to break all these existing regulations into pieces somehow—to get the system behind it to collapse, and then rebuild, rebuild, rebuild."

Does that mean Kenji Yumoto really has faith, in the end, that Japan is actually a legalistic society capable of being changed by citizens themselves; not, as its critics say, an interlocking arrangement of closely held and unaccountable political powers?

Kenji Yumoto, graduate of Todai Law, ponders that question a moment. "I don't think so—I don't know, really. Maybe this society is a cultural one.

Sometimes money is what holds the power. And other kinds of powers. Formal law, laws enforceable in the courts, don't regulate everything here. Sometimes, well, 'arrangements' are the way Japan works.

"You know, we can discuss, inside the university, anything we want: politics, the powers of bureaucrats, *amakudari* [descent from heaven—see chap. 10], the imperial family. But not in public. Even Todai graduates, once they graduate, they shut their mouths, no matter what they think. I have friends who get harassing phone calls, letters from right-wing hate groups or whatever, because they let themselves say too much outside the campus."

Higher education," wrote historian Kazuyoshi Nakayama of Yukichi Fukuzawa, "or university education, according to Fukuzawa, was appropriate for a few gifted persons who were willing to work for the independence of the country. Simply put, general education was for the independence of each individual, while higher education was for the independence of the country."[7]

While it would have been impossible for either man to foresee the era of a Japan that relied upon economic output for its independence to the extent that college degrees were needed for almost 40 percent of the population, Fukuzawa and Arinori Mori were not that far apart in their basic vision of the university at the center of Japan's national modernization—no further apart in fact than Kenji Yumoto and Osamu Taniguchi in the fundamental intent of their youth, to "change Japan from the inside."

Taniguchi pursued his own vision from his own special position as a member of the first entering class of the Keio Daigaku Shonan Fujisawa campus—sometimes with an audacity that would amaze a Todai contemporary. In one seminar class on intercultural communications, for example, Taniguchi found himself and his classmates bored to desperation by the lecture style of their professor. And he determined to do something about it.

"We all found that the lectures were putting us to sleep, and the materials she gave us, we read them and discussed them in class—and we all knew that we could do that much on our own. So, I first did some Japanese-style *nemawashi* [opinion-gathering] among the students as to how we thought the seminar could be changed into something that we wanted. And then I went to her office alone and told her to change it."

Walked into her office alone to tell a professor she was too boring; "told her to change it"?

"Right," laughs Taniguchi. "She said, 'You're the first person who has ever told me that.' But she took my opinion as interesting, and she thought what I was suggesting really would make the course more valuable, and so we talked on and off for about a week. And I told her what I thought she should do. And she asked me to become a teaching assistant in the class, to change things a bit in our direction. So in this seminar, I was able to serve as a kind of discussion leader, and I also evaluated the rest of the students along with her. Now," he concludes exuberantly, "she acts only as an observer as we conduct the course ourselves: When there is a need for new material, or the correction of views, or guidance, then she lectures.

"After all, when Keio founded this campus, they wanted to get back more to the fundamental ideas of Yukichi. And I guess this is what intercultural communications really means."

Changing Japanese university education?

Can't be all that hard, obviously.

A few months later, however, as we sat talking in the back of the campus's empty auditorium, a fuller picture of life at Shonan emerged. Not only is the school small, with a teacher core that is generally young (in their forties) and selected just for this campus, but the student body is full of "returnees"—a special designation that has presented Japan with real problems, in the form of young Japanese who have lived abroad on corporate assignments of their parents, yet who must, when they return, be brought quickly up to speed in the Japanese educational requirements so that they can take the college entrance exams on an equitable basis. (In 1994, there were a total of some 14,500 returnees, ranging from primary grades to college, and the number grows annually. Nearly fifty thousand Japanese children, ages seven to fifteen, were living abroad that year.) In Taniguchi's department, 25 percent of the students are returnees. And many of the students, returnees and otherwise, commute to campus by automobile each day—signifying a degree of student body affluence and independence almost unthinkable in other Japanese universities.

The computers, the databases, the e-mail are everywhere, and they do help otherwise reticent—or simply overwhelmed—students communicate not only with teachers but with one another. While the core courses of the first two years as elsewhere are in the form of mass lectures, and some of the professors, computers or no, insist on the old Confucian techniques of "shut up and listen," "in some points, yes, Keio is dedicated here to coming up with new solutions to old problems." This, after all, is what got Taniguchi fired up about going to college. "I think that the background of our generation is changing. I mean, my parents' background wasn't very typical. [Taniguchi's father spent more than half his career working overseas.] And if we compare my parents' social background to ours, there is again a great difference between those two. So I think Japan is going to change in many ways. We don't have to work for a company; we can work for ourselves these days."

Japan will change in many ways. We don't have to work for a company anymore. Can it be any wonder that a young man of Taniguchi's age finds himself as inspired, as worked up, as, say Yukichi Fukuzawa or Arinori Mori? There's a chance to make a difference here after all!

But as we chatted on, strolling about the gleaming campus, through the high-tech library, I thought I perceived uncharacteristic expressions of doubt; moments of hesitation signaling that not all was going as swimmingly as it appeared. At last, I had a chance to ask this pioneer of the initial freshman class of Keio Shonan Fujisawa, and of the first graduate class of his department, whether he thought the campus had changed much just in his own four years there. A note of unease emerged. "I think so. In bad ways. I think it's reverting to the old-style system. Because maybe for us, we never had elder students on this campus. We were the very first, so we had to do everything on our own, everything 'the first time.' But now the entering class has *senpai* [senior grades above them], and already you can see them passing a lot of information about lectures and about teachers back down the line to the younger ones. So all they have to do is follow the old ways, like at Todai or at Hitotsubashi. Just get copies of the lecture notes, just read them and pass the exams. The computer part of this scheme is still good, yes. But it's the students: it's not that they're too quiet; it's that they are just not aggressive. It's because of the testing system; it's because of the disciplinary system pounded into them from early days. The *senpai* give them the information now on how to pass the tests, how to get the degree. So it's just getting more like the other schools."

No matter how it is changing, there is real worry evident on this campus. The men all know that, as certified Keio graduates, they will all ultimately be employable no matter how bad any national recession is; it's just that the big companies will not have as many new jobs on offer in this recessionary season, and there could be tough competition for the best places even for these elite grads. But it is the women who will have the most justified concern about careers: Of the national total of 1994 female college grads, 15.2 percent remained unemployed in 1995.[8] But then, there isn't much new about that, either: Women have always borne the brunt both of recession and of professional discrimination. And who knows—maybe they'll find a Keio grad to marry, anyway. . . .

Something else was amiss in Taniguchi's deportment during this visit; this time he had a little less *sang-froid* than when we talked before. In April, the heart of the *shushoku* [job-hunting] season, I called him once again, to see how his plans to change Japanese education are progressing. "I've had to give up my plan for a psychology degree. The field is too narrowly professional, and once I'm in it the chances of coming back toward an educational career are about nonexistent at this school."

There was a short silence, of great eloquence. The dream was gone. "But I've still got plans to change education!" he assured me. "I'm going to finish my master's in intercultural education, and then hunt for a job with a big corporation like Mitsubishi Shoji or Asahi Television. Then after twenty years I can retire and come back to the campus, and then start reforming education. But right now," he admitted with more than a little worry, "I'm job hunting. And it's very tough."

The Japanese university has crushed him. A young Japanese, with his dream to make a difference, will wind up as just another part of the national corporate machinery. In time, his dreams will all fade away as his role in the national struggle to make Japan "strong"—through ever-growing production, marketing, industrial expansion, and the social ordering that all this makes necessary—begins to drive him.

Poles apart in schools and outlooks; the one a consummate if fledgling insider and the other always looking outside; the one with his plans and the other with his dreams—they both wanted to make a difference. Both fell to earth, pulled by the same Japanese system of gravity. Yumoto will be a businessman; Taniguchi will be a businessman.

The "changing education from the inside" that inspired both never could have occurred because elite Japanese universities are actually a trap. They pull you in with the promise that you can "change things only from the inside," and then they change *you*. This is accomplished by conditioning—forcing—you to accept a career system, even one that begins with employment in a foreign company, that guarantees its own ruling legitimacy by making sure it is *never* threatened or changed more than cosmetically. Moreover your personal fate is linked precisely to its success.

"What impressed me in comparing our studies at Todai to our studies at the University of Chicago School of Law," Yumoto once told me, "is that in the United States, we studied only the letter of the law. Here at Todai, we seemed always to be studying the spirit of the law." Perhaps this begins to sound like a noble, if not very professional, sense of priority—until one recalls what American Todai Law student Louis Ross reported about his discoveries of principle in Japanese commercial law: No matter what it actually says, the strong are automatically vested with power over the weak—merely as a consequence of the natural order of things. Far from principle or justice or mercy, the message here is really one of ultimate pragmatism. Nothing can go right for you unless you first have, and keep, power.

"Japanese citizens are not really citizens," as James Fallows puts it in different words in *Looking at the Sun*.[9] "Through its post-Meiji history, Japan has differed from other 'industrialized democracies' in that its fundamental policies, including the emphasis in school curricula, were not democratically determined." The Japanese "are mobilized, organized, and superbly well trained by the state and its institutions, but they have not really participated in its governance."

Perhaps one day, when they are safely orthodox and chastened and attuned to the responsibilities of the establishment, these two young elites will participate. But by then their missions will have become quite different. Yumoto and Taniguchi were never meant to touch the schools, their systems, their curricula, their purposes, in the same ways that the schools touched them. For both young Japanese, it was always like reaching for the sun.

Notes

1. All biographical materials on and quotations by the two subjects of this chapter are gathered from a series of interviews conducted separately from late 1993 through late 1994. I have changed their names here to assure their candid responses to my questions.

2. Ivan Parker Hall, *Mori Arinori* (Cambridge, MA: Harvard University Press, 1973).

3. Ibid.

4. Peter F. Drucker, "The New Society of Organizations," *Harvard Business Review* (September–October 1992).

5. *Yukichi Fukuzawa on Education: Selected Works* (Tokyo: University of Tokyo Press, 1985).

6. "Universities Rotting Within," *Japan Times*, March 14, 1995.

7. *Yukichi Fukuzawa.*

8. "More Than 13% of New Grads Can't Find a Job," *Japan Times*, April 26, 1995.

9. James Fallows, *Looking at the Sun: The Rise of the New East Asian Economic and Political System* (New York: Pantheon Books, 1994).

6

The Leisure Class

You see, all these rights and laws women didn't earn.
—Professor Mitsuko Duerr

Her name is Saki. She is well into her eighties. And the late-autumn Tokyo sunshine that falls like an elegant brocade around the shoulders of her kimono makes her almost a portrait of the slender, dignified femininity Westerners think of as the Japanese woman.

She moves with a timelessly elegant independence and serenity, which could not more deeply belie the realities of her life. When she was still in her mid teens, finished with her nine compulsory years of school, she was ordered to work in her uncle's shop until a marriage could be arranged by her parents. Saki never met her groom until her wedding day, when she became the property of his family and assumed her station as a servant in his home.

Saki's days as a young bride began at 4:30 A.M. when, driven by the carping commands of her mother-in-law, she rose to cook breakfast rice over a wood-fired stove—and served every other member of the family before she herself could eat. She then launched into an exhausting repertoire of chores that went on until nightfall, which took her back to the kitchen again to prepare dinner. In the hours between, her "training" as a wife progressed under the tutelage of a mother-in-law armed with a yardstick, which was cracked swiftly across Saki's shins if she let her toes even accidentally touch the ribbon borders of the *tatami* floormats everywhere beneath her feet.

Saki bore two sons. The youngest would die at Guadalcanal. But ever since they had secured her services as *oku-san* (wife, as opposed to mere bride) in the family, as well as assistant in her husband's business, times began to improve. Several years after her mother-in-law died—women of her generation often did not live beyond their late forties—Saki's eldest son brought his own bride home, and the circle was completed. Saki had worked her way up the seniority ladder to an absolute command of the household—and of its new bride—which she wields to this day.

Elsewhere on Tokyo's crowded streets we might see Tomoko, young enough to be Saki's great-granddaughter. Tomoko is an economics graduate of Keio University and an assistant in one of the planning sections of a prestigious major corporation. She plays the piano, skis, and enjoys a rendezvous every now and then with old college classmates at Ginza wine bars, when overtime does not keep her late at the office. But she always returns at a decent hour so as not to upset her parents. She knows they're already anxious over just when she and her fiancé Takaaki will finally set a date for their marriage.

Tomoko is in no hurry. Of course her parents do not know that she has already had an abortion, or that she takes the long view of prospects with Takaaki, a fish she considers already caught. She likes her job, banks more than a third of her pay, and shops occasionally in the city's stylish salons and finer department stores. While she is forbidden by her employer to wear jewelry at the office, it is not uncommon for her to wear six hundred dollars' worth of elegant but simple fashions to work. Tomoko hopes to get out and see some of the world—Hawaii, Singapore, perhaps even France— before she weds, finds an apartment of her own with Takaaki in the crowded suburbs, and resigns her job to start her family.

She fully expects that the salary, annual bonus payments equal to five months' pay, regular promotions and raises, overtime, extra family and commuting allowances, health insurance, and retirement plans that Takaaki can count on for the rest of his career will support her and her children with no threat of interruption throughout her life. In fact she plans to return to work herself once her children are in school, to put away money for their college education and for a "real" home—a house—someday.

Saki and Tomoko, though here composites of several real persons, are two genuinely representative contemporaries of present-day Japan. The women are generations—universes, really—apart in experience and lifestyle. But in a surprising number of ways their values are not dissimilar.

On however small a scale both are members of authentic elites, highly respected by society. Both belong to small but influential cliques that each woman would instinctively refer to as her *uchi,* her inner group. In Saki's case it is her family and her long-departed husband's business; in Tomoko's it is her section in the corporation. In both cases, livelihoods, business successes or failures, and the future welfare of many people depend on their groups' fates, and on these two women's respective roles in guiding and supporting them. More important still for our purposes, they are the mothers—the ultimate sources—of the elites that Japan's educational system, and the Todai system have prepared or will train to take over Japan, at one level or another. And this makes them important elites themselves.

The span of intergenerational change seen in their circumstances is almost incomprehensible. It is unthinkable that Saki as a young woman would have been sent to college; it is unthinkable that Tomoko would not have been. And that is a fine illustration of what Japan itself means when it insists that it is both "changing," and surviving largely unchanged, down to the present. For though the modern age has brought far more changes to the lives of Japanese women than it has to men, both Saki and Tomoko would agree with each other on much, including the fact that, to a large extent, they are both in control in Japan.

A s in most other times and places in history, men and women in Japan in the 1990s are not very honest with each other.

Ryosai Kembo is the classic descriptor for the correct station of women in Japanese life. The dictionary translates it as "a wife who is good and obedient to her husband and wise in rearing her children." However quaint, those qualities are in fact demanded of all of the nine million wives—more than half of all the mothers of young children in Japan—who are also holding down jobs outside the home. These women represent the 20 million adult females who, wise, obedient, or otherwise, now number four out of every ten Japanese employees.[1] There is more than sweet homily at work in this phrase. There is raw cynicism: Japan cannot function economically or politically today without the front-line commitment of its women as well as its men, and the nation's economic and government elites must respond to their needs. Yet neither employers nor government administrators can be seen as acceding to women's demands for equality without risking a damaging loss of control over them and their families. To these elites, that would mean the loss of control over society itself. Ever so carefully the two ends of the social pole, images and realities, must be kept balanced.

- Thus Japan's feminists insist that the modern society represses women and the modern economy exploits them. But now more females than ever are in the job market, earning more and scoring greater progress toward wage and career equality than ever in history.
- Thus the male power establishment claims that it is working at a fever pitch to extend institutional fairness and equality to all women. But such laws as they pass have no enforcement clauses, do nothing to prevent sexual discrimination in hiring, and in large part do not even acknowledge the existence of sexual harassment.
- Thus women insist that their career opportunities are deliberately forfeit when they leave work to bear children, so they can never return to

compete for promotions with men. But they exercise far more authority over their families, long outlive their husbands, control the vast majority of the nation's private expenditure, and enjoy much more leisure and discretionary income than males.

• Thus men insist they are refocusing their personal priorities from jobs to the home. But the divorce rates are growing at record paces, families are having fewer and fewer children, and the average husband now commits less than eight minutes per day to housework and child-rearing.

Japan, in short, is beginning to ring with an accusatory public diatribe between the sexes that seems to echo America's. But comparisons work only on the surface. Beneath it, where men, women, and their children live together, battles surely rage and psychic casualties can be fearsome: Women are unhappy over their empty sex lives, men are psychologically crippled by dominating mothers. Both are complicit in victimizing their own children with nearly inhuman educational pressures. Yet truces in these battles are legion. And, encouraging to those who hope for real change in Japan, women actually appear to have some odds of winning, at least over the short term and in matters that affect them most immediately. Whether that will continue to be true over the longer term is questionable, as we shall see. But, for the present, the conditions of national life leave women of both Saki's and Tomoko's generations holding some very strong cards.

Intending no irony at all, Mitsuko Horiuchi gives the perfect example why the same women who are 40 percent of the work force in the world's second-largest economy, and who regularly cast more votes than men in the world's second-largest electorate,[2] have neither economic nor political power in their own country.

Then-director for women's affairs of the Prime Minister's Office, Horiuchi not long ago explained to journalists the cabinet's vigorous New National Plan of Action of the Headquarters for the Planning and Promoting of Policies Relating to Women (which included appointment of a man, naturally, as minister for women's affairs). Describing a drumfire schedule of budget meetings, consultations, policy reviews, and information programs to launch the plan, Horiuchi revealed that she herself had been staying at her desk as late as 3 A.M. to get all the work done. "Personally," she confided to a solicitous reporter, "I have three children. But I live with my mother. My mother takes care of all three; otherwise, I don't think I could continue to do this work."

More than relaying an anecdote, Horiuchi unintentionally was affirming that for all the hubbub of programs and illusions of forward motion, the Japanese elite track to power remains lastingly divided into two: one for men, one for women. Tailored to each sex, they are extremely difficult to traverse from either side. Membership—ultimately leadership—in the elite groups that are open to men requires that almost all allegiance be given to the job, not the family. And so women who want the same power as men must adopt the same set of values, in one way or another subordinating their families to their enterprise. If they don't have mothers of their own handy at home to raise their children for them, they are shut out. Often, they are shut out even when they do.

It needs to be recognized that Japan has gone a long way, through its action plans, policy changes, new laws, and other mechanisms, in terms of responding to women's demands for workplace recognition. And it is prepared to go further because the labor economy now demands that women be placated at least enough to make them cooperative workers. (In the early 1990s, for the first time since the end of the war, more than half of all Japanese women fifteen and older were holding down jobs.[3]) But this is not a struggle for the rights of women. In fact this is just another government plan for slow and carefully controlled modifications in the social status granted to women. And it works extremely well.

But why? Why does this apparent power of the modern Japanese woman —measured by the yardsticks of purse, political consciousness, and electoral pluralities—not bring women genuine power? Because they are part of a social system that does not grant men the power of independent choice either. And it is on this systematic suppression of choice that the very success of the nation rests.

For example, women's work is always seen in a specific social light. A working American housewife or mother is almost always considered to be supporting her family. But the Japanese wife who works is almost always *not* working to support a family, but to supplement the comprehensive family welfare that is *provided by the husband.* In her early years, her income helps pay for a better education for her children: a target that supports national goals. In her later years, her income helps increase her family's savings for retirement: a target that also supports national goals. But she is never considered a family breadwinner, a role vested exclusively in her husband.

Mainichi Shimbun, one of Japan's largest daily newspapers, prints more than six million copies a day and deploys literally hundreds of reporters at home and overseas. In 1981 Naoko Abe was one of the first women ever to join its elite career editorial staff—one of only two females among the 120 journalist recruits offered a job that year. A university graduate, she was the first woman assigned to the Kyoto Bureau, and later to the prestigious Political Section, in the 120 years of the *Mainichi Shimbun*'s existence.

A lot more women have joined the staff since she did. Only one, however, has ever drawn an assignment abroad. Abe, who is married, had spent three years in the Foreign Department when I spoke with her and holds hopes of becoming the second. Could she now expect posting to a high-visibility, career-building correspondent's job in, say, Bosnia? "Never. They just recently told me that they're just not ready to send a woman to a place like that. I don't think they would send me to [any] third-world country, for example."

This is more than protective paternalism. It is another piece of evidence that equal careers for women, and even more for wives, are not acknowledged as important to the organization, to the society, or to the family. This allows employers to continue to ration equality of opportunity within their organizations, and it allows the government to ignore women's claims to equal representation in the society: a society that has been defined as an economic class, and in which women have been perpetually designated as second class. Though they made up more than half the industrial work force in Japan as long as eighty years ago,[4] and a great deal of the immense industrial fortune of their country has been built on their voluntary labor, women still earn only half the wages of men.

Of course, the net effect is exponential self-reinforcement:

• A man's involvement in the lifetime employment system is understood as crucial to his family's security, as the wife cannot substitute for him.
• His role as the sole breadwinner legitimates protecting him from female competition, because his career advancement is a matter of his family's survival.
• Since the average woman in actuality has almost no opportunity for a career, there is no reason for her to stay and try to build seniority for promotion with the same employer the way a man does.
• Nor will that employer want her to build seniority: younger women are always cheaper and always available.

And since almost all Japanese affluence—job security, career advance, health insurance, retirement plans, family allowances, tax preferences—already passes to the family through its male head, there is no reason to reapportion any to females. Those young women who are unmarried rely for their ultimate security on their fathers, and those who are married on their husbands. Therefore, the wisest thing a woman can do is get married and stay married: The difficulties facing a divorced wife or mother with no career possibilities and only hourly work at half the pay a man gets[5] in this system are obvious. The consequent rarity of families headed by a single mother (only about 1.1 percent of all Japanese births are to unwed mothers, and many of them may, in fact, under Japanese code, have a common-law husband; about the same percentage of Japan's total number of families are fatherless as a result of divorce) means that little pressure exists to grant women an equal franchise in the lifetime employment system.

There are female success stories in Japan, to be sure: in government administrative jobs in particular and in politics; among entrepreneurs, in the worlds of fashion and communication and show business one can find successful, wealthy, even powerful women. But they are always relatively few. It's meant to be an all-male club.

To the mystification of Western feminists, the obvious economic and voting power of Japanese women in the postwar age not only brings no change in their status, but not even any real agitation for change. The women's movement in Japan boils down to the discussion of terms of the government's plans. Or, as Horiuchi puts it, "There are 52 nationwide major women's organizations; they form a liaison group, and that group has representatives who sometimes come to our (cabinet) office, and who also submit written requests to the prime minister to improve the status of women in Japan." All "action" is in reality the appeal of petitioners to rulers. Thus all camps are comfortably secured within the government's huge tent. An injustice is corrected here, a complaint addressed there—and soon another action plan will be announced.

But in very few instances—only in occasional, specific, carefully worded decisions on actions brought in individual cases to the courts that defend the judicial power of the male government establishment—is the enormous reality of women's importance to the economy and the society allowed to underscore the constitutional and political *right* of women to equal treatment.

- Women's pay in companies with more than thirty workers remains on average half that of males. Wives and mothers who return to the work force are almost forced to take part-time jobs, where comparable pay rates are a third lower than for full-timers.
- Women who work only as part-timers constitute more than 30 percent of the female work force, yet are denied fair treatment in government pension benefits paid for through their jobs.[6]
- Women in clerical jobs in business outnumber men almost three to two, and hold more than two of every five jobs in the professions and technical fields—yet they account for far less than 10 percent of all middle managers.

• The very employment of women in major corporations is biased. Personnel rules place almost all of them, right from their entry, in slots that bar access to the "career track" for which almost all males *are* hired. And women virtually cannot be promoted through the ranks of middle management.

• In elective government in the 1990s they have done no better: As of 1993, only two women were mayors in Japan;[7] 2.8 percent of all members of the country's 47 prefectural assemblies, and less than 7 percent of the 763 National Diet members, were female as of that year.[8] The government failed again in 1992 to meet its stated goal of a 10 percent representation for women in the hundreds of important advisory panels where policy goals are hammered out, but finally did tip the 10 percent mark in 1993—at least in part by asking some of the women to serve on multiple panels. It was next aiming for 15 percent by 1995. That would be half what the United Nations has urged on Japan as its initial goal.

But women do play a vital role among Japan's elites. Then what is the sanctioned track for young elitist women like Tomoko? It is, with important modifications, quite like the elite track that produced Saki: marriage and the family.

It helps to begin our explanation by redrawing some of the old clichés about Japanese women and then to fill in this picture of how much their lives have changed in recent years: more changes, coming more quickly, than anyone including women themselves really comprehends.

A woman's life expectancy at the time of World War II was only about sixty years. By the end of the 1980s it was just over eighty-two years,[9] the longest in the world. Therefore in the span of just one lifetime, an entire extra generation of life has been given to theoretically every Japanese woman. Rich or poor, married or single, this is the one most important fact in the condition of women everywhere in Japan. On average, a Japanese urban woman reared in a middle-class family (80 percent of the national population is urban and a larger percentage than that believes it is middle class) can look forward to spending thirty-eight years as a largely independent "good wife and wise mother," from the time her last child enters school to the time her husband passes away. That span of years is longer in total than is her life until its start.

She will receive twelve years of primary and secondary education in her youth, and it is more likely that she will go on to university or junior college—almost four chances out of ten—than will a Japanese male.

She will almost certainly work—at any moment over 60 percent of all Japanese female adults are working, either as employees or in family businesses—and she will marry later, at twenty-six-plus, than women of earlier generations. She will also bear fewer children: no more than two, but just as likely only one.

Before she marries she will live with her parents, banking or shopping away a large percentage of her income. After she marries, she will most likely leave her job, probably when she is expecting her first child. She will receive free prenatal and postnatal care from the government, contributing to one of the lowest infant mortality rates in the advanced world, and inexpensive child care will be available if she wants to return to work early. More likely, though, she will stay at home at least until her youngest child grows to school age.

Then she probably will return to the work force on a part-time basis, to save money for her children's education. After they graduate, she may or may not work on, for extra family savings toward retirement or for her own gratification. The odds are that she will at some time avail herself of adult education, whether to learn hobbies such as flower arrangement and tea ceremony, to strengthen her skills in a foreign language, or to pursue college-level courses for self-edification.

After age thirty-five, with children off to school and husband in a career stage that demands more and more hours at the job, a very large percentage of the day will become her own to command (relatively few women have, like Horiuchi, a mother or in-laws living in their homes). Housework including meals can all be done in less than four hours. Virtually the entire household budget is under her management; almost all shopping decisions are hers. Part-time and volunteer work beckons during the day, as do tennis lessons, lunch with friends, shopping, TV soap operas, and classes in calligraphy or French. In the evening her returning children reclaim her attention. It will be more or less like this for her, eventually minus the children and then finally her husband, for four decades or more. While her husband, the average Japanese male, put in a total of 2,500 working hours in 1992—with one out of every six men topping the 3,100-hour mark (the equivalent of 388 eight-hour days)[10] and courting actual damage to his health from overwork (there are estimates that it causes more than 10,000 deaths annually) —"Three meals and a midday nap" was the popular turn of phrase for the new daily priorities of the new Japanese woman.

What we have described here, in other words, is Japan's new Leisure Class.

Of course to some extent this is a cynicism, unjust both to low-income families where wives work because they have no choice and to highly motivated, university-trained women who are denied careers they have dreamed of all their lives because they are forced to choose between a profession and a family. But, to a greater degree than most conceptual thinkers on Japan have yet seen, it *is* true.

Middle-class, urban women enjoy a position of almost unimaginable privilege in Japan. Consider:

• They are ceded lifetime security—indeed, guaranteed it, by all the social and bureaucratic structures that define and control them, *as long as* they play the game by society's rules. They are allowed, even encouraged, to protest inequities. But, short of domestic disaster, as long as they follow the outcome of consensus they need never assume the heavy male burdens of household breadwinner. (And all they need do, except in cases of severe abuse, is cooperate minimally with their husbands to be protected by powerful social sanctions against the vicissitudes of divorce.)

• Women control all household budgets in the nation, including the world's largest preserve of individual cash savings. Almost all spending, saving, and investing priorities of the home are theirs to decide, which has brought everyone from stockbrokers to postal-savings clerks to court them and left vast percentages of the consumer industries in bondage to their whims. It is not an accident that home appliances emanating from Japan are so plentiful, so imaginatively varied, and of such quality that they have become familiar sights in homes all over the world as well. Japanese wives are discriminating shoppers, with a lot of time available to educate themselves as consumers. They are a demanding test market for manufacturers.

• As women's roles in the work force have grown so important to the economic expansion of Japan, they have indeed acquired stature under the country's "power is a function of production" rubric, touched on in an earlier chapter. They must now be counted as vital elements of the economy as well as de facto directors of household consumption. This has given their priorities a certain new weight in the society's economic scheme. For example, day-care center capacity throughout the country now actually exceeds demand—and a new law has been passed that grants up to a year's parental leave from work.

• Women remain comfortably exempt, except in cases of farms and family businesses, from the necessity to take any role at all in aiding their husbands' work or careers. Japanese elites never take their wives to social functions associated with business; they never even entertain at home their colleagues, supervisors, or customers, which would oblige their wives to play the Western role of official hostess. In a male-only lifetime employment system, the wife is almost completely immune to all pressures related to "the job"—including, most importantly, the threat of losing it.

• While it remains true that the only gateway to this new leisure class (other than inheritance) is marriage, and that most women by far do marry in Japan, it is also important that the rapid shift from extended to nuclear families has freed housewives from a vast amount of the responsibility they held under the old *ie,* or patrilineal household, system. No longer need they be concerned with the grating punctilio or sheer physical labor required in intricate family politics and ceremony or with the reverence and priority owed senior brothers-in-law and their wives. Nor—most importantly—are they burdened with the nagging presence of a mother-in-law. In Japan the demands of the position of "housewife" have very greatly abated.

• It is also true now that women who marry within the middle class are quite likely to be marrying a handsome inheritance. Not only are their parents-in-law the most affluent and successful generation of Japan's celebrated savers, but if they are homeowners they may be passing on land assets that are literally worth more than a hundred times what they fetched when purchased a generation or more earlier: even, perhaps, millions of dollars. And since the average family size has fallen steadily in the postwar period, there will be fewer siblings for their husbands to share those inheritances with.

• The late marrying ages of both sexes in Japan (females after twenty-six; males at nearly thirty) give women not only a great deal of "free time" to select their spouses but also something of a warranty: By the time he is this close to thirty an elite male has long since passed his highest educational mark, entered the business where he will be employed for life, and had the time to show some maturity and some promise of what his career is likely to yield. In some prestigious large firms, in fact, more than 50 percent of all marriages are between employees. Further, because of the constant age difference between sexes at time of marriage and the dwindling demographic contours of the population, at present there are more potential suitors than potential brides. Altogether, it's a great buyer's market for Japanese single women.

• As a result of these profound Japanese changes, today's women have been allowed to shelter themselves from much in life that is unpleasant, or at least demanding: poverty, unemployment, the need to help a family survive. Neither they nor their mothers have ever had to send sons or brothers to war. The world as externalized in the Japanese social schema is a man's place; women are not expected to concern themselves overmuch with questions of foreign relations, defense, the environment, or the course of larger events. While many women do think, talk, and write about these things, most lead rather sheltered lives in regard to public questions. They have it, that is to say, both ways: Their position in the home is privileged and protected, while their position in the economy is being improved steadily if slowly—without their having to take much hand at all in bringing about the improvements. To the "pure homemaker," in fact, almost nothing in the outer world, beyond her relationship to it as a consumer, has anything at all to do with her daily life. (This is why homemakers' groups frequently seem so collectively naive and easily manipulated in, for example, such matters as "approving of" long-continued government bans on imports to Japan of foreign rice: It is these same bans that force them to pay from four to six times what their contemporaries elsewhere in Asia pay.) Bluntly, people who have never had it so good are seldom genuinely concerned about changing the world around them.

• As women marry later and later in life, and as the pressure of tiny homes, high costs of living, and horrendous educational expenses for their children grows, families have responded by producing fewer and fewer offspring. The statistical average now is down to only about one and a half children per couple—less than the replacement rate for the national population. Japan's populace is already aging with alarming speed. It is as much the government's concern to avert a looming demographic catastrophe by persuading women to have more babies as it is a genuine spirit to recognize women's rights that has led to progressive national policy and legislation for child-care leave, the expansion of child- and day-care facilities, and other family-support encouragements. In what might be termed irruptions of administrative angst, in fact, some local governments are already paying subsidies to families that have produced "extra" children,[11] and it has even been suggested that the national government establish such fecundity bonuses for women.

• None of this means that Japan is the best of all possible worlds for all women. However, a certain amount of irresponsibility is abetted, both by men's consideration of women as beneath the responsibility of public roles and by women's disingenuous acquiescence in that view. Most notably, and most crucially, this tells in the failure of the intermediate community in Japan. Because men have almost no time to devote to community affairs, it is left to women to engage in local activities of all descriptions. Middle-class urban women, however, with no pressing need to fight for anything more than principle, have largely accepted the proposition that men are the only ones really qualified to lead. For this reason (that is, because men are always away at their jobs and largely absent from the community), virtually all initiative in community groups comes from the government, not the people. Citizens are conspicuous by their acquiescence in the public decision-making process. This has a more dangerous effect than might at first be supposed: Since almost all budget for the community comes from central government, virtually all authority on spending that budget also comes from on high. Because of this vacuum—the lack of participation of common households in community political affairs, on the one hand, and the dominance of elite male administrators accustomed to *presuming* the decision-making power on the other—almost nothing stands between the Japanese people and the directives and political intents of the central government. It is a danger that largely can be laid at the feet of Japanese women.

This is one more way in which the circle of the Japanese system of control is self-perpetuating.

This is an arena, however, in which the purposes of Japan's government and its women will before long inevitably collide. The impact will be wrenching, and it will be felt throughout society. It is possible that it will set back progress for Japanese women literally by generations. The outcome is sure to mean personal heartbreak for many thousands of Japanese; for a great number, it already has.

Japan is about to age, almost disastrously. In 1990, 12 percent of the population was age sixty-five or older—representing a doubling of the national ratio of seniors to the rest of the population in just twenty years. The government forecasts that, by 2020, the percentage will more than double again, leaving Japan with the largest proportion of old persons in its population of any advanced nation. More than one in every four Japanese will by then be sixty-five years old or older.[12]

This has the potential to bankrupt the country. Japanese government social-welfare payments (including pensions and health-insurance outlays) reached some 120 billion dollars in 1994, accounting for almost 20 percent of the national budget: more than the outlays for public works, defense, education, or science.[13] That figure is expected to double, to $240 billion, by decade's end, driven by the huge increases in the senior population.[14] Cross-referencing the rise in the senior population to the growth in outlays to sustain them yields a calculation that the government's welfare bill alone will rise to as much as a third of the national budget by 2025, mainly just to take care of the elderly. If no adjustments are made in retirement age or social programs, in a single generation from now 2.2 working men and women[15] will have to produce all the tax revenues needed to support one retiree. A mid-1994 government report estimates that the tax burden for those workers still remaining in 2025 may rise to 50 percent.

These figures do not, of course, equal more than a fraction of what the costs will be to Japan's economy overall. Some estimates are that 40 percent of the gross domestic product will be consumed in supporting senior citizens by 2025.

There is much discussion of raising retirement-age eligibility under

Japan's version of Social Security and of raising taxes soon. (Indeed, the government will not only raise the consumption tax from 3 to 5 percent in 1997, but may also attempt to levy a new, specially purposed 1 percent in payroll tax on the employed population. All these new incomes are still forecast to be insufficient to prepare for the social expenses of the aging of Japan.) As unpopular as these steps are and will be, public reaction is likely to be just as strong to the government's ultimate preferred solution: obliging the nation's daughters to provide shelter, sustenance, and care in their homes for their husband's parents or their own, or both.

Statistics portend a dark future for the elderly. Most middle-aged couples who will reach retirement age after the turn of the millennium say they do not want or intend to live with their children in retirement. But when the infirmities and illnesses of old age overcome them, six in every ten of them say that they do indeed hope to be cared for by their children.[16] Most of the rest prefer to be taken care of in their declining years by "a spouse." This overlooks the obvious non sequitur: Women already outlive men by six years and are expected to outlive them by seven years in 2025.[17] Who will care for all the widows in their late seventies, their eighties, and beyond? And what will happen when these disabled elders—there will be over five million of them by the same year—*do* come to rest in their children's homes: homes that may be much too small to accommodate invalids, and where the homemakers themselves will be in their fifties and sixties?

The answer is that the burden of caring for these millions will fall on women. Ninety percent of all Japan's caregivers now are women, and four out of every five of these are ministering to a spouse, a parent, or a parent-in-law. The majority of these disabled seniors are bedridden, and the burdens are very heavy indeed: 40 percent of all women caring for seniors in their homes now were forced to quit their jobs to take on the task.[18] Obviously, the aging of Japan will push many hundreds of thousands more women out of the work force before they are ready to leave. And so it will actually reinforce the system in which industries eject women workers with mounting seniority and replace them with young, cheaper recruits. Future change in Japan, in other words, is going to *reverse* the drives for equality of working and career women, rather than strengthen them.

There is much public talk in government circles of ameliorating this looming burden. Already, localities are giving grants to elders to make living in their own homes easier, and local women's groups are organizing self-help support associations for sharing in-home care. But it is disingenuous to suggest that this problem can be solved comfortably within communities themselves. Only the national government can create and fund the efforts on the necessary scale to prepare for the vast growth in numbers of the aged who will need institutional-quality care in their last years—and the government does not have the money. The infrastructure of nursing homes for the elderly is already inadequate. Tokyo, a city of almost twelve million, has only a few thousand public and private nursing-home beds today.

There is an official pledge of enormous programs to begin filling in this deficit soon with care centers, new residential homes, and new programs to serve the dependent elderly. "But what the government is actually doing," according to a Sumitomo-Life Research Institute analyst who has produced studies on national aging policy, "is working on ways for women to provide all this care. They are sponsoring the creation of home-enterprise systems, and pushing companies to grant more leaves to employees for home care-giving." Of course, the bases of these types of "solutions" are indeed women, caring for the elderly at home.

In fact what the government is most likely doing is promulgating a falsehood. According to this analyst, "When I talked with the senior official for these matters at the Ministry of Health and Welfare, she admitted to me that while her ministry is telling the people that it will create lots of nursing homes to care for the elderly in future, their real aim is to make the younger generations take care of their parents at home. So they are saying different things: on paper—to the people—they are saying 'Don't worry.' But the facts are something different."

The facts are that, bowing to the pressures of the moment, Japan is engaged in creating the illusion of forward progress for women, but it is not dispensing *power*. And the illusion is already becoming threadbare. As a tough national recession hit Japan in the first half of the 1990s, job recruitment openings for women were arbitrarily, throughout entire industries, cut by more than twice as much as those for men. One wonders where these women will acquire the retirement-savings income necessary to support themselves in their old age. And, in the uncertain future of the next century, women will have to fight for themselves on yet another front: to oppose the determined efforts of the nation's power elites to force them back into servitor status of the same character as in the ancient household hierarchy, and to pre-empt their newly won leisure time, for purposes much more useful to meeting the national goals.

Notes

1. Japan Economic Institute, Report No. 44A, December 3, 1993, p. 7.
2. Director of the Office for Women's Affairs of the Prime Minister's Office Mitsuko Horiuchi, Press Briefing, March 3, 1993.
3. "More Than Half of All Japanese Women Now Working," *Nikkei Weekly,* September 13, 1993.

4. Lynn Thiesmeyer, review of *Japanese Women Working,* ed. Janet Hunter, *Asahi Evening News,* August 29, 1993.

5. *About Japan Series: Japanese Women Yesterday and Today,* Foreign Press Center Japan, March 1991.

6. "Boost for Women Sought in Pension Overhaul," *Nikkei Weekly,* November 15, 1993.

7. Office for Women's Affairs, Prime Minister's Office, "Women in Japan Today," January 1993.

8. "Few Women in Politics, Report Says," *Japan Times,* September 2, 1993.

9. *Nikkei Weekly,* November 15, 1993.

10. "Government Study Addresses Excessive-Work Habits," *Nikkei Weekly,* January 17, 1994.

11. Horiuchi, Press Briefing.

12. Interview with Research Fellow Takako Katsuragawa of Sumitomo-Life Research Institute, Inc., February 1993.

13. "Costs Climb for Nation's Social Programs," *Nikkei Weekly,* November 1, 1993.

14. "Taxes Seen Rising to 50 Percent of Income," *Japan Times,* May 25, 1994.

15. "Plan to Raise Pension Age to 65 Draws Fire," *Nikkei Weekly,* October 18, 1993.

16. Katsuragawa interview.

17. *Nikkei Weekly,* November 1, 1993.

18. Katsuragawa interview.

7

Who's on Top: The Women Elites

If you talk with thirty-year-old women who are single, they are not very happy. Actually every one of them with whom I met is very eager to find someone to marry. It's just the trouble whether they can find someone worthwhile.
—Professor Takie Sugiyama Lebra, in a 1994 lecture

Of course, females have a little advantage over males: In case things don't work out, they can always depend on their husbands. A woman can just give up the idea of a career.
—Mikako Okuma, former career staff member, Mitsubishi Research Institute

If anyone would seem a beneficiary of the "new equality" Japan now claims it guarantees to women, surely Takako Katsuragawa would top the list. A graduate of Sophia University—the same school that produced reformist Prime Minister Morihiro Hosokawa *and* his wife—Katsuragawa went on to attend the Matsushita Institute of Government and Management, and then became the first woman to be accepted as a staff research analyst, in the same career status as her male colleagues, at a prestigious Tokyo think tank.

She loves her job, has already produced important work while still in her twenties, finds that her employer treats her with scrupulous equality, and has just married a young man with a promising future and an egalitarian willingness to share all household chores. In all prospects she would seem set for a sparkling professional future. Except that she plans to quit as soon as her first child comes along.

Katsuragawa represents the paradox of her generation of Japanese female elites, the first to sail out across the newly opened horizon of Japanese legal equal-opportunity mandates. She is glad to see that women like her at last are recognized in principle as equal to males and thinks it vital that women now be given the same career prerogatives as men. She knows that there is a new landscape of social support for working mothers, such as lengthy child-care leaves that are available to both spouses, and easily accessible day care.

But she is adamant about planning to resign and return to being a house-wife, abandoning her new career, as soon as she has her first baby.

Why? "Maybe I'm a very conservative person," she laughs. "But I be-lieve the mother just has to be at home until her children are three years old. So she can give them lots of love."

Katsuragawa may or may not be the despair of labor administrators, on one side, and feminist crusaders, on the other, who have so tortuously achieved the compromises that at last open elite career paths to young women like her. But she and the many thousands of her university-graduate contemporaries turning away from such hard-won gains just as the doors to equal opportunity seem to be opening illustrate the truth of the social situa-tion of women in Japan. Among elites as well as the working class, most see their futures in starting a family, not in following a career. As Katsuragawa cheerfully acknowledges, "Most all women want to get mar-ried. And after getting married, and after becoming pregnant, they'd like to quit their jobs. Caring for the children is more important than work."

But that's not all they're planning on doing.

There are truths here more evident than instinctive domesticity. One of them is that Japanese women typically seek marriage not just for the com-panionship of a husband but for what is to them a social imperative, produc-ing children. Even for educated women, even for those from comfortably affluent families where self-support is not a concern, the marriage market is what counts. It can be hard for an outsider to understand just how strongly this drive weighs even on the most intellectual of women. When interview-ing a female scholar who is a Ph.D. candidate in the Law Department of the University of Tokyo—the elite of elites—I was startled to hear her admit freely that a major reason for her choice of academic career was to find a husband who will also be a scholar, "so that we can share our lives.

"In Japanese tradition," she explained, "to become a good housewife is the final goal. Many women in Japan who have graduated from university want to work in corporations. But most think that to take a job is just one step toward getting a good marriage partner."

Parents can be almost frantic in their insistence that daughters marry and produce families. Daughters reflect that imbuement, making it one of their own highest priorities. Elite women who have not found a potential mate by their late twenties are almost obliged to accept matchmaking introductions to complete strangers, arranged by their families, just to show that they honor this "obligation." A strong atmosphere of angst begins to cloud the psyche of many women who pass age thirty unwed.

Part of the reason is the ipso facto prevalence of the nuclear family in Japan itself. Because divorce occurs, for example, at only a little more than a fourth the rate in America (where the population is twice as large), society sees almost everywhere either extended or two-parent families and has almost no familiarity with households headed by single mothers that seem to be successful alternatives to marriage. Actually choosing to be a single mother, under any circumstances other than extreme duress, is thought a social aberration (and would be financially difficult in any case because of the low career potentials for women). In one opinion survey of a thousand pregnant women conducted in 1990[1] only eight percent of those polled found choosing single motherhood "acceptable." Though no Japanese law forbids it, fertility specialists routinely refuse to perform artificial insemination on single women.

But these rationales are tautologies. The main reason that even elite women overwhelmingly stress marriage and motherhood above professional career in their own life choices is that achievement in the professional world, though it may receive emphasis in headlines and the public debate, still has almost nothing to do with the real principles underlying the elite status that Japanese society *is* willing to grant women.

To put it succinctly, a woman is not considered well adjusted, let alone successful, by any social arbiter—government, the media, business, her own relatives—until she has married and produced her own family. Marriage "was and still is," in the words of Takie Sugiyama Lebra, "considered a mandatory condition for a person to attain full human status and to enjoy life."[2]

The duress of social stigma is understandable in any society. But why such an overwhelming stress among modern, educated women themselves on attaining the role of mother, wife, and mistress of a household? For one compelling reason: While the exclusion of women from elite careers on almost every front for generations has made it impossible for them to attain political power in the external world, they have learned how to accrue political power through their control over the *interior* world of the family. It is, as seen in an earlier chapter, in the position of homemaker that women have gained the status of a new leisure class, have taken command of the realm of consumption, and have gained real power over the conditions and decisions affecting their daily lives.

There is, then, a genuine dichotomy of power in Japan along the axis of gender. The opposite side of the coin of women's exclusion from formal, institutional power is women's ascension to domination of informal, domestic —and equally real—power throughout the society. Modern women elites like Katsuragawa pay greater homage than they know to their female forebears in recognizing that legitimate elite status, for Japanese women, comes mainly through their control over a household.

At first this power will be confined largely to the realms of her own home and neighborhood. But for the elite woman, or those aspiring to be one, the choice of a suitable husband is extremely important because as the couple matures, and the husband attains higher and higher rank in his career, the power he acquires will extend to the wife in important ways. "The internal activities of the family," writes sociologist Matthews Masayuki Hamabata, "are intimately related to the position of the family within the [national] economy and the polity, and the way those two realms are organized is intimately related to the internal activities of the family, at least within the upper class in Japanese society."[3] In other words, among upper elites the whole family participates in the national power structure.

Just how it does that is explored below. But the main reason it is so requires a review of Japanese history—and the recognition that even the most modern and rational of societies does not spring full blown from the pages of sociological theory or popular democratization, but rather develops out of its own most powerful traditions. It was only slightly more than a century ago that the Meiji government, reforming Japan at a time when much of the national economy was still based on family industry and elite-family control of capital, took command of the family itself. As it reached for modernization in a single, unsettling leap, the new government reincorporated the family as a Confucian institution through which men, their wives, their children, and their property could be controlled by a central authority. This reorganization of the family along formal lines is called the *ie* system.

To understand the impressive degree to which Japanese women find power in the family today, we need to discuss how the *ie* system made the household a unit of government and transposed marriage into a type of economic and political alliance. The *ie* had always had something of government about it: It was the old household system of the ruling *samurai* families before Japan's emergence into modern times. Complete with complex schematics of main houses and subhouses, it was based on the web of relationships spreading beneath the family patriarch and on the relative ranks between older and younger sons. Since the warrior classes ruled the old Japan through the control of feudal holdings by clans, with power passed through intermarriage and inheritance, the blueprint for these extended, highly formalized families to serve as quasi-governmental organizations had in fact already been drawn when the modern age began.

When the Meiji government came to power in 1868, its biggest task was to displace the old rule of the warrior class. But it found the *ie* system a very comfortable model to draw on for its own new systems of control because the *ie* was a strict hierarchy with strong Confucian traditions of loyalty and obedience to the head of the household. Though the new leaders did not need the tangled webs of *samurai* alliances and rivalries interfering with the political imperatives of modern nation-building, these domestic hierarchies of the household were, it turned out, just the qualities a young rebel government that seized power in the name of the ultimate Japanese patriarch, the Emperor, did want to inspire. Rather than rolling up and discarding the past then, the Meiji government used it—by making the *ie* system into the law of the land. Commoners, who until then did not even have the right to possess a family name, were legally obligated in 1871 to adopt surnames and the same domestic life-styles and family organizations of the warrior caste, those of the *ie*.

Under the Meiji government, and all governments until after World War II, the *ie* was an organization in many ways like a business: the sum total of all the nuclear families of all the men of a single line of descent, living under the authority (and, often, in the house) of the senior patriarch. Only males could inherit property from generation to generation—and only the eldest male. All women, whether sisters or brides of the brothers, were propertyless and formally powerless in the *ie*.

It is important to understand how far-reaching this system, which produced Saki (the venerable great-grandmother described in chapter 6), was: It embraced all families, high and low, in the empire. As the only option for women, marriage under this system became a mechanism for forcing them to submit to the male authority of whatever *ie* they married into. A bride was, in a sense, leaving her own family completely to enter her groom's. In fact that is still true today.

However, the *ie* was originally not only a family arrangement, but an economic one: It was as important for control of the family's property and businesses as for control of its members. The more seniority Saki acquired —and especially after she had produced an heir—the more deeply she became involved in the family business, and the more her husband and other family members, depending on the type and size of that business, relied on her to help run it. She acquired real managerial authority over the family's material assets as well, in other words. And the marriage itself was thus transformed from a dependency into a partnership.

Within the *ie* and through it, then, women found all their roles in life, from wife and mother to community and family member—and all their status. In their senior years, in fact, when they themselves became the mothers-in-law, women in the *ie* possessed considerable social stature and power both inside and outside their homes.[4] A man who tried to displace his wife with no justification at this stage was running terrible social, even professional risks. He could keep mistresses if he had sufficient extra money, but there was no question of a divorce.

The society that had forced her obeisance became in turn very dependent on the woman. By observing its punctilio women became the real keepers of the traditions of the *ie,* and more than small factors in its ultimate turns of fortune. Men and women could in fact be called real equals—though any American woman observing Saki's life casually would hardly interpret her situation that way.

What the *ie* did to metamorphose Saki's life patterns into Katsuragawa's was to formally disappear. It was legally abolished by the Occupation authorities as a vestige of feudalism. That they were understandably oblivious to the inner harmonies and balances that had made the *ie* system so effective in socializing both men and women, and organizing the society for stability through the tumultuous changes of Japan's modernization, made no difference. In law it was done away with—but only in law. In pattern and tradition, in consciousness of status and seniority among related families, the *ie* as the guiding concept of the larger family remains in many ways to this day. Even many middle-class housewives are more keenly aware than their husbands, for example, of just who is related to whom in their families, by marriage or blood, and to what degree.

And the *ie* is much more than a persistent collective tradition for well-to-do and powerful elites. Hamabata, writing in the same commentary of present-day bureaucratic and industrial upper-class families, notes its continuing influence not only over the social aspects of family life but over the political as well: "Indeed, the *ie* [at this level] looks less like a family and more like a corporate group with a variety of options available to it to fill positions and thereby guarantee organizational survival."

But its demise as a legal system was not the only change. At war's end something else happened that had an equally dramatic impact on women: The family was urbanized. Like a cyclonic vortex, the rapidly growing cities and industrial zones sucked hundreds of thousands of young Japanese women out of their extended families of mothers- and brothers-in-law, *honke* (main houses) and *bunke* (subhouses), and the family's businesses, and set them down in new suburban zones. There they were left alone as homemakers with children, while husbands commuted off to new jobs, and new allegiances to their own lifetime employers.

This has had more effect on the power roles of women than even their transformation as consumers in the new economy. Divorced now both from her husband's business and from the minute standards of family and neighborhood behavioral expectations—and left utterly alone with her youngest children almost the entire waking day—this was a woman liberated from many of the powerful social matrices that had bound her for centuries, *yet left by tradition with the absolute authority of command over the family's affairs.* If she still answered formally to her husband, within her own household she became free. The history of the social emancipation of Japanese females is largely the story of the exploration of this freedom.

It has had its beneficial side for women of the new elites, as seen in chapter 6: new leisure, new self-determination, new awareness, new affluence and new-found power. But it has had a darker side as well, which modern Japanese women are not quite so eager to speak about. In a way, they have handed over their children as hostages to buy that freedom.

Japanese mothers, including elites, may indeed be willing to lay down their own career aspirations to give their children good homes; to produce sound, happy, well-adjusted offspring in the closeness of a loving and attentive family. But in practice it is not as simple as that. What so many mothers, deprived of the traditional stairway to social status through ascension in the *ie* and cut off from any equivalent achievement in a career, are in fact striving to do is produce *successful* children. Sons and daughters become extensions of a woman's social aspirations. And the only way she can succeed, in society's eyes, is by turning out children who are themselves successes in the educational system.

For her to achieve entry of a son to one of the top universities of Todai, Keio, or Waseda is the equivalent, to a homemaker, of a husband's promotion to company vice-president. So strong is this female brand of social competition that even young women today, who *have* managed to find new entries onto corporate career tracks, will switch their priorities to the future "careers" of their children—even before they are born.

This is a very subtle trap for women. Its successful outcome, the educational triumph of a son or daughter, is roundly applauded by everyone from family to government to society itself, and by extension this becomes a *national* applause for a mother. Each year the newspapers and magazines are filled with pictures of smiling candidates who have succeeded at the entrance exams. Successful careers and good marriages are secured in a single tick for such triumphant offspring, everyone recognizes. Yet it is too easy to ignore whether this achievement, which comes at such painful cost and terrible risk, is what the child himself actually wants. From the outset the child is socialized by its mother to strive for just this victory. Mother, child, and educational system all form one great team, to strive for this family "success."

In just this way, then, almost all elite mothers collaborate actively and enthusiastically with Japan's elite power structure to capture yet another generation, which will emerge imbued with the same values and capabilities needed to reinforce that power structure itself. Few mothers, until recently, have stopped to ponder the truth that this same power structure they work so hard to push their sons into is what produces the barriers to female participation that have shut *them* out to start with. Largely because of feminine ambition, Japan's elite selection mechanisms start not in the classroom, but in the cradle.

Although no longer in law but in a tradition authenticated through social recognition and through the vast web of social and economic hierarchies that runs Japan today, the modern family that is the echo of the old *ie* remains in concept something like a unit of government. The male is the head of the family, representing it to the external world. Within the *uchi* (the "inside") the woman has risen to head of the nuclear household, where her own authority can be nearly absolute and an attractive alternative to unmitigated competition for power with males in the outside world. The child is answerable absolutely to school as well as to parents; the father is answerable absolutely to his employer. The employer in turn is answerable not only to the marketplace but formally or informally to the government, which is composed of the elites that this family system itself has competitively produced through the educational system. Only the woman enjoys an answerability, to her husband, that is largely abstract and defined only by broad, simple principles.

There are, however, still other nexuses through which elite females extend their family's influence and protect it. To outsiders the existence of these intimate networks can come as a surprise, as it did to sociologist Hamabata, attending a cocktail party with upper-crust Tokyoites: "I learned at the party that Mrs. Murata, whose husband's firm was in electronics on an international scale, and Mrs. Itakura, whose husband's firm was also world renowned, were not just good friends but cousins. Their mothers were sisters. Through small talk, I also discovered that the young people's households were in food products, pharmaceuticals, and finance. Furthermore, they were all related through their mothers; that is, their mothers and aunts were sisters. This was the first revelation: a kin network across industry through women." A revelation indeed. This second tier of Japanese elite social organization is one largely invisible to outsiders. But it is a primary cultural channel through which women continue to build status and influence as managers of the most crucial affairs of their families.

Hamabata's revelation would seem at first as surprising as learning, on attending a social gathering of the American Chamber of Commerce in Washington, that more than ten percent of all the husbands and wives there are related by blood or marriage. But a comparable situation, in Japan, would likely produce little surprise. You would not be shocked to learn, for example, that the sister of Empress Michiko is married to the son of the chairman of the chemicals giant Showa Denko, whose own brother is president of mammoth utility Tokyo Gas—and whose daughter is in turn married to the son of the late Prime Minister Eisaku Sato. (Sato himself, of course, was actually the full brother of the late Prime Minister Nobusuke Kishi, whose own grand-uncle was Yosuke Matsuoka, who had been Japan's foreign minister during the war.)

There would also be little to remark in the fact that a brother of the Empress is married to the daughter of Baron Kichizaemon Sumitomo of the Sumitomo fortune; nor that *her* sister married Morinosuke Mitsui of the fabled Mitsui clan. It also would surprise us little to learn that the brother-in-law of the Empress has a sister who is wed to the grandson of the late Prime Minister Hamaguchi.[5]

The reformist former Prime Minister Morihiro Hosokawa also knows that the political knack runs in his family; his grandfather was wartime Prime Minister Fumimaro Konoe and his great-grandfather, as well as holding the presidency of Gakushuin Peers' School, was at one time the chairman of Japan's prewar House of Peers itself. Hosokawa's other relatives anchor him to the imperial family as well. He has a brother whose wife is the daughter of Prince Mikasa and a distant cousin who is the wife of Prince Hitachi, the brother of the present Emperor.

Anyone who arrived for the event in a Toyota, meanwhile, would certainly be familiar with the illustrious family whose company manufactures that automobile. Yet he or she may not know that its chairman's father-in-law was a director of the Mitsui Bank, and his daughter-in-law's father served as vice-president of the Mitsui & Co. trading giant. His own brother-in-law, meanwhile, is a former construction minister and governor of Shizuoka prefecture, while his sister-in-law is the daughter of the former head of Shimizu Kensetsu, one of the nation's largest construction firms.[6]

Though attendees at this gala might not think anything especially important about all these relations, in fact there is. They constitute *keibatsu,* or the extended family cliques into which Japan's upper-class *ie* are fused. Politics, the administrative elites, industry, commerce, the arts, the academic world: All are woven into the dense tapestry of this serial Japanese family portrait. Even Masako Owada, who in 1993 was drawn into the royal family from the "commoner" classes to the great approbation of the Japanese public by becoming engaged to the Crown Prince, counts among her family relations two managing directors of large corporations, a university professor, a former corporate president, two Imperial Japanese Navy admirals, a former commandant of the Japanese Maritime Safety Agency, a noted social critic—and of course her father, a former deputy foreign minister.[7]

What these ties may or may not mean to business and political alliances at the highest levels of elite power structures is not our point at the moment, though. They are important to understanding what motivates the life choices of women elites (or of aspiring elites) because they illustrate how families compete for power through forging marital alliances, as well as how vital is the role of women and how strong are their own chances for status elevation in the context of this marriage game. In this realm the contracting of "good" marriages by young women, and the guidance of their children to and through the "right" schools, both combine to build a stairway to expanded power and status for females of a scale that could almost certainly never be attained by unmarried or childless women. Nor by wives who do not manage their children's ascent high enough up the educational ladder to secure the rank of "suitable" marriage material.

At the very highest levels the competition can be intense, as this depiction of a Ladies' Auxiliary gathering that Hamabata attended makes poignantly clear. "The light chatter—carried out in the most formal Japanese—about children, their educations, and matters of life-style belied an undercurrent of serious worrying, as each woman realized that she, her children, and her household were being inspected by the other women in the fluid process of judging household status. Status, affirmed by alliances created through marriage, made marriage a consistent topic of conversation. Marriage also defined one of the major realms of responsibility for these wives."

As expected, the university plays a vital role here as well. Political scientist Chitoshi Yanaga summed it up this way: "Bright young graduates of the best universities are always in demand as husbands for daughters of influential business and political leaders. When one already has a good pedigree, it is possible to improve it socially and financially by acquiring a degree from an elite school. Marital ties are often established to enhance the position, prestige and power of the families as well as the individuals involved."[8] That is, men play the marriage game too. And the way they get their turn at it is by passing the entry gates to the "best" universities.

The women that Hamabata writes about are from, or very close to, the cream of Japanese elites, consisting of no more than a few hundred families. It is certainly not fair to imply that hundreds of thousands of young women of the upper middle classes (or their mothers, on their behalf) are all scheming to marry their ways to power and influence. Or that they are being dishonest about their real life and career goals; many women would genuinely like to have fulfilling careers. Certainly none that I talked with framed their expectations in the blunt terms of marrying simply for upward mobility. It is probably more true to say that feminine traditions of the family as the framework that controls—and protects—the fate of the individual woman exerts a stronger pull on their underlying sense of values than they realize.

At the very least Princess Masako, who delighted the nation by becoming the bride of the Crown Prince, demonstrates that there is some growing parity of priorities among the sexes. She was considered an "ideal modern woman" by young Japanese adult females at least in part because she had graduated from Todai herself, and was a career administrator in the Foreign Ministry. One could simply accept at face value the words of a University of Tokyo woman student who told me "in Japanese tradition, to become a good housewife is the final goal." Still more charitably, one could accept the puckish assessment of sociologist Takie Sugiyama Lebra of today's contemporary feminine aspirations: "to find someone to marry. It's just the trouble whether they can find someone worthwhile."[9]

If women in all these roles, formal and informal, are genuinely this influential in Japanese society, it is even more important to ask whether advances in their position in the formal half of society are also real. Can we genuinely expect them to assume institutional power, to become chief executives, and high government officials? Princess Masako, a cultured, highly professional, and genuinely liked young diplomat in the Foreign Ministry, seemed to many in Japan, both in the establishment and outside it, an exemplar of the kind of compromise Japanese women might at last be excused to affect between their private aspirations and their societal obligations. At the very least, the imperial household seemed to be giving its official stamp of approval to career women as legitimate marriage partners in elite families—something never before directly conceded by the national patriarchy.

It is hard for outsiders to imagine just how great a leap of progress this symbolizes. A good example of how things have changed generationally for women at Katsuragawa's level, for instance—and how they have remained the same—might be to look at her family itself. Thoroughly modern research analyst Takako Katsuragawa met her husband while working in the election campaign of her own mother, Hisae Kitamura, in the family's hometown of Takasaki, Gunma prefecture. This makes her a rarity. Takasaki is just sixty-five miles from metropolitan Tokyo, but half a century away in perceptions: Hisae Kitamura says she is only the second woman in ninety years to serve on the city council. She has her own blunt assessment of what is holding her female contemporaries back. "They don't like educated women here. I talk to a lot of executives in Takasaki society, and they just do not want wives who are at the same educational level as themselves. If they have four years of college, their wives should just have two. Their sons should all go to university if they can, but the daughters should just satisfy themselves with junior college. A university-educated woman has a hard time just finding a husband here. This is especially true of Gunma prefecture. But it's probably true in all of Japan."

Sumiko Iwao, a Keio University professor who has studied, lectured on, and written widely about women's issues, believes that women have moved to a new plane of material and intellectual independence, sidestepping much of the repression that flows from Japan's male-oriented social bias.

Today's women, she finds, "have a surprising degree of autonomy and freedom in their lives. Japanese women by no means want to be like men, spending inordinate amounts of time at the office and leading culturally impoverished lives. They know that with their wide circle of friends and freedom to work, raise children, pursue a hobby, join a volunteer group, or simply have a good time, they are far better off than men."[10]

We have seen that middle-class women certainly do have a new independence as the modern leisure class. However, this is not the same thing as progress toward real equality, and the record indicates a rather different story. Comparing women's advances in leadership roles, for example, is instructive. While the number of female entrepreneurs has expanded by more than a fifth over just the past decade, making women the chief executives of nearly 4.5 percent of all companies, the lower house of the national legislature was in 1993 still only 2.7 percent female, which placed Japan behind 127 other nations on this scale of sexual equality. Even in locally elected assemblies, only 3 percent of the membership was female.

This means that Japanese women can advance in areas of the society where initiative and individual talent and ability are the major criteria for success, such as the entrepreneurial world, the arts and entertainment, and they can receive the material rewards. Even in the powerful government bureaucracies, some few women have achieved real positions of power. But the avenues to politically based power—the realms where political support organizations, campaign funds, and influential connections count most, and where the stakes are access to Japan's roles of public prominence—remain largely blocked. The consequences were illustrated bluntly by Professor Takako Sodei, who pointed out to a welfare symposium discussing women and old-age care in Tokyo that "welfare programs for old people are [now] being formulated in 3,300 municipalities across the nation. Almost no woman is involved in this work. If that is the picture, it is impossible to realistically work out any serious program."[11] She is precisely right. And it is precisely women whose fates are being decided, in these councils where they have as yet little or no voice.

The university is of appallingly little help here. "It's sad, but it's true" is the reaction of one of the universities' own success stories, a graduate who was one of the first women ever permitted to enter the prestigious

Mitsubishi Research Institute as a career-track elite. "The universities shouldn't be separate from society. They should be bringing up students knowing they are going to live within the society, and teaching them something about the best ways to change it for the future. I don't know why they are failing."[12]

They are failing because it is not a matter of theory over the "best ways" to make changes. Where real power is at stake, women progress slowly because they are trying to effect a real revolution. They are trying to take power from the grasp not just of men but the real power-holders who exercise this kind of detached control over them and their families, and who happen to *be* men. Revolutions truly are not dinner parties. Because the institutions these power-holders sit atop are almost completely male, and because the lifetime employment system for elites gives them an intimidating social as well as professional prerogative, women reaching for the power to impose equality are actually fighting the organizations *upon whom their own men depend so completely for the sustenance that supports wives and families to begin with.*

For these complex reasons, real confrontations are understandably slow to unfold. Because of the successes of people like Takako Katsuragawa, it is easier for women to believe that things just as they are indeed are getting better for them. Many of the reasons this appears to be so were discussed earlier: the tremendous expanse of leisure time and disposable income for women; the basically favorable marriage market; the expanded access to higher education; the government's cognizance of their importance as childbearers, care-givers, and socializers of the future generations. Other reasons are less visible but just as potent. Divorce and single motherhood are still so rare as to affect women's sense of mental and economic well-being and protection very little, and their society's universal moral perspectives on such phenomena even less.

Women do not see as readily that they are flowing with a course of events, not changing it. Nor can they see that only through real confrontation will they have any chance of wresting the necessary power from male elites to control their own fates.

Hisae Kitamura, Katsuragawa's mother, provides a different real-world model for the kind of struggle women will have to wage if they really want to lead their communities. Kitamura is herself a housewife, and her husband is a banker. But she is also principal, owner, and founder of a kindergarten teaching over two hundred children.[13] "I went back to college after my two daughters were old enough to start school, and got a teaching license. I worked at a nursery school first; then I discovered many things I hadn't recognized before. That a child's early education depends a lot on the principal's way of operating the school, for example. And I thought, well, there's no other way for me to be part of a good school than for me to become a principal myself, and run my own nursery school." Kitamura finished two more years of college requirements for her license at night school, then opened her own kindergarten.

She appears to have always been the kind of woman who is determined to do things her own way. After she had spent many years building her school, a local political boss began to get involved in PTA and school politics in her neighborhood, making her feel as if her prerogatives were being infringed upon. She decided to fight on his ground. A hundred days before local election campaigns began, she decided that the best way to wage that fight was to run against his hand-picked man for the city council. She filed as a candidate for office. "If I were only a housewife, probably I'd have just gone on putting up with it. But I run a school. I decided the atmosphere where children are brought up is actually a miniature version of society. And if they were brought up in an environment like this, with one big boss and ten smaller leaders all bowing to him, they can't be brought up right.

"People were afraid of this man, so at first nobody would help me in setting up my election office. I had to bring in a campaign manager from another district. And my office was pretty empty. I campaigned door-to-door, in the snow." Visiting dozens upon dozens of houses each day, working from eight o'clock each morning to ten o'clock at night, Kitamura wore out three pairs of shoes. "I found myself talking mostly to women. Of course I didn't say 'I'm trying to get him out.' I put the emphasis on having a female voice in the city council. I talked a lot about children, and their education. I promised a voice for women, and to support a clean city and a richer cultural life.

"When I was in the middle of it, I thought I had no chance to beat him, fighting him all on my own. Even people who knew damned well that he was the wrong guy—this is the way our society works, somehow—they still came out for him. But at least I was one whose voice would be heard.

"Maybe it was because of the freshness of a woman candidate, plus the kindergarten establishing my credentials as an educator—or maybe it was because people just held some special expectations for me. But I won."

In her four-year term on the city council, Kitamura says she learned a lot more about how things really work. Despite hearing that some of her colleagues called her a "geisha" behind her back, she says she found interesting doors to power opening for her. She claims she managed to secure school insurance association coverage for the four thousand children in private kindergartens in the Takasaki region who did not have it before she made it an issue. She found that "bureaucrats from the city's administrative offices would come to me, and say 'Why don't you bring in more of your requests; we'll try to do whatever we can to get them through.' " In the short space of her term of office, in other words, she discovered that fighting for office—and winning—is the way to gain cooperation from the elite, and thus gain access to the power that controls Japan.

After her term was completed, Councilmember Kitamura decided, at the persuasion of former Prime Minister Yasuhiro Nakasone (who hails from Gunma), not to stand for re-election but instead to run for the Gunma Prefectural Assembly, which, she said, in the century of its existence has never had a female member.

She lost.

Notes

1. "Baby Experience in Short Supply," *Daily Yomiuri,* May 15, 1991.

2. Takie Sugiyama Lebra, *Japanese Women: Constraint and Fulfillment* (Honolulu: University of Hawaii Press, 1984), p. 113.

3. Matthews Masayuki Hamabata, *Crested Kimono: Power and Love in the Japanese Business Family* (Ithaca: Cornell University Press, 1990), p. 31.

4. Much of this discussion of the *ie* draws on Lebra, *Japanese Women.*

5. John Roberts, "Power by Associations," *Tokyo Journal* (October 1988).

6. "Nihon no Shin Meika," the vernacular weekly magazine *Shukan Yomiuri,* October 4, 1987.

7. Chart "Owada's Family Tree," *Daily Yomiuri,* January 7, 1993.

8. Chitoshi Yanaga, *Big Business in Japanese Politics* (New Haven: Yale University Press, 1968).

9. Takie Sugiyama Lebra, lecture delivered at International House, Tokyo, May 28, 1993.

10. Sumiko Iwao, "The Quiet Revolution: Japanese Women Today," *Japan Foundation Newsletter* (December 1991).

11. "More Women Lawmakers Needed to Cope With Aging Society," *Asahi Evening News,* December 20, 1992.

12. Interview with Mikako Okuma, former staff researcher, Mitsubishi Research Institute, February 1993.

13. Interview with Hisae Kitamura, principal of Kodama Yochien, February 1993.

8

Family: She's Got the Whole World
in Her Hands

*The commitment (to children) exists at all levels of Japanese society
and among all its institutions. Education is seen as key to industrial
development, national cohesion, international political stature,
personal development, moral character-building, cultural continuity,
and the creation and maintenance of interpersonal relationships.*
—Merry White, *The Japanese Educational Challenge* (1987)

*Mothers are often considered the primary agent for socializing
children, especially when the children are very young. In contrast,
little attention has been paid to the fact that mothers are also
socialized into becoming "good mothers."*
—Mariko Fujita, " 'It's All Mother's Fault': Childcare and
Socialization of Working Mothers in Japan" (1989)

To almost anyone from a developing or even a developed nation, it must seem that a Japanese child born today begins life in the very best of times. Japan has the highest life expectancies and the lowest rate of infant mortality in the world. The social conditions in which young families live in all rural and most urban areas are stable and wholesome: Crime rates are low, the illicit drug problem is statistically minimal, government services are efficient, low-cost national health insurance is available to all. The constitution, national security policy, and Japan's low political posture in global affairs virtually eliminate the fear of involvement in war or the chances that any child will someday be drafted into involuntary military service. The country's consumer markets are rich and rapidly expanding with novel and luxurious goods. Telephones, color TVs, automobiles, and modern home appliances are almost taken for granted in even the humblest households. The national economy may bear the scars of a wildly excessive era of speculation in the late 1980s, yet inflation remains under control and it still at least seems true that virtually all young adults are guaranteed the opportunity of achieving a lifelong position in the comfort-

145

able Japanese middle class. A salaried worker is bringing in some $53,000 a year, while the average household (due mainly to mother's working) has a disposable income of $68,000.[1] On top of that, the average of Japanese savings per household is some $176,000,[2] though methods of reckoning private savings differ between Japan and other countries, and this is a very broad "average."

Yet in many ways it seems that the same newborn is facing an uncertain future. The lifetime employment system is coming under increasing pressure, and job promotions are inevitably slowing all up and down the career path, as is economic growth. Decent homes in the cities seem virtually impossible for young couples to ever hope to afford; tiny condominium apartments or long commutes are the only alternatives. Almost all the desirable jobs are in densely crowded urban zones that require up to four hours of commuting hell each day. Streets and public transit systems are vastly overtaxed with automotive and human traffic; such basic public infrastructure as sewerage systems, sidewalks, and public parks are woefully inadequate in many parts of the country, even in cities. Taxes are rising, and prices in Tokyo and Osaka are the highest in the world, averaging anywhere from 40 to 60 percent more than in the largest U.S. cities. And today's and tomorrow's entry-level work forces face the disturbing prospect of being taxed ever more oppressively throughout their working lives, to support a retirement generation that will double in size by the time their careers are two-thirds—or even half—over. Economic stagnation, even poverty, are large problems in some rural areas, and their populations are drained as teenagers and young workers leave home to find better jobs in the cities.

Can it be any wonder, then, that from both the positive side and the negative, the average young mother sees no reason to try to fight an educational system that enlists her from the outset in raising a child in a way that will advance the family's prospects as well as the offspring's in toeing the educational-system line? A "good wife and wise mother," indeed, is just as much a part of the team engaged in the competitive struggle for educational achievement as are the son and the daughter and the teacher and the school system. The shrinking size of the average family (the overall lifetime reproduction rate in Japan now being down to around 1.5 children per woman), the continuing urbanization in tiny homes and sharply rising costs of education that have led to this low reproduction rate, and the long hours spent at work by most fathers all focus ever more pressure on mothers to be "career managers" for their one or two children from ages as young as two.

If they have any doubts about that, society quickly dispels them: "The first three years of children's lives are considered particularly problematic in Japanese culture," writes sociologist Mariko Fujita. "Not only is it a period of character formation, but it is also a time when children's health and physical strength are considered precarious. . . . Whether or not the child can later build successful relationships with others depends on how much time, affection, and love the mother has given to the child. In other words, the idea makes the mother solely responsible for the personality development of the child, excluding the father from that responsibility."[3]

This, of course, implies that life for working women—especially for women who cannot afford to leave the job market during those first three years—can be an absolute hell. A woman will almost certainly lose her place on the career track if she leaves work to provide this early nurturing. Day care is often available to her as an alternative, and the family in truth may genuinely depend on her income. Yet in the eyes of society, she is damned if she does (work) and damned if she doesn't during these years.

Over the past decade the government has felt itself pressured to provide for more day care, as a visible symbol of and an actual commitment to women's working-equality rights—not only because women hold such a vital place in the low-wage end of the labor market, but because the effort to support working women as a way to encourage them to bear more children has grown somewhat frantic. There are now about twenty-two thousand public and private day-care centers in Japan,[4] but their management has become a critical tangle that still leaves many hundreds of thousands of children in the arms of their mothers—and their mothers out in the cold:

• More than 80 percent of the centers close by 6 P.M., as they themselves are staffed by working mothers.[5] But urban working women face the double problem of possible overtime at the office being demanded on days that cannot be forecast, and inconvenient commuting times on suburban trains and buses between the centers and their jobs downtown. One survey conducted by a union federation has shown that as many as half a million children up to age six may be on waiting lists for centers, simply because their mothers cannot assure that they will be able to pick them up by closing time.[6] Such mothers must either forego work, work out some sort of child-care arrangement with neighbors, turn to relatives for help, or try to find whatever employment they can nearer to home.

• Day-care centers are highly selective in admissions policies. "Admittance to day care is not automatic," writes Fujita. "The day-care office of each municipality must review whether the parents of a child are qualified for day-care service. What the parents must prove is that the *mother* is unable to take care of the child and that no one else in the same household (for example, a grandmother) is available for child care. The regulation presupposes that the *father* is working and therefore unavailable for childcare. Moreover, it is not enough for the mother to declare that she is working. She must obtain proof from her employer, or from her doctor in case of illness."[7] Of more than 1.5 million children in day care in 1992, reported the *Asahi Evening News,* only forty-four thousand infants who were under one year old were admitted, "because of low ceilings on the number of infants accepted."[8]

• The Health and Welfare Ministry, which oversees and partly budgets the public side of day-care centers, responded to mounting criticism in 1993 with a plan to increase subsidies to centers that would stay open later than 6 P.M. But this still appears to amount to something of a sham: While the national government is obliged to pay half the expenses of the public system, in reality, according to Professor Hiroyuki Nakanishi of Hosei University, it expends far less, leaving the remainder to be shouldered by municipal and local governments. The head of the nursery section in one residential ward of Tokyo, for example, estimated that his office was supplying more than three-quarters of the funds actually needed to operate government day-care centers. Moreover, Nakanishi says the productivity expectations of the ministry, in terms of caregiver-to-children ratios, are impossibly high.[9] The outcome, then, really is a kind of smokescreen in which the national government can constrict or loosen supply of day-care services in any region by deciding how much financial support to appropriate. The end result is that mothers of the youngest children are still pressured most heavily to remain at home—which, of course, neatly knocks them off the career track, and allows their return only to the secondary job market.

Nor is the time spent by children in day care always merely custodial. The system finds opportunities to begin building its pressures on mothers and children even here. Fujita, who herself placed her toddler son in a day-care center, reports on the strong sense of competition between mothers to be "correct" nurturers engendered by the teachers there. "The teachers, consciously or unconsciously, set up an atmosphere of a 'school' despite the children's young age. . . . First, the [monthly meeting of teachers with all mothers] is organized around the behavioral problems of the children that the teachers observed during the month. The teachers identify these problems. For, example, some children are very restless during meals. The teachers give the names of these children not to each mother privately, but openly to all the mothers. The teachers also list the names of those children who do well and those who have problems in performing daily tasks such as changing clothes or washing hands.

"Second, during the meeting, the teachers ask the mothers to talk about behavioral problems their children have at home. Somehow, the focus is always on *problems* instead of the positive aspects of the children's behavior. For each problem, the teachers act as counselors, giving mothers their advice, instead of creating discussion among the mothers. Hence, the flow of conversation is between the teachers and one mother, while the other mothers wait their turn quietly.

"Third, at the end of the first six months of the school year, the teachers distribute a report describing the problems and progress of each child. Since the report is distributed to all the parents in the class, every mother knows not only how her own child has been doing, but how all the other children have been doing as well. . . . By focusing on problems instead of praising the children and by acting as counselors, the teachers take the upper hand and establish themselves as the authority, over the children's mothers, in childcare."[10]

They also, it might be observed, launch these toddlers, at least within their mothers' minds and at least by implication, down the great school-and-society competitive track.

When children themselves first enter formal education—elementary school —the strains of competition are generally muted: Teachers work much harder, from the first grade on, to encourage a feeling of group solidarity, of acceptance, of protection from failure and from the differentiation between poor and good performers, in these early years of social acclimation. Earlier chapters have already related these efforts to the socialization of Japanese toward group-oriented ethics and cooperation; this chapter explores how in turn much of this protective atmosphere is dissolved into the other face of Japan's schizophrenic socialization, the naked race for academic preferment, at the level of middle school.

Even from the outset, some children with ambitious parents are driven toward the competitive edge, by being sent into prestigious nursery schools, which themselves require passage of an entrance exam, and later into after-school attendance in *juku,* or cram schools, which will give the children an advantage for enrollment in the better grade schools and then junior highs, which lead to the better high schools, which lead to the better universities. Families can spend from $2,000 to $20,000 to gain these advantages for their young offspring, and many would call it a bargain. Some private universities have high schools and middle schools attached, and entry into the private grade schools they operate constitutes the boarding of an "escalator" on which children can ride all the way to college without taking the onerous, wide-open competitive entrance exams.

But not everyone would consider the costs of the educational "mainstream" reasonable. A government white paper published in 1994 ascertained that the "average" cost of raising one child from birth to university graduation totals $235,000. A couple working full time, with two children, can expend over half a million dollars to see them both from neonate through to the baccalaureate sheepskin.[11] The adversity of having, as the government would like to see, more children per family than the average is illustrated by the case of a couple from Fukuoka, in western Japan, surveyed in 1993 by a popular magazine. Both work full time and remit more than 35 percent of their income to their three children studying at prestigious private universities in Tokyo. Just in the previous year, their educational outlays for their children, two of whom were entering freshmen and had to set up residence in the capital, had totaled $102,000.[12]

Naturally, all of this lays a good foundation for considerable stress among Japanese mothers. Indeed a Tokyo survey discovered that four out of every five married women—half employed and half unemployed—experience stress attacks from "often" to "once in a while," trying to negotiate the financial and social rapids of their children's educational and career-entry progress.[13] These two subjects occasioned the most worry, but close behind came their children's health and their children's future marriages.

The latter two could legitimately occasion as much distress as the former, it seems. The health of Japanese children, for example, has been shown statistically to be in a broad, disturbing, if not yet crucial, decline:

- Obesity is increasing among young schoolchildren; around 9 percent of ten-year-olds exceed the weight average for their age by 20 percent.[14]
- Eyesight is growing worse at all school levels: A fifth of all primary-school pupils, nearly half of middle schoolers and an astonishing six out of every ten high schoolers tested at less than normal vision in 1993.[15]
- In Japan's larger cities, more than half of all children age four and younger have symptoms of allergies.[16]
- Twenty-two percent of junior-high students and 13 percent of elementary-school children tested by the government in 1991 showed signs of clinical depression, resulting from exam stress and family problems.[17]
- Seven of every ten ten- and eleven-year-olds reported themselves in 1992 to be suffering from constant exhaustion, due to their late study hours.[18]
- The average Japanese schoolchild now spends less than two hours out-of-doors each day, due to pressures of study, school activity, and absorption in TV and video games.[19]

As usual (and perhaps this time with some justification), the popular media has focused the public's attention on this problem, labeling it with the made-up term *moyashiko*—bean-sprout children, or youngsters who are "raised in the dark and are weak." While school worries and the epidemic conversion of children into bookworms are easily enough identified as the pathology in many of these cases, in others it is only suspect.

In any case, the classroom clearly may not be the only unhealthy environment for Japanese children today. One preliminary survey of television violence done in the early 1990s showed that Japan, not America, had the most cases of mayhem and murder on prime-time TV dramas. Almost 100 percent of all such shows on Japan's five main networks contained violent material in a single week surveyed by a Todai sociologist; the ratio for America was 58 percent.[20] Whether or not that in turn is contributing to more crime in society is open to question, but it surely gives a parent pause to hear that in a recent half-year police reporting period, nearly 50 percent of all crimes in Japan were committed by minors, with over sixty-one thousand juveniles arrested or detained.[21] These cases were mostly bicycle thefts and shoplifting. But the number of juveniles involved in substance-abuse seems to be sharply rising, even while the number of teenagers in Japan is sharply falling.

The fourth source of stress identified in the survey mentioned—the marriages of offspring—would likely give at least a case of sweaty palms to any parent with two or more children contemplating matrimony: The cost of weddings in Japan is extremely high. In ceremonies and receptions often held in the nation's better hotels, or in luxurious wedding palaces that specialize in staging these elaborate festivities, an average of some $45,000 worth of hospitality is lavished on the more than eighty guests of each reception, all feted with six-course meals, costly gift-mementos, and speeches and songs from the newlyweds' friends, family, and even bosses. The total tab, for everything from invitations through honeymoon to setting up a new household, works out to a standard $98,000 per blissful couple, with parents expected not only to worry over whether Kenji and Keiko chose the best possible matches for themselves and their families, but to pitch in a third or more of the up-front ceremony costs, and almost any percentage at all, from zero to one hundred, of the rest of the expenses.[22]

Japanese women have reported, in some surveys, a desire to have more children than they actually do (it has been estimated that one of every two married women in Japan has had an abortion). But with child-rearing costs like these, the average amount of living-room space per person in families' homes less than half of that in the United States,[23] and the stress involved of a woman, married or not, raising the children virtually alone, can it be any wonder why today's Japanese women are excusing themselves from the national drive to produce more Japanese?

Perhaps women can be forgiven for focusing so sharply on supervising the lives of their children for another reason: the absence of working-class husbands from the family. Divorce rates are something less than one-quarter those of America, as divorce is still considered scandalous and many women have resigned themselves to staying in troubled marriages at least until the children are grown and gone. But more than 40 percent of Tokyo housewives polled in a municipal survey said they have given serious consideration to divorce, but have decided to stay on for the time being; of women in their forties and fifties, in fact, the percentage jumped to more than half. (More than three-quarters of married males, on the other hand, said the thought had never crossed their minds.)[24] But despite the risk of social objurgation, and the even more serious risk of loss of financial livelihoods (the average settlement in 1993 was a mere $48,000 in lump-sum alimony and property settlement),[25] the rate of divorces is growing much faster than in America now. And of all divorce suits filed in courts, 70 percent are initiated by women. The second-most frequent cause listed by them was abuse by their husbands; domestic violence is believed by many to be much more widespread in Japan than reported or admitted. The chances of remarriage for a divorcee with young children are slim, but those without children, and increasingly those of middle age and older, are generally able to find new partners if they want them. This may be the reason increasing numbers of empty-nest mothers are embracing divorce as "the way out."

Apart from spousal abuse, the most obvious reason for marital incompatibility is marital absence by the husband, an absence obviously enforced largely by the working environment. Not only do huge numbers of white-collar and blue-collar husbands find themselves working the overtime stretch daily, either paid or unpaid, or out on the obligatory drinking rounds nightly, leaving husbands with only an hour each day to talk with their wives and less than thirty minutes with their children, but work-based *residential* separations of families are so common now as to affect 1 percent of all salaried male employees in the country: almost half a million couples.[26] The syndrome is known as *tanshin funin,* loosely, workers living without their families. It comes about when salarymen are transferred from headquarters or big-city posts near their homes at ages when their children are deeply involved in the educational race; 85 percent of these men say they have agreed to leave their families at home and move into bachelor quarters near their new assignments for periods of up to four years, because they did not want to dislodge their children from the schools in which they had invested so much work and family money to enter. The husbands dare not turn down these assignments, as all know that they are the next, ineluctable step on the promotion ladder, which come most often to men in their late thirties through their early fifties. The number of men affected, as large companies come under more strain to balance their personnel resources in the great recession of the 1990s, was growing at the beginning of the 1990s at a rate of 10 percent per year.

While the practice may not be particularly hard on housewives who see their husbands so little anyway, it can be even more damaging to the marriage than the daily grind of home-around-midnight, gone-by-7:30-next-morning that most of these men are bound to. (Indeed the *tanshin funin* salaryman, shopping for his own groceries at night, mending his own shirt buttons, dragging his clothes to the laundromat, has become something of a sympathetic figure in a pop culture otherwise more given to depicting salarymen as Simpson-esque boobs.) That is because it is the wife who learns firsthand that, with a reasonable modicum of income at hand, she truly can afford to execute her desire, should it have already begun to grow, to live without a husband at all.

L ooking carefully at contemporary family life in Japan, one can learn more than that, beneath their stoicism, many middle-class Japanese of all ages and stations live their lives within the confines of something like a carpeted, draped, and air-conditioned purgatory: not uncomfortable enough to warrant escape, but harsh for those who decide to buck the rules. One could think about the effect of these punishing pressures and paces on the whole nation. And one could consider whether, emanating from the world's second-largest economy, they have anything to do with the lives of middle-class families of other countries as well.

We all know that there is a reason for the long hours forced on Japanese husbands and fathers: Japanese manufacturing productivity has risen, on their backs, by an annual average of nearly 7 percent over the past three decades, compared to less than 3 percent in the United States. As a result, through a quirk of speculations in the global currency market, on one day for few hours in April 1995, the gross domestic product of Japan—the size of its national economy—achieved exactly that of the United States itself when measured in dollars.[27] Not only has Japan caught up, but, measuring comparative industrial investment rates, it is bidding fair to surpass America soon as the largest economy on earth.

We know also why the pressures of education exist on Japanese children, and we can come close to comprehending the reluctance of Japanese society to grant women any true level of equality with males. The former prepares more workers for the tasks of being Number One; the latter removes the tinge of urgency from the social-equity policy calculations of Japanese bureaucrats.

But how often do people in America, say, pause to think that the entry of U.S. women into the work force has in fact raised the average of working hours for *Americans* by 20 percent over the last two decades[28]—and that this may have some connection to Japan? How many consider that the resultant pressures on family *and* professional life, leading to huge growths in reports of stress on the job and in everyday American life, might be due directly to competing with Japan economically, as Masao Miyamoto has suggested in chapter 2? And not just for some global, distended, near-theoretical markets, but specifically for America's own markets?

In the mid-1990s, it is a commonplace of political debate to remark that the average American middle-class worker has enjoyed almost no actual income gains above inflation since the mid-1970s.[29] If this had not aroused a political rebellion in the United States before 1994, it was not only because the actual effects were hidden by fewer children per family, more housewives entering the labor market, and greater social-welfare support for the retired, but also because *cheaper imports from abroad helped ease the rising cost of living.* Cheaper imports and their impact on domestic competitors' prices have, in other words, had the effect of a hidden form of cost-of-living adjustments for Americans, making life better without it having required employers to extend anything. And that is why successive American administrations have embraced imports, in the form of the free market, so heartily: They help to hide an unpleasant political and economic truth that might otherwise have repercussions at the ballot box.

But this is a truth with more than one dimension. What has been really hidden is the stark reality that Americans have exchanged the comfort levels, the leisures, and family-time values of their middle-class affluence for simple goods. No nation, by far, runs a higher trade surplus with the United States than Japan. For companies in America to compete with the efficiencies Japan has gained by harnessing its own families to the national economic drive, the United States has in effect had to do the same. In a sense, middle-class Americans work longer hours now, are more tired and stress-afflicted, and suffer more damage to family life because they are now trying to keep up with the Japanese, as well as others for whom Japan's predatory marketing practices in America have opened the gate. With no national debate at all about the social costs to their own lives, the Americans have simply been forced to plunge into a new race, similar in concept and importance to the old arms race with the Soviet Union of the previous four decades: a productivity race, which has come to threaten the extinction not of a nation, but of its way of life. No end appears in sight; instead one is almost reminded of the hit of the rock charts a decade ago, whose refrain, then considered quite amusing, was "I think I'm turning Japanese."

Notes

1. "Slow Income Growth Slowing Rebound of Japanese Economy?" Japan Economic Institute, November 11, 1994.

2. "Elder Society Won't Be All Problems," *Asahi Evening News,* October 4, 1992.

3. Mariko Fujita, " 'It's All Mother's Fault': Childcare and Socialization of Working Mothers in Japan," *Journal of Japanese Studies* (winter 1989).

4. "No Place to Park the Kid," *Asahi Evening News,* January 28, 1993.

5. "Moms Rap Day-care Centers," *Japan Times,* November 18, 1993.

6. Ibid.

7. Fujita, " 'It's All Mother's Fault.' "

8. *Asahi Evening News,* January 28, 1993.

9. *Japan Times,* November 18, 1993.

10. Fujita, " 'It's All Mother's Fault.' "

11. "Boost Child-care Support, Paper Urges," *Japan Times,* April 9, 1994.

12. "Moving Further Out of Reach: Tokyo Universities," *Aera* magazine, February 2, 1993.

13. "Stress Plagues Japanese Women: Survey," *Nikkei Weekly,* April 18, 1994.

14. "Obesity on Rise among Japan's Children," *Japan Times,* October 5, 1992.

15. "Average Student's Sight Worsens, Growth Rate of Mean Height Drops," *Daily Yomiuri,* January 5, 1993.

16. "Survey Finds City Dwellers Most Likely to Suffer from Allergies," *Nikkei Weekly,* July 4, 1992.

17. "22% of Junior High Students Suffer Depression," *Asahi Evening News,* December 27, 1991.

18. "Survey: Most Sixth-Graders Tired, Stressed Out," Asahi News Service, April 9, 1992.

19. "Fear of Burnout for the Rising Sons," The Times Service, London (reprinted in the *Asahi Evening News*), January 24, 1993.

20. "Prime-time Shows Knock 'em Dead," *Japan Times,* June 24, 1992.

21. "Minors Commit 50% of Crimes," *Asahi Evening News,* August 13, 1992.

22. "Wedding Spending Survives Slump," *Japan Times,* November 23, 1993.

23. "Our Average Qualifies as Average," *Japan Times,* January 6, 1991.

24. "42% of Tokyo Wives Have Contemplated Divorce," *Japan Times,* January 28, 1994.

25. "Divorce Rate Hit Record in 1993, Survey Finds," *Japan Times,* June 20, 1994.

26. "480,000 Men Apart from Families," *Asahi Evening News,* February 6, 1994.

27. "Yen's Surge Raises Prospect of Japan as World's Largest Economy," *Nikkei Weekly,* April 24, 1995.

28. "Are We All Working Too Hard?" *Wall Street Journal,* January 4, 1990.

29. See Kevin Phillips, *The Politics of Rich and Poor: Wealth and the American Electorate in the Reagan Aftermath* (New York: Random House, 1990).

9

Weapons

The Emperor urged teachers Friday to encourage creativity among students.

—*Japan Times,* October 17, 1992

Education is a weapon whose effects depend on who holds it in his hands and at whom it is aimed.

—Josef Stalin

Personal development and self-discovery are closely linked to an acceptance of one's social role and its requirements. The goal [in middle school] is the development of an "outer-directed," compliant adult with a situationally based sense of morality.

—Rebecca Erwin Fukuzawa, "The Path to Adulthood According to Japanese Middle Schools" (1994)

The career prospect die is largely cast," observed a special U.S. Department of Education report on Japan's schooling system several years ago, "for the great majority of students when they enter high school." That is surely true. But it would have been truer still for the American bureaucrats to acknowledge that the real "killing ground" for decisions over the lifetime careers of all students begins even further back, in junior high school. Junior high is the last level of compulsory education, and great emphasis is placed here on *which* high schools the students will be allowed, or even encouraged to try, to enter. Teachers play a large role in this decision, as do examinations that have already been virtually decisive —even while being unofficial.

Misperceptions by Western visitors paying casual visits to Japanese junior and senior high-school classrooms are common. Seeing orderly rows of silent students stand and bow to the teacher when he or she sweeps into the room, and watching the seamless, almost rehearsed quality of the drills as the class goes through its dignified, no-nonsense paces, they almost never seem to realize what they are witnessing: first, an effect of the Heisenberg Principle, in which the mere presence of a foreign witness cues the class members to perform in their most presentable, formally Japanese behaviors; second, the enormous pressure in the deep background that keeps everyone present, save the teacher and visitor, anxious over his or her own future. Little wonder that a 1990s Japanese government white paper on the nation's youth turned up the fact that more than half of all middle-school students—as well as high-school students—would prefer not to face what they know is coming: "they do not want to grow up."[1]

Middle-school students go to cram schools (*juku*) more, participate in outside activities less, spend more hours in school, and study longer outside school than any other group of students, from kindergarten to college. Though about half of all middle-school libraries stock *manga* (the ubiquitous Japanese comic book), their students find less than eleven minutes per day on average to read even real books. Because junior high is where the system switches from "mellow" to mean all at once—from the accommodating, nearly familial embrace of grade school to the front lines of raw discipline and competition for a place on the career ladder. "At the middle school level," writes scholar Rebecca Erwin Fukuzawa, "the characteristics of the ideal student shift . . . [from] the relative freedom of early childhood [to] the concerted demands for adherence to the heavy social responsibilities of adulthood. [Here,] academic classes do not need to be made relevant, entertaining, or even intellectually stimulating. At this level study is a sober business."[2]

Why? Because here is the starting line of adult Japanese society. Here children enter the factory-like assembly lines of modern mass Japanese education, each made aware that the eyes not just of teacher and parent but the whole system are watching and evaluating—and judging, for keeps. Here the three major motivating devices that force compliance and hard work come into play: *hensachi, naishinsho,* and *juku.* In these three short years, the adolescent teenager can make or break himself or herself for life.

*H*ensachi is a word that strikes fear and frustration in the hearts of fourteen-year-olds across the nation each year. It means standard gradepoint deviation, which for each and every student is discovered through anything from a single test to a series of tests, all unofficially given, prepared by commercial corporations just as are American SATs, and paid for by the students themselves. The deviation scored is the real key to success or failure in "casting the die" of high school choices for everyone.

Here is how *hensachi,* a system used in almost all public high schools in almost all Japanese prefectures, works:

Sometimes in the final year of middle school, sometimes earlier, sometimes once and sometimes as often as once a month, junior-high students take these commercially prepared mock tests, which supposedly parallel typical high-school entrance exams for public and private high schools. Mostly they have been administered by their own teachers, during class hours, but the *hensachi* tests are not officially recognized by the school system so often they are taken outside classroom hours, or perhaps even in *juku* classes. Each test costs the participant about $13.

In the autumn of the final year of middle school—ninth grade—teachers, parents, and students hold private conferences to discuss which high school Kenji or Keiko should apply to enter. Essentially, this amounts to a guess as to whether the student can pass the high school's entrance exam. It's a crucial guess because if the student fails, he or she must repeat the ninth grade before having a second chance to take the exam. In public high schools, most of the actual exams are drawn up by prefectural education officials and are standardized; and since 95 percent of all middle-school graduates go on to high school anyway, virtually everyone other than the most incorrigible goof-off knows he or she can at least make it into a public high school.

But that's not really the point of these tests and interviews. What most of the students want to know is, how top-ranking a *private* high school can they hope to enter? Because that's where almost all the gateways to Todai and other top universities are: in the elite high schools. At the conference, the teacher spreads out all the mock-test exam scores and derives a *hensachi* figure for the student: a deviation score from the mid-point average for all his or her contemporaries. In actuality the teachers will have been made aware by each of the private schools being considered what *hensachi* range (obviously, above the average score) its successful exam-takers have had in the past. If the student's own exam scores do not match up to the level of the school he or she has targeted, it is highly likely that the teacher will try to talk the family out of what will be more than likely a futile attempt for their child to pass the exam to gain entry to paradise. (If a student has chosen a lower-ranking school than his scores show an aptitude for, however, the teacher will encourage raising his sights.) The point is that while none of this is officially binding—or even official—the teachers are steering students to different levels of high schools, and the students follow their recommendations most of the time.

The background to *hensachi* is this: The official operating policy of the Ministry of Education, and thus of the intervening levels of educational bureaucracy down to the school itself, is that all students are not only inherently intellectually equal and of the same approximate learning ability but must be treated the same. None should be differentiated by natural ability into any curriculum schedule variant from the others. Thus, whether in classes that have the average of thirty-four students apiece or in classes crowded with up to forty-five, the slowest learners are always kept with the fastest. Curriculum-wise, the same material, in the same amounts, must be covered by junior-high teachers in classrooms all over Japan (some say that, on any given day, every public-school child is learning the exact same lessons as all others across the nation; that is something of an exaggeration). Obviously, the discipline of pacing keeps teachers focused constantly on "bringing up the rear" of slow learners, and just as naturally the fast-trackers suffer by being held back.

Knowing all this, half or more of the parents send their children to cram school in the evenings and on weekends, where they can really pull ahead of the school class itself—and so eventually earn much better scores on the *hensachi* exams. Cram school is an automatic head start, in other words, toward the best high schools and thus toward good universities and colleges. This probably accounts for why 60 to 80 percent of all Japanese students spend some time in *juku*. At least half of all middle-school students attend and that figure will likely rise if the nation drops from a partial six- to a full, five-day-per-week school schedule as is now under consideration —many more students will merely switch from school to *juku* on their newly "free" Saturdays. One other big pressure for cram-school study is that the Education Ministry, studying entrance exams at both the junior and senior high-school levels, has repeatedly found that many schools ask test questions *above* the level of the standard curriculum material for the junior high schools from which the candidates come. In 1993, for example, it was learned that 58 percent of private high schools were demanding answers to at least one question that was not included in materials taught in public junior high schools. (The comparable figure for entrance exams to get into private *junior* highs from public grade schools, meanwhile, was 48 percent.)[3] Everyone knows the chances of passing such exams are well nigh impossible for students who have not been pursuing advanced education outside class at the cram schools. This has caused no end of bickering between private and public high schools, with the latter charging the former with purposely overtesting as a way to steal the best-prepared students.

There is also a problem in the standardization of the commercialized *hensachi* tests. Since they are so prevalent throughout the system, questions and answers—even copies—can be unscrupulously sold by successful applicants to anxious candidates outside the campus—in precisely such venues, for example, as the *juku,* where the two meet while they are both cramming for the respective high-school and college entrance exams.

The practical result, I learned from Shige Matsuzawa, a young Kanagawa prefecture (which includes Yokohama and many large Tokyo suburbs) assemblyman struggling with the education problem, is devastation in the public high schools and the continued skimming of the cream of the crop by private schools. "Only one-quarter of our public high-school graduates now go on to college of any sort," he sighs, "while the nationwide average [for public high schools] is 34 percent." The reason is that, since his district is close to Tokyo and the nation's top universities, it has a large number of highly regarded private high schools, who draw the best and brightest from middle schools both in Kanagawa and other, neighboring regions.

So "in our public high schools, the students ending up there are dispirited, there is little grade competition, and they have no elevated plans or goals."[4] In a prefecture with 165 public high schools, the equivalent of two high schools' worth of students each year are dropping out. Progressively, schools at the high end have become more and more elite; while those at the low end, where—their fates sealed by low *hensachi* scores—the students know they have likely already "failed" to fulfill their families' expectations for university and career achievement, have become more and more ghettoized. Little wonder violence and bullying are a constant worry here—leading still more parents to keep their middle-school children's educational noses to the cram-school grindstone, so they will not have to face the physical threat of them winding up in a public high school. Of course, many public high schools, and high-school teachers, do a good job, and all is hardly misery. After all, not everyone can get into private schools. It is still quite possible, with the necessary work, to go from public high school on to college or university.

But so grim has this type of problem become that, in 1993, the Ministry of Education tried to root out *hensachi* exams altogether by forbidding them during classroom hours. Yet in 1994 most students were still taking them, in one form or another, because teachers said they had had no warning on how, reliably, to replace this counseling evaluation tool. And now, with the number of adolescents declining drastically (three hundred thousand fewer pupils and ten thousand fewer teachers a year since 1993),[5] competition among high schools has merely intensified, leaving public high-school teachers fighting for the very jobs they know will be cut as their classrooms get emptier.

Everyone likes certitude in Japan's institutions. Teachers want to know that when they recommend a certain high school to a certain student, there is a good chance of success because, in some small measure, the very recommendation by the teacher is taken into account by the private high school (in fact, some schools will admit the most highly recommended students without even administering their own entrance exam). No teacher wants to suffer the humiliation of recommending too many students who, when faced with the actual entrance exams, cannot pass them. That creates still more agony all around: The teacher loses face, the family loses face, and the student loses face as well as a year of his or her life. Thus do the ties of Japanese education, all pointed up the pyramid of the Todai system, bind everyone ever tighter.

In a way, however, the Education Ministry's attempts to downgrade or abolish *hensachi* exams as the yardstick for recommendation to various levels of high schools has made school life even more treacherous for the students. Now they know that evaluations of them will rely more than ever on *naishinsho*. Naishinsho is the unofficial name given to secret reports the schools keep on every student. These reports contain both grades and subjective evaluations of the student, entered by teachers throughout middle school. Virtually no student, or his or her parents, is allowed to see the *naishinsho* (though some scattered schools and districts have begun to rebel against this custom, allowing students access), thus making it into a dossier. Ironically this was originally meant to break the grip of *hensachi* grades on admissions to select high schools, either ameliorating or amplifying them with teachers' opinions on the positive and negative aspects of a student's determination, sincerity, and cooperation. These dossiers are provided to high schools in advance where the students decide to take their tests, and their families know that many schools weigh these subjective opinions carefully: In fact, in Tokyo 30 percent of all junior-high students are accepted or rejected for entrance exams at the private high schools of their choice based on the middle school's recommendations alone, as summarized in the *naishinsho*.

Students are naturally afraid of these reports, both because they know the dossiers are gaining increasing importance as decision-making tools in accepting or rejecting them at desired high schools and because they do not know what is in them. The secret evaluations are ultimately based on the teachers' goodwill or caprice, as well as professional judgment. The *Asahi Evening News* published a poll of junior and senior high school students which showed that 57 percent of the respondents believed that *naishinsho* contents are affected by students' personal conduct toward teachers.[6] One Tokyo junior-high instructor made the mistake of explaining in writing to his students how he would assign evaluations, saying he would lower grades for such behavior as chewing gum or eating in class, or "acting in an unpleasant manner."[7] In the spring of 1994, in reaction to the ministry's efforts to de-emphasize *hensachi* scores and amplify the impact of the contents of the *naishinsho,* an educational publisher produced a book advising junior-high students how to persuade teachers that one possesses the "correct" attitude. "Look teachers in the eye when you talk to them; attach colorful charts and illustrations when you submit homework reports; volunteer to serve as student association president" were among its tips to the ambitious as well as the worried. In five months the book sold thirty thousand copies.[8]

This subject of the struggle for place in the best high schools is now turning, of course, into a struggle for place in the best *junior* high schools, as we saw with Todai graduate Kenji Yumoto a while ago; it now is said that only 60 percent of all grade-school graduates actively seeking entrance to private middle schools are being accepted.[9] But more important, it leads us to a broader revelation that explains very clearly not only why the Japanese system is able to sort out with such efficiency its best candidates for elite educations, but how it manages to bring along all the *rest* of the students with such academic degrees of success that (excepting dropouts, whose only other pathway is night school) virtually all its students—even the poorest—are literate, numerate, and fully prepared in terms of self-discipline for the job market when they graduate. The first proof of the institutional success of the Japanese educational system is that, until 1992–93, the economy was so successful that there virtually *was* a job waiting for every graduate of every level of the system, even for dropouts. In 1954, only half of all middle-school graduates went on to a high school at all.

The second proof combines the airtight discipline of the schools and the unremitting insistence that every student, no matter how slow *or how fast* a learner, be brought along at the pace of "educational standardization," throughout all the grades of public school.

But the third proof is by far the most vital. Japan actually, we see, has a dual educational structure, consisting of the formal (public and private schools) and the informal (*juku,* or cram schools, and private tutoring). And the Education Ministry counts on this. As 80 percent or more of all Japanese students are at one time, or at many times, involved in this informal system, it is vital to the nation, the student, the family, and the observer trying to understand what is going on.

Juku initially gained a foothold in Japan because, as noted above, the increase in pressure on students from middle-class families seeking to qualify for college entrance has grown enormously. For those attending public high school, it is now almost impossible to pass a college entrance exam without some form of outside instruction. For those attending junior high school (of whom, the most recent figures show, about 70 percent attend *juku* for at least a year) it has become impossible to enter the best high schools en route to college, simply because junior-high teachers are not allowed to coach advanced students, and everyone must learn at the same pace. *Juku* is the way for the fast learners to overcome this handicap: Most *juku* students are expected to absorb material at a rate three times faster than it is taught in public school.

Even though the number of schoolchildren in Japan is declining sharply, there are from fifty thousand to a hundred thousand cram schools in Japan. Moreover, despite some well-publicized bankruptcies that followed the collapse of the bubble economy, the number may in fact still be growing, because the number of students coming to them is actually growing.

Why is this? Because, with the increasing affluence of middle-class families, and the decreasing average number of children in each of them, parents have been more and more willing to devote money to giving their children this "extra edge." On average, parents of junior high-school students are spending more than $1,500 a year on *juku,* private tutors, or special educational texts for each child. Indeed, some 60 percent of all mothers working part time report they are doing so mainly to bring in the extra money necessary to send their children through *juku.*

But the more children that attend *juku,* the more that *have* a special advantage on the entrance exams to coveted schools. The schools now find themselves with too many qualified applicants to admit them all. So, every year they raise the bar, by writing more difficult entrance exams. Thus the competition for good schools tightens, and still more children file into the *juku,* adding still more qualified competitors at exam time. It really is a vicious circle for students and parents. An article published in the weekly magazine *Gendai* in the spring of 1993 claimed that the cost of running this "second stream" of private education came to a total of ¥3 trillion per year, which at today's exchange-rate average amounts to something like $30 billion. More than half of this amount goes to *juku*; the rest to private tutors and to special-text publishers serving both, and for incidental expenses like transportation. Tuition for private schools also comes out of private resources.

All of this is footed by families. And here is where we see the ingenuity of the Japanese educational system: While it foists the cost of educating its elites onto the private families of the students, it meanwhile is able to spend the lowest percentage of national GDP of all industrialized countries, 3.8 percent, on funding public education,[10] yet is able to concentrate virtually all of it on the "average" or lower-ability student to maximize impact. The longer standard school year after 12 years, totals 16 years of comparable American public-school attendance. The combination of all these factors explains why Japan's overall educational systems and policies are so successful.

In addition, the pressure on mothers to work part time to raise these moneys for their children's "outside" education guarantees Japan's employment system a virtually inexhaustible supply of cheap, willing, and expendable workers. From this vantage point too, it can be seen how well and truly the Japanese system fits the demands of both government and industry—which it is what it is designed to do.

Meanwhile, the pressure on students and families is still growing. Spreading outward from the cities in concentration, *juku* attendance is now increasing quickly even in smaller towns (where enrollment has expanded from 66.3 percent of students to more than 77 percent in just seven years), and even in rural areas: 62.2 percent of all students living in the countryside will also attend a *juku* at some time in their lives.

It is often true, then, that the struggle to get into the right high school can be as grueling, or more so, than the struggle to pass the entrance exams into universities and colleges. But, at both levels, it is becoming disturbingly clear that the ever-accelerating vortex of competition exacts greater costs than those measurable in time and money. A recent survey of high-school students shows that a full 23 percent of respondents are pessimistic about their own future;[11] in another survey, more than 60 percent said that if they could be reborn, they would choose a nationality other than Japanese.[12]

Social life in junior and senior high school can exercise a distorting influence not only on students but society itself. The most obvious example is the sexism, sometimes institutionalized, in which only boys count in the race up the ladder to the best schools. Several secondary schools with good placement reputations at colleges have been warned that they are admitting too few female students: The reason is that with low levels of female attendees, the schools will not be required by the Education Ministry to offer home-economics courses, which boys would otherwise have to take, subtracting from their study time for more "important" subjects. In a survey of 101 sports clubs at ten different high schools, all were reserved for male members—except for their 198 "managers," 196 of whom turned out to be females, who do everything from scorekeeping to laundering the boys' uniforms and sewing on their buttons.[13]

Erich Berendt, professor at Chiba National University for twenty years, sometimes teaches night school at a famous women's university named Tsuda and is amazed at how female students flower intellectually when out of the presence of males. "They recognize that they have a chance to take leadership roles within university life that only boys would normally take if they were in a co-ed school. They know that, in other schools, the Japanese male is expected simply by virtue of being a male to be the head of university clubs, class groups, student associations, whatever. They go to Tsuda because it gives them the opportunity to share leadership themselves. And they say, when they have this chance, the most amazingly intelligent things. Yet at Chiba, where things are co-ed, they'll automatically defer to boys, even the ones who are assholes; they still expect the boy to take the lead. It says to me something very powerful about the roles built into the Japanese educational system."[14]

But much more immediate are worries over violence in school, including physical punishments meted out by teachers (formally illegal) to keep troublemaking students in line; these punishments are sometimes quite severe—even severe enough to cause death. Another source of violence is that among students, most often the result of bullying between classmates. There are also other grounds for concern over what this pressure-cooker is doing to adolescent and teenage Japanese, including the rapid spread of sexually transmitted diseases, pregnancy among teenage girls, and even child pornography.

One of the great, dark secrets of school in Japan is *taibatsu*—corporal punishment. Outlawed nationally, it occurs constantly, and cases of extremes appear in the popular press regularly:

- A junior high school science teacher gave 100-volt electric shocks to five of his pupils for forgetting to bring their textbooks to school.
- At a high school, forty of eighty-four male students in the first-year class had their hair cut short for receiving poor scores on a test.
- At another high school, a teacher ruptured the spleen of a male student when he kicked him for reading a comic book in class.
- A soccer coach at a junior high school burned the hands of two members of his team on a hot stove because they did not sound off with morale-boosting team cheers.
- A junior high teacher hit a fourteen-year-old girl so hard for failing to enter the classroom on time that her eardrum was broken.
- Two teenagers at a private school for troubled youths were suffocated to death by being locked inside an unventilated metal container in the heat of the day, as punishment for smoking.
- A fifteen-year-old girl, racing to get through her schoolyard's front gate in time for the start of classes, died from a crushed skull when a teacher slammed the heavy metal gate on her.
- In just one town, a suburb of Tokyo, one of every three junior high school students was found in a survey to have been physically punished, even though half claimed they had done nothing wrong.[15]

Every year, at least a hundred students in Japan receive fractures, sprains, or bruises from corporal punishment. Yet, in the seven years to 1993, only two public-school teachers had reportedly been dismissed for illegally abusing students.[16] Most students who suffer injuries less severe never report the incidents to their parents, so in effect school, student, and teacher are involved in a massive cover-up of physical punishment.

Why all this violence against adolescents and teenagers by their own teachers, in their own classrooms and schoolyards? Because school rules, for dress and for behavior on and off campus, are so severe it is almost impossible to avoid breaking them at some time. The Christmas Day, 1991, issue of the popular weekly *Spa!* magazine ran a feature story on especially egregious examples of these nonsense rules:

- At a Nagano Middle School, students are instructed when walking in hallways to keep a distance of at least ten centimeters between themselves and the walls at all times, and to make all turns at corners on a sharp ninety-degree angle.
- In Nara, the maximum length of a piece of toilet paper to be used in a visit to the restroom is thirty centimeters. The maximum length of time allowed in a restroom stall in a school in Aomori is seven minutes.
- At a school in Hyogo prefecture, when boys and girls talk at least three people must be present, a distance of at least two meters between all parties is to be maintained, and such conversations must be terminated within three minutes. But that's probably still better than at a school in Tokyo, where a boy and a girl wishing to engage in unofficial conversation must submit a written request beforehand.
- In Kanagawa, if two male students find themselves alone in a classroom, all windows must be opened so that either one or both can be summoned by shouting.
- Again in Tokyo, boys and girls who are classmates on the campus must, when passing each other on a public street, maintain a distance of at least three meters.
- At another school in Tokyo, undergarments worn by females must be of plain white, heavy cotton material.
- At an Osaka school, pony tails are prohibited.
- In Chiba, any students with naturally wavy hair are obliged to have it artificially straightened. And any hair with a natural reddish or brownish tint must be dyed black.
- In Hyogo, graduates of one school are forbidden to hold any class reunions for six years after graduating.

And so it goes. From the color of socks to the length of skirts and haircuts to the regulations on wearing of uniforms, utterly nonsensical proscriptions abound, aimed at students who are ostensibly in the process of learning to become adults. With the opportunities for violations of these rules, and the pressure on teachers to enforce them, it almost seems natural that rebellion among students and frustration among pedagogues will frequently grow to the point of explosion, to the point of violence, assault that contravenes the law, and even manslaughter.

Anyone who has ever wondered how the Japanese seemingly maintain such perfect discipline, and respect for teachers, in their junior and senior high schools on what appears a universal basis should consider carefully the triple pressures brought to bear through *hensachi, naishinsho,* and *juku* on any child who has internalized the university or college aspiration —probably about 60 percent of the average student body at the average Japanese secondary-education campus. And those who wonder how this motivation is extended seamlessly to those who are not college-motivated can gain insight from the following excerpt of the essay "The Path to Adulthood According to Japanese Middle School," by the scholar Rebecca Erwin Fukuzawa, from the pages of the winter 1994 *Journal of Japanese Studies.* This extract is cited at length because it demonstrates the Orwellian dynamics of the teacher-student interaction, reminiscent in a fascinatingly microcosmic way of the Stalin show trials of the 1930s, and thus makes disciplinary process plainer to outsiders than any purely academic discussion could.

> Discipline procedures for more serious incidents involved the teachers of the whole grade. When teachers at Nishi [Junior High—a fictitious name] discovered that close to one fourth of the first-year students [that is, thirteen-year-olds] had been *chewing gum and eating candy in school* [emphasis added], they mobilized as a grade. One day at 5:00 there was an announcement over the PA system requesting about eight boys to report immediately to the teachers' room. When several of the students summoned did not appear, their homeroom teachers began calling their homes. In the meantime, the other teachers began to extract informal confessions from the students already gathered. At close to 6:00 they reached at home the boy who had allegedly given out most of the gum. His homeroom teacher got on the phone and ordered him to get to school immediately.
>
> After all the students were assembled the teachers began questioning the students and discovered that gum and candy had been trading hands for several weeks. The teachers dismissed the students at about 7:00 and stayed until 8:00 planning what they would do the next day.
>
> The next morning in the homeroom period at the beginning of the day, each teacher passed out slips of paper to all the students in the class with instructions to confess whether or not they chewed gum or ate candy at

school, and if they did, who they gave it to, who they received it from, and the dates for each transaction. During free periods that day the teachers collated the data from every student on a big chart, cross-checking the information. Some students reported giving or receiving gum or candy from students who did not confess. The teachers marked these students who did not confess for special questioning. Then they divided students into groups of 10 to 15 by sex, homeroom, and receipt or bestowal of the contraband. The next day after school the library was arranged into a temporary courtroom and groups scheduled for questioning. The four homeroom teachers sat in a line at long desks facing the line of 11 to 16 standing boys or girls. Along the side at another table sat teachers attached to the grade, the head of the guidance committee who came in and out to hear parts of the proceedings, and myself. . . .

The following is an excerpt from my field notes of the interrogation of a group of girls who received something.

Kasuga-sensei: "We'll begin the investigation of the facts. Each of you in turn please tell us who you received gum or candy from and when."

(The first girl states that she took candy from a friend twice.)

Kasuga-sensei: "What did you think when you accepted the candy? Did you know that it was against school rules?"

"Yes," she replied in a small voice, "so I took it home to eat."

Nezu-sensei: "How about the second time?"

First girl: "I ate it at school."

Nezu-sensei: "You knew it was wrong yet you ate it. And the second time your willpower to resist what you knew was wrong lessened. You see how small things anesthetize your conscience into thinking that breaking rules is not a big thing. We're really disappointed in you. Next time how can you tell us you won't accept sake *(alcohol)?"*

(The girl sniffs back a few tears. The second girl brought gum but didn't confess to bringing it yesterday. She says she was asked by a friend to bring it.)

Nezu-sensei: "Well, if you were asked to bring sake *would you bring it?"*

(She says no.)

Nezu-sensei: "How can you say you won't? Both candy and alcohol are forbidden in school, but you brought candy didn't you?"

Amano-sensei: "Bringing gum is bad but lying about it is worse. Lying is the worst thing in the world. Really shameful and traitorous. It's the worst thing a person can do . . . ."

(As they go on, the teachers emphasize how such small things escalate into smoking cigarettes and drinking alcohol.) . . .

Kasuga-sensei: "Such small things show that your hearts are rotting. . . ."

Nezu-sensei: "Rule violations bring shame to both you and the whole school. If people in the neighborhood see you, they will judge you not as an individual but as a Nishi student. If Nishi's reputation grows bad, and word spreads, high schools won't want to take Nishi students. How can you jeopardize the chances of the upperclassmen to get into high schools with such selfish behavior? Would you like to go to X Gakuen (a private high school in the neighborhood with a terrible reputation)?"

(They all answer no.)

Amano-sensei: "The first time you received gum or candy, wasn't there a small voice inside of you saying no?"

(All the girls raise their hands. There is lots of sniffing and wiping of eyes.)

Amano-sensei: "You have both a good heart and bad heart. This time you listened to the bad one. A murderer is the same; he listens to the bad one. You all haven't got that far but you're fueling the growth of the bud of a wicked heart. Show the best of yourselves! You are girls so you will eventually become mothers. If you can't differentiate between good and bad, how can you possibly raise a child properly? Such moral confusion will be transmitted to the next generation. This is why we teachers want you to reflect on what you've done. Get rid of that budding evil in yourself. In your life now you probably do lots of things half-heartedly, cleaning at school, committee duties. You have not been concentrating on what you are doing. Mend your sloppy ways now. For your sake we are angry at you today."

(Most of the girls are almost sobbing.)

Kasuga-sensei wraps up the session: "So from today try to rethink how you live your daily life. Let this be an opportunity to enrich your life."

After the group interrogation, students wrote a reflection essay with a note from either parent. In their notes some parents questioned the school's discipline. In response the teachers called an emergency parent/teacher meeting to explain the school's policy and their actions to parents. Teachers were pleased at the outcome of the meeting; many parents frankly expressed misgivings about school policy, but when the teachers explained their position, the extent of the problem, and their rationale, they felt they had won the support of even the most critical parents.

And so, like expert prosecutors, the teachers had wrapped it all up: personal guilt and shame, punishment, family pressure, sexism, the binding of the students to the goals of the school and the mores of group and neighborhood under threat of exclusion, and absolute authoritarianism of the educational institution over even minor aspects of personal behavior. This they dumped on these traumatized thirteen-year-old girls, who for taking a few illicit bites of candy and gum had been indirectly compared to potential murderers. Thus do the wheels of school discipline in Japan grind so fine.

One Sunday evening in November 1994, the mother of Kiyoteru Okochi found her son dead, hanging by his neck from a tree in the family garden. Okochi, who was thirteen, had been the victim of constant bullying by a small group of classmates at his junior high school. They had forced him to steal money—a total of $13,000—from his family over the previous year and turn it over to them under threat of violence. Kiyoteru had believed the threats because, as he explained in a note, the four classmates had thrown him into a river and held his head underwater once when he had tried to refuse. But at last their demands grew to several hundreds of dollars every day, and Kiyoteru could not keep up. Instead, leaving behind words of appreciation for his family, he hanged himself.

It was not an isolated incident. Within less than a month, seven more junior high students, and even two grade-schoolers, killed themselves because they could no longer tolerate the bullying at school. Some hanged themselves, and some jumped from high rooftops. Many left notes, but some did not. In fact, during the 1993–94 school year, national police reports said, one schoolchild committed suicide every three days.[17] In 1992, 159 victims of bullying took the final exit.

Others do not kill themselves but, instead, are killed by their classmates. In 1993, a thirteen-year-old boy who finally refused to sing again a song his older classmates demanded he perform for them was beaten and rolled up inside a heavy gym mat, his feet sticking out of the top. When he was found, he had suffocated. Others have been stabbed; still others beaten to death.

And others have been merely physically assaulted: girls who have their hair cut off or their underwear ripped off, and boys who have been wounded in the genitals, in cases investigated by private detectives. Police themselves, in the first ten months of 1994, investigated sixty-six cases of bullying as criminal matters, but the schools, in 1993, reported a total of twenty-two thousand cases of lesser severity. While this figure is falling, so is the number of students in the population, and many educational and child-psychology experts believe that these numbers may represent only about 10 percent of the actual total of bullying cases each year. In one

Education Ministry survey released in early 1995, almost four out of every ten junior-high students responding reported that they had been victims of bullying. The incidence per ten thousand students was on the highest rise in seven years.

Any parent of two or more children can tell you that "bullying" is a highly subjective term. Kenji calling Keiko "a pig" may not be very kind, but among thirteen-year-olds it hardly constitutes brutal intimidation. Yet the quality of bullying in Japanese grade, middle, and high schools is more akin to picking off, and turning against, the weak—and driving at them mercilessly, day after day, to the point of ostracism, verbal abuse, extortion, violence, and sometimes even outright murder. It is of the kind found in prisons, where the whole population is itself under extreme pressure of deprivation, minute discipline, constant observation, and the ambiguous threat of immediate punishment anytime, anywhere, of any intensity, for any infraction. Japanese bullying is of the same tone that derives from locking too many animals in too small a cage and feeding them too little. It is a permutation of the brutality of a system within which one suffers, helplessly, injuries to body, dignity, and self-control. School bullying has become of such concern that the government has felt compelled to take high-profile action. In early 1993, just after a fifteen-year-old boy threw himself under a train, the Health and Welfare Ministry announced that it would hire and station in schools around the country fourteen thousand welfare workers to counsel children and families and serve as a "bridge" between them and the schools, to break the code of silence that students themselves follow in so many bullying cases. In late 1994, the Education Ministry (possibly to steal a march on the Health and Welfare Ministry) announced that it would budget nearly $5 million to bolster counseling at schools, and the cabinet itself was lectured by Prime Minister Tomiichi Murayama on the necessity to cooperate to stem the growing tide. How it was to accomplish that, he didn't say.

Perhaps having the counselors—"someone to talk to" in authority—will help. More than a quarter of all middle-schoolers report that they do not have friends they can talk with about problems. It is believed that most of the minor bullying cases occurring at schools go unreported by the victims because they do not wish to disturb their parents, they are afraid that complaining will bring only more bullying, or worse, that the school's reputation will suffer if word of widespread bullying gets out, and such a school would be likely to lose its ability to directly recommend its graduates to desirable high schools or to colleges. Everything in this pressure-cooker world seems to work against the victim; children have become victims of bullying merely for trying to help shelter their friends who were themselves victims of it.

In the meantime, at least some of the victims have taken their own defense into their hands by "school refusal." In the 1993–94 school year a record number of seventy-five thousand elementary and middle-school students stayed out of class for thirty days or more "because they did not want to attend." While dropout rates are far lower in Japan (less than 3 percent) than in the United States and are falling—perhaps understandably, given the ever-tightening job market in which college graduates are beginning to snap up jobs formerly filled by high-school grads—the "school refusal" problem has obvious ties to violence, and the threat of it, on campuses. There are many tranquil schools in Japan, and many more where the violence is confined to the athletic field. But at too many others, with teacher and campus violence, and bullying growing all around them, too many young Japanese and their parents are becoming acutely aware that education affects one's chances in life in more ways than one.

Surely a test of any society's health is its willingness to look squarely in the mirror and note *all* the things, both good and bad, seen there. There is rising evidence that in Japan, citizens not directly involved in the problems of public and secondary education—that is, all those who are not caring parents of children caught up in the whirlwind—are willing to do little more than carp and complain about "the younger generation," which only a few years ago was identified popularly in the public media in terms something akin to "aliens" as adults began to suspect that young people may not be as dedicated to the driving nationalist motivations of Japan's economy as the older generation has been. Whether or not they are—and most truly have no choice—there is a lot in that mirror that Japan has almost broken its neck trying not to see. This will only make it harder for the nation to fathom rising rates of violent crimes, the spread of drugs and guns, and the appearance in their midst of monstrosity cults such as the religious group that has been prosecuted for committing gas warfare against the population in 1994 and 1995.

The nation was shocked on New Year's Day, 1994, when it woke to discover that five teenage girls had joined hands and jumped from the eighth-floor landing of an apartment building in a Tokyo suburb, leaving three dead and two injured. On the landing, police discovered the plastic bags of paint thinner that they had all been sniffing just before the leap. Drug, alcohol, and inhalant abuses have been spreading among Japanese youth, faster than most people have realized. Japanese police, for example, in 1992 reported arresting 14,700 teenagers on suspicion of inhaling or distributing thinner or other intoxicant chemicals.

An estimated 10 percent of the thirty-four billion cigarettes sold in Japan are smoked illegally by minors.[18] Up to 17 percent of high-school students in the Tokyo and Osaka regions are problem drinkers, according to surveys reported by medical specialists,[19] and more than 60 percent drink at least occasionally. Almost 3 percent of middle-school students have experimented with thinners, marijuana, sleeping pills, stimulants, or other drugs, and one in six has reported shoplifting.[20] An unbelievable one-quarter of all middle-school female students at selected schools across Japan said they had engaged in talking about sex with strangers through commercial telephone clubs. Seventy percent of high-school students have watched adult videos, and nearly thirty thousand teenage pregnancies were aborted in 1993.[21]

More frightening still, among girls aged between fifteen and nineteen who had abortions in the Tokyo area, 25 percent were infected with the sexually transmitted disease chlamydia, a rate two and a half times higher than that among older women.[22] Health experts point out that this means teenagers are having sex without condoms, exposing themselves in large numbers to AIDS. Among capital-region high-schoolers, an estimated 20 percent of the males and 17 percent of the females have had sexual contact, half without benefit of condoms. The public suffered another titillating shock in the fall of 1993, when police rounded up 101 female students, mostly teenagers, and lectured them for selling their panties to purveyors who would sell them in turn to aficionados of a popular Japanese sexual peccadillo, sniffing women's dirty underwear. But one college teacher researching the effects of the sex industry on Japanese young people estimates that as many as six thousand girls in Tokyo are selling their underwear to these merchants—and likely more than four thousand more female teenagers are either working part time at telephone sex clubs or posing for soft-core porno and nude photographs.[23]

The Todai system may indeed be getting what it wants from the ranks of Japan's young, but the toll taken on those still waiting down in the recruit pool—the nation's schoolchildren and teenagers—is growing larger with each passing year.

Notes

1. "Apathy Plagues Youth, Report Finds," *Japan Times,* January 15, 1992.
2. Rebecca Erwin Fukuzawa, "The Path to Adulthood According to Japanese Middle Schools," *Journal of Japanese Studies* (winter 1994).
3. "Schools Found Testing Above Students' Abilities," *Asahi Evening News,* May 3, 1993.
4. Interview with the author, spring 1993.
5. "Team-teaching Project to Begin in Fiscal 1993," *Japan Times,* August 21, 1992.

6. "School Report Card Giving Kids the Blues," *Asahi Evening News,* December 6, 1994.

7. "Bad Behavior Affects Grades," *Asahi Evening News,* October 20, 1994.

8. "Book Teaches Students the Fine Art of Ingratiation," *Asahi Evening News,* October 3, 1994.

9. "Nation's Education System Is Under Examination," *Japan Times,* January 20, 1994.

10. "Nation Gets Best Results for Least Education Funds, OECD Says," *Japan Times,* September 26, 1992.

11. "In What Direction Are Japanese Youth Heading?" *Asahi Evening News,* July 9–10, 1994.

12. "Japanese Children Glad to Be Japanese," *Asahi Evening News,* May 21, 1991.

13. "High School Sports Clubs' Female Managers Often Act as 'Mother' to Their Male Peers," *Asahi Evening News,* November 25, 1992.

14. Interview with the author, December 1992.

15. "Students Complain of Corporal Punishment," *Asahi Evening News,* June 1, 1993.

16. "Violence Taints Academic Achievements," *Japan Times,* February 3, 1993.

17. Anthony Head, "Japan and the Safe Society," *Japan Quarterly* (April–June 1995).

18. "Minors Light Up Due to Lax Rules," *Asahi Evening News,* February 12, 1993.

19. "Problem Drinking Surges at High Schools," *Asahi Evening News,* September 30, 1993.

20. "Theft, Drugs, Alcohol Turn Up in PTA Poll," *Japan Times,* August 18, 1994.

21. "Study of Teenage Pregnancy to Examine Issue Worldwide," *Japan Times,* October 13, 1994.

22. "Teen Girls' Sex Diseases On Rise," *Daily Yomiuri,* April 22, 1992.

23. "What It Takes to Make the Girl a Tramp," *Asahi Evening News,* September 29, 1993.

10

Making It

Key industries were nurtured by the government, in return for which business submitted to the multitude of official rules and regulations that provided jobs for bureaucrats. In its oligopolistic characteristics, informally coordinated by the [University of Tokyo] school tie, Japan's government ministries were complementary to the oligopolies of the private sector, which had their own Todai graduates.

—Leon Hollerman, *Japan, Disincorporated* (1988)

The bureaucracy is now more powerful than the government, with bureaucrats holed up in their ministerial fortresses, drunk on ministerial nationalism and following a course aimed at preserving their power at all costs. These fortresses must be demolished.

—The late Naohiro Amaya, former Ministry of International Trade and Industry deputy minister for international affairs

A warm spring afternoon graced the gardens of the National Diet Building across the avenue, beyond the windows, as I settled into my scuffed office chair for green tea and conversation. What I had come to talk about was how the mechanism of strategic planning for the Japanese economy worked. What I ended up hearing instead, from the mid-level official of the Economic Planning Agency (EPA), the cabinet body that issues the annual white papers on the economy and on the national standard of living, was a primer on how top-level bureaucrats from Japan's top-level universities get where they are destined to go—to the seats of power—and how they run the country, and why the way they do it is so dangerous to Japan and America.

"We don't actually plan," admitted my informant candidly from the outset, "so much as we coordinate. Japan is not a centrally planned economy, of course. It is the various ministries that each set what they think are the proper budget levels and projects for the year, or the years, ahead. They don't agree with each other, because each has its own view of and ambitions for the future. We have no power to moderate any of their views. So it ends up, sometimes, being quite sticky for us."

"Sticky," he explained, in that this absence of consensus in effect leaves the job of trying to create one squarely in the lap of a hapless group of Economic Planning Agency intermediators who are actually powerless to influence the actions of any of the competing ministries. "Let's say—as happened not so long ago—that the Ministry of International Trade and Industry forecasts a 4 percent growth rate for the national economy for the fiscal year ahead, because there are certain large-scale industrial initiatives it would like to see pursued in a period of strong growth, and it wants backup in the form of rosy forecasts. But the Finance Ministry, which is trying to extinguish deficit financing (Japan already has a cumulative government deficit equal to more than half its gross domestic product, one of the largest of all advanced nations and almost as high as America's), as a matter of its own policy, says it predicts only a 3 percent growth rate, and the government should not count on unrealistic expansionary revenues coming in from the tax base. More than likely, we at EPA would end up with a formal forecast somewhere around 3.5 percent—simply because that's halfway between their two positions."

Japan's growth forecasts are much lower at present. But it is more than elite administrative egos that are being ameliorated in this maneuvering. It is genuine ministerial struggle over control of the vital policy throttles of the whole government. And it has serious consequences. In early 1994, for example, as the nation struggled through its worst postwar recession and forecasters in the private sector were convinced that economic growth in the year ahead would be little more than 0.5 percent, a top-ranking EPA bureaucrat was himself asking permission of the deputy cabinet secretary to advertise a government-certified projection of 3 percent growth.

Why? Because that particular administrative executive was "on loan" to the EPA from the Finance Ministry, which through a constant flow of temporary personnel assignments to its top ranks has come to acquire great influence over the agency itself. And the Finance Ministry that year wanted to use its strategic EPA influence with the cabinet to make it appear that the government was expecting tax revenues in the coming year to grow by some $12.5 billion more than any self-respecting economist could possibly forecast.

The reason? Such window dressing, if successfully executed—and no matter how loudly hooted down by other economic forecasting specialists throughout the nation—would formally absolve the ministry from planning to issue the deficit-covering bonds that would otherwise be needed to close the gap between 0.5 percent and the 3 percent guesstimates, and because a 3 percent figure would allow the Finance Ministry to forecast a much larger growth in incomes than everyone knew would occur. The ministry did not want to issue those bonds not only because it did not wish to drive up Japan's national debt further, but because it knew it might have difficulty finding buyers for them among Japan's cashed-pinched banks, which would not find the bonds' low interest rates very appealing.

It did not matter that businesses large and small could drastically miscalculate their own investment and sales targets for the year based on such a bogus official projection, perhaps severely damaging or even bankrupting themselves. Nor did it matter that there might be a real 2.5 percent, or worse, hole in actual revenues when the year ended: The ministry was prepared to go on dressing its windows to cover that black hole in the budget, too. Everything about the EPA's projections would have been false —except for the power that the Finance Ministry would be using to manipulate both the Japanese economy and its international finance and trade partners through it.[1]

But the danger to Japan was not as large as it appeared. While the Ministry of Finance certainly could not guarantee a 3 percent growth rate it *could* influence, if not outright command, Japanese banks, insurers, brokers, and financial institutions to prepare for much less. The cat would be let out of this bag quite early, and so most businesses would have learned soon enough to stick to their private evaluations in navigating through Japan's troubled financial realities.

The manipulation of public imagery, and the realities of division of power, however, were not the only lessons to be gleaned from a visit to the Economic Planning Agency. In fact a little thoughtful analysis of what goes on here alone shows us a great deal about how the products of the Todai track work to control Japan: not only how great the power of the elite university diploma is, but how it works in practice and in command, both well and badly.

The story told here demonstrates, in fact, seven truths:

• The administrative elites of Japan rely upon the top five universities, especially Todai, for the resources of esprit de corps, loyalty, conformity, and responsibility necessary for an elite corps' success in besting competing corps of administrators and of politicians in the fight for power;

• The real governing processes, no matter who the players are, are deeply informal and therefore depend upon the character and relationships of leaders and led, much more than on formal dispensation;

• The conflict of agencies among the bureaucracies, both public and private, is as severe and divisive as that among political groups—or perhaps more so, as politicians rely so heavily on the administrative elites to form and execute government policy;

• The real purposes of governing administrators and agencies are often almost completely hidden from a public of whom they are deeply contemptuous;

• The power to manipulate information, internally as well as externally, is the key to success in the constant striving of elite groups against one another, on many levels and scales;

• There are in fact giant loopholes through which Japan's "competent" administrators can and do crash, resulting in failure and error that are damaging to the whole country. One has but to look at the "bubble" economy of the late 1980s and its collapse into Japan's worst postwar recession to see that administrators do not always know (and are not always able to retain complete control over) what they are doing;

• The dangers of these self-arrogated powers reach much farther than most Japanese and outsiders alike realize. They threaten the very position of Japan in the community of nations, and they ultimately threaten most the crucial U.S.–Japan relationship because of the great lack of awareness that exists outside this nation of just how much of the power of the Todai system is directed baldly at an endless aggrandizement of Japanese national power.

How these factors all make up the government of elites in Japan, and how they all grow from the roots of the Todai system embedded in the nation's education ground, can be understood easily once we consider the framework of power in the nation where all these elites operate, and through which all these agents interact.

A good visual analogy to this framework would be the familiar geodesic dome: a structure that appears from the outside to be built of parts both diminutively small and identical in all separate dimensions, yet which adds up *in toto* to a capacious, strong, maximally efficient structure with just enough room inside for all the pieces that make up modern Japan.

Japan's Iron Triangle

1. The Bureaucracy

Each year, France's revered Ecole Nationale d'Administration turns out a hundred graduates: the cream of the nation's academic elite, who will have their pick of the top career tracks in the French national bureaucracy. These are the young people cut out to be future leaders of France over the coming forty years, anointed by their success in grueling scholastic competition.

Each year, more than fifteen hundred Japanese four-year university graduates will emerge the victors in a brutal national civil service examination that will winnow them out from among some forty thousand of their peers, elevating them to the golden circle of candidates for the first-class careers available throughout the government. For the very best career tracks in administrative, legal, and finance posts, more than 40 percent of the candidates—about four hundred—will be from Todai. Hundreds more will qualify from the remaining Big Five schools, the University of Kyoto, Waseda, Keio, and Hitotsubashi.

But, in the end, of the eight hundred or more in total of these examination heroes making it through the filters of serial interviews at the big prestige ministries and into the elite civil service, about half will still be Todai grads. The Finance Ministry will take far more than half its fast-trackers from Todai; the Foreign Ministry, the Environment Agency, the Posts and Telecommunications Ministry, the Defense Agency, and other big bureaucracies—the Labor Ministry, the National Police Agency, MITI—will take large shares as well.

And all the remaining spaces will be filled in from the graduates of the Big Five, plus the very narrow list of the country's remaining first-class prestige schools: the former "imperial" universities, Tokyo Kogyo, Kobe, perhaps a few others. After that, the gangway to heaven is lifted up for another year. By this time the examination strife for the future seasons has already begun at high schools and junior high schools and even kindergartens all across urban Japan.

Is this really a search for the nation's most brilliant leadership talents? Why does the predominance of Todai men at all levels and generations in the leading ministries, such as Finance, matter? Because these are a large part of the corps of elites who will run the country—not just administer it; not just execute policy or resolve its failures or generate its ideas for future implementation, but *run* the country.

The ministries, of course, and all the other parts of Japan's government, hire thousands more people than this, and large percentages of them are college graduates. But only these, the first-class civil servants who have passed the exams and the interviews—the cream of the crop of the Todai system—will make the decisions about Japan's present and future course. They will research and write the nation's civil, criminal, commercial, and tax laws, help guide them through the Diet, supervise all levels of local government down to the very placement of roadside bus stops, create foreign and defense policy, and make sure that the country's industrial, commercial, and financial enterprises remain or keeping striving to become the strongest on earth.

They are, henceforth, part of the first leg of the so-called Iron Triangle of

Japanese leadership—the bureaucracy—and they are arguably the strongest of the legs, above the bureaucrats working in enterprise who are their counterparts from the Todai system, and even above the nationally elected people's representatives in the Diet and in the cabinet. They are the team players, and they all come from the Todai system because all these parts of the geodesic dome must fit together *perfectly* to make Japan work. They need not necessarily be brilliant (though many are), but they must all have the same values, be team players and be capable, on the same level, of quick study, consensus-building, and diplomatic ability to decide and command when consensus is impossible.

"The type of person being recruited," writes Hollerman on the historic congruence of Todai-based oligopolies of the government ministries and the major enterprises, ". . . must be capable of conciliation and persuasion [in an age of rapid change]. It remains true, however, that younger career officials are recruited from a dedicated, self-selected group that from an early age has aspired to enter the ministry. The candidates from this group are dedicated to the traditions of the ministry and to its established point of view. They look to their seniors for cues to correct behavior and thinking, and try to please them."[2]

Taken as a whole then, this is no elite of creative thinkers and brilliant strategists. This is an elite that must work together, share an ethic of service to the purposes of the ministries, industries, and authorities they guide, and always be mindful of an ancient household adage of the Tokugawa, the clan of Japan's feudal shoguns: "The eagle is at pains to hide its talons." Those whom everyone knows to have the dominating power, that is, must learn to exercise it without revealing it too nakedly. In getting one's way in Japan, that would be a sure method for turning the conciliated into the enemy. And no one who is bound to spend his whole career working his way up the same ladder of the same ministry, no matter how powerful, is anxious to make enemies that he will meet again in the future.

2. Enterprise

Why would he necessarily be afraid to meet at some other time, in an almost guaranteed climb up through the echelons to leadership of Japan's most potent power brokerage, someone he has allowed to become an enemy? Because Tokyo, headquarters of the world's second largest economy, is a very small town. And he can never hold *the* preponderance of power.

The men he must meet and deal with, outside as well as inside the ministry, are either Todai men themselves or are closely attuned to the structure of the oligopoly of power they belong to. (I was once given an instructive illustration by a senior executive of one of Japan's biggest consumer-goods companies. The executive was summoned to the office of a mid-level ministry official for a two-hour dressing-down because of an alleged infraction by his company of an unwritten administrative rule. Though he himself is a Todai man, this executive had to sit quietly through a denigrating lecture from a junior bureaucrat. "It's because the bureaucrat was a Kyodai man. I know: I looked it up in the graduate directories before I came to his office. If he had been a Todai man, I would have shouted back at him.")

To understand why in that case this interchange might have ended as a more humiliating power match for the ministry official than he expected (unless, of course, he himself first took the precaution of checking the graduates' directories; Kyodai and Todai share a long-standing rivalry) we must explore how the organization of mainstream Japanese industry—the second leg of the Iron Triangle—matches the oligopolist power structure of the ministries, with an elite that is itself a product of the Todai system.

Keiretsu

When Japan was an emerging modern nation, it imported its manufacturing economy almost whole from the West—whose modern economies had been evolving for more than a hundred years. Japan had to do it in a hurry, and so state involvement-sponsorship of business network organization, coordination of the financing, the actual work, and the export roles of enterprises involved the new government of the Meiji era deeply.

At the end of the Great Pacific War in 1945, when Japan had to be industrially restarted from its ashes, it was natural that the nation's enterprises and its government would again take shortcuts to get business back on its feet. This is why the postmodern patterns have looked in so many ways like the prewar modern ones, with lead banks to supply capital loans, the organization of giant trading firms to find all the resources abroad that Japan famously lacks, and to find the customers to absorb the expanding stream of products at home and abroad.

One result was that major enterprises of the prewar groupings—those bearing famous names like Mitsui, Mitsubishi, and Sumitomo—found themselves clustering once again loosely about one another, at first filling one another's wants and later working as close-knit *keiretsu* (industrial groups) financed by major banks and insurers. As these businesses started once again from the postwar ground up, they were financed by loans distributed by banks under the direct guidance of the government. And so

Japan's weak capital markets played little role in financing or controlling their ownership.

Instead, the members of these gigantic families of corporations largely purchased one another's shares and sold large increments of their equity to the same banks and insurers from which they borrowed their capital, making sure they were actually owned and controlled by "stable institutional investors"—that is, by one another. Versus these insiders, even today individual stock-market investors own an average of no more than 30 percent of their total shares. The result of this has been that corporate managements in the *keiretsu* are largely answerable only to one another's executives—not to private shareholders. This in turn has led to two other important consequences: First, most board members now are managers of the corporations where they themselves work, as the shareholders have been content to let the lifetime employment managers run the companies virtually unimpeded. This means that they make up a plutocracy of executives produced by the Todai system. Moreover, the largest source of outside directors on the boards has been from "brother" companies. On average, 10 percent of the leading *keiretsu*-family shareholders of each corporation have their own members sitting on the boards of these owned companies. Given all this criss-crossing of shareholding and board assignments, there is about five times as much interlocking directorship as in the United States.[3]

On top of that is another dimension to Japan's big *keiretsu* groupings. Traditional patterns of business in Japan have resolved along lines of generally greater reliance on outside suppliers for components and services than in other industrial countries. "In automobile production, for example," writes Michael Gerlach, "about 80 percent of the costs of a Japanese automobile come from outside suppliers, in contrast to only 50 to 60 percent in the United States, West Germany and France."[4] But cost competition is furious among the Japanese, and for that reason the largest firms have built huge pyramids of suppliers beneath themselves, to serve mainly or only themselves. Capital ties, financial and technical assistance, and the dependence of supplier companies on one main customer in the pyramid above them, as well as some personnel interchange in the upper levels, serve to bind these pyramids into huge functional conglomerates, which the *keiretsu* parents control tightly by simply dictating the prices (and margins) they will pay for supply.

As a result, while there are only six major *keiretsu* in Japan, they actually include not only their brother firms horizontally but literally thousands of firms beneath them. Thus the 188 companies that show up in the listings of these *keiretsu* memberships (Mitsui, Mitsubishi, Sumitomo, Fuyo, Sanwa, and Dai-Ichi Kangyo—the last three named for their lead banks) number controlled about 50 percent of all Japan's natural resources, primary metals, cement, chemicals, and industrial machinery businesses; 40 percent of the nation's total bank capital; more than half its insurance capital; 55 percent of its real-estate business; and 57 percent of all sales in the distribution field.[5]

It is most advisable, then, to visualize the dominant enterprise structure of Japan as direct and concrete lines of control extending from the boards of the top parent companies down through these 188 and to many hundreds more of subsidiaries, partnerships, and contractors below each. Leaving aside the other 90 percent of the country's listed companies, executives furnished by the Todai system run it all.

Let's take, as an example, the university backgrounds of the directors of the lead companies of the Mitsubishi *keiretsu*:

University Backgrounds of Mitsubishi *Keiretsu* Directors

Co. name	Total of directors	Todai	Kyodai	Keio	Waseda	Hitot-subashi
Mitsubishi Bank	45	26	—	9	2	5
Mitsubishi Trust	40	18	1	8	3	2
Meiji Life	34	10	—	4	6	6
Tokio Fire and Marine	43	18	—	4	6	3
Mitsubishi Corp. (trading)	55	19	2	11	8	6
Mitsubishi Construction	41	7	—	4	4	—
Mitsubishi Estates	33	10	—	5	—	5
Mitsubishi Rayon	20	5	4	—	—	2
Mitsubishi Kasei (chemicals)	32	10	6	1	1	5
Mitsubishi Petrochemical	25	11	2	2	—	—
Mitsubishi Gas Chemical	26	10	—	2	2	—
Mitsubishi Oil	27	—	7	6	4	3
Asahi Glass	31	10	—	2	3	2
Mitsubishi Paper	23	8	1	—	3	—
Mitsubishi Steel	20	4	—	—	4	—
Mitsubishi Materials	45	11	4	—	3	6
Mitsubishi Cable	24	5	3	3	2	—
Mitsubishi Heavy Ind.	44	21	3	—	3	—
Mitsubishi Kakoki (tools)	11	—	—	3	2	1
Mitsubishi Motors	44	8	2	—	—	3
Mitsubishi Electric	37	10	6	—	3	—
Nikon	24	8	—	3	3	3
Nippon Yusen (shipping)	30	12	3	4	2	4
Mitsubishi Warehousing	22	8	—	—	—	3
Kirin Beer	35	10	6	6	5	4
TOTALS 25	811	266	47	79	63	63

Source: *Yakuin shiki ho* (Toyo Keizai Shinposha, 1995).

Of 811 directors of Mitsubishi's top 25 *keiretsu* corporations, 518—or 64 percent—are products of the Big Five Japanese universities.

Thirty-three percent of the same total of directors of that same *keiretsu* are Todai grads, making the supreme decisions for their corporate pyramids. And the picture is much the same—one could call it a copy, actually, in the other *keiretsu* as well.

Nor are these the only groups in Japan's business and industry of which it is true; neither Sony nor Matsushita Electric Industrial are members of the six big *keiretsu*—but in themselves they have grown so large that each now heads its own pyramid *keiretsu* of supplier companies. (Among the additions to their corporate families have been America's famous former Columbia Pictures and, for a while, MCA.) The glue that holds these suppliers and clients together itself is based on an understanding of hierarchy and social-power flows, institutionalized in the very laws of the country.

American graduate student Louis Ross, studying antitrust and commercial law at Todai's Graduate School of Law, illustrates: "When it comes to case law, I'm learning that the larger party to the contract between two companies usually always wins. And there are reasons: for example, there is no allowance for discovery in contract law here. I asked my professor, finally: why isn't the contractual relationship in Japanese law more specific in what is written down? And this is how he explained it: 'Louis-san, if I give you a book, and you promise to give it back to me, you'd give it back, right?' And of course I said yes. And he simply said, '*Yappari.*' [Of course!] Well, I thought about it for a moment—and then I said 'Of course I'd give it back to you, because you're my *sensei* [honored teacher]—and because I'd be in big trouble if I didn't give it back.' And he smiled. I'd learned the lesson."[6]

Japan's analysts will insist that *keiretsu* influence itself is waning; that the connections between suppliers and buyers within each *keiretsu* are loosening already. That may hold some ineffable element of truth. But it is also true that the *keiretsu* are copied in hundreds of medium-sized and small enterprise structures as well, embracing many thousands more companies than the 188 mentioned here. And they are being born all the time: As Gerlach points out, NTT, the nation's giant telecommunications carrier, which acted as a domestic monopoly until 1988, was partially privatized to give new capital room to compete and grow in the quickly expanding telecommunications industry. As a result, "NTT faced a major set of new competitive challenges . . . and new opportunities."[7] Before it had even been fully privatized—while the government was still its major shareholder —NTT swung into action to build itself a new *keiretsu,* with the "creation of new business ventures across a wide variety of business lines. By June 1989, NTT had eighty-one new subsidiaries in which it owned in excess of 51 percent of the shares, and another fifty-six affiliated companies in which it controlled between 20 percent and 50 percent of the total shares. . . . In addition, NTT dispatched *several thousand* of its own employees to these companies" [emphasis added].

Of the parent company NTT's forty board members, fully half are Todai graduates.

So it isn't so much that these mega-corporations are the halcyon fields of the executives who managed to make it through the Todai system. It's that the culture that the Todai system taught them—group harmony, self-effacement, the avoidance at all costs of open differences with colleagues, the implicit recognition of the authority of seniority and personal loyalty to group leaders, full-scale internalization of the organization's ethics and value systems, and the ultimately nationalistic rationale for total victory of the company, the *keiretsu,* and the country, no matter what the cost—is the single dominating value system in institutional Japan. That is because all down the corporate ladder, behind these executives, are generations of younger, less senior employees, holding all the key leadership positions and waiting to advance. They are all products of the Todai-driven educational system. Moreover, across the thin bureaucratic boundary that separates enterprise from administrative government, all their contemporaries, the government-bureaucratic managers, are in place too—all having flowed from precisely the same mold.

Todai at Work

As mentioned above, enterprise and bureaucracy both function as parts of Japan's educational system: All these generations, from department general managers down to recruits, constitute not only a single vast power framework with the integrative form and function that constitutes government itself, but a vast archipelago of ethical reinforcement, regeneration, discipline, and instruction. Each interlaced bureaucracy makes up a kind of career-long graduate school.

The first years of this "school" begin with the new recruit being assigned to the basic unit of corporate organization, the section. In most companies this unit has from five to fifteen members, including noncareer female clerical employees. The section is normally constituted merely by having all its members' desks pushed together in a line, side-to-side and back-to-back. At the head of this line is the desk of the *kacho,* or the section chief—the most important management rank in the day-to-day functions of the company. Other section members sit, in line with their duties, in a generally descending order of rank with the most junior closest to the door.

There are no real job descriptions for the subordinate workers below the chief and his assistant. Job assignment is fluid. A recruit is seated next to the second most junior member of the team, and he begins to learn the job, basically, by watching what this comrade does. At various points he may be given explicit instruction, and certainly will ask questions, but a great deal of his basic knowledge of what the section does is supposed to come simply from watching it work and interacting with its members, both on and off the job. He will start with simple tasks, like filing, and then eventually will be given specific assignments of increasing responsibility, but always with the next most senior members watching over him. "Rather than telling people what to do," as one managerial commentator has said, "the process emphasizes watching and assisting; it especially encourages employees to figure things out for themselves."[8] Mistakes will sometimes be made, but this too is considered a cost of the learning process—it is up to the section chief to limit the damage and see that subordinates' mistakes do not turn into costly disasters.

A section chief's job, then, is not only to direct the work of his unit—buying grain low in the American Midwest and selling it higher in Korea, or spearheading the design of a new video camera—but, just as important, to oversee the instruction *and* the performance of all his subordinates even as the work goes on. He must match the most capable of juniors to the most suitable tasks for each, and he must do this in the context of the Japanese group: less by issuing commands than by leading members toward consensus. Discussion is expected to be free and frank, but in the end the section chief is responsible to superiors for the work of his unit, and he must, in one way or another, get his people to do the job the way he has decided it must be done. This accounts for much of the after-hours socializing the section does together, usually but not always lubricated with alcohol. Mistakes have to be pointed out in instructive ways, members with tough assignments have to be encouraged, delicate egos have to be massaged carefully. Stories abound of the classic *kacho* of corporate lore, who throw pieces of chalk at underlings seen to be goofing off or volunteer to find suitable marriage partners for section members who have no luck themselves. The chief has great latitude in the exercise of his authority, but he always establishes that authority incontrovertibly. The section may have reached a consensus to handle a difficult task a certain way, but the consensus is always to do it the section chief's way. Thus, he is the ultimate teacher for the first half of one's career.

Getting the job done through the miasma of all this informality and indirectness is not the only challenge to the business bureaucrat once he reaches the plateau of section chief himself—usually, by his late thirties or his forties. In their excellent book *The Invisible Link,* M.Y. Yoshino and Thomas B. Lifson examine the organization of the nine giant trading companies called *sogo shosha,* which handle more than half of all Japan's imports, and show succinctly how the section chief's accountability as a teacher affects his own career prospects. "The *kacho* knows that he is being evaluated by his [own] superiors to a great extent on his ability to develop the skills of his section members, without allowing them to make very many serious mistakes. Accountability remains with him for the mistakes committed by his subordinates. The importance and prestige of a leader derives from this function of being the custodian of group effectiveness, not from his abilities as an individual."[9]

Tough assignments, in other words, are the "exams" of this graduate school, and close attention is paid by the leader because a student's failure can weigh heavily against the career prospects of the teacher himself. It is an interactive and interlocking system of enforced educational conformity, just like Japan's colleges themselves, where teachers will go out of their way to avoid giving failing grades because the faculty considers them a reflection on the instructor himself.

The way a section chief learns to build and maintain this "harmony," through which he supervises and teaches subordinates without appearing to be doing so directly, carries the section chief into the realm of competition and advancement in his own career as an advancing manager. Section and department chiefs learn to work with one another in more than an institutional way: They learn to trust one another through giving and accepting commitments, to get things done in concert that cannot be achieved by one section alone. Manager Tanaka might ask Manager Saito for his help or advice in accomplishing the job. If Manager Saito supports Tanaka, then, in a way, a favor has been extended: a favor that must be reciprocated. Perhaps Manager Tanaka will someday bring a valuable piece of restricted intra-company intelligence back to Manager Saito; that will help settle the debt. Or some other way will be found for Saito to ask for a repayment. "Commitment and understanding are . . . preconditions of the system of exchange [of support between managers] to operate, and as long as they are present at the minimally acceptable level, the system will operate. Credibility and obligation are the more dynamic elements." To succeed as they move higher up the ladder, even managers must learn: learn the personalities of managers who could be or are their own rivals, and learn how to gain their cooperation by offering their own. "This improves the ability of one unit to subordinate temporarily its immediate interest to the interest of another subunit, in order to enhance overall organizational interests in the long run."[10]

The manager who successfully learns these lessons—enhancing organizational interests through interaction—is passing his own tests for promotion up the ladder. "And [Manager Tanaka] will move on . . . to other assignments. In this longer run he will carry with him relationships and reputation he has built with [Manager Saito] and all others with whom he has had obligation exchanges. The career-long employment system is a major element in the ability of the administrative networks to work. In all cases *sogo shosha* managers are aware that they can expect to be dealing with each other as members of the same firm for the rest of their careers."[11]

Thus, lifelong learning of the most pragmatic kind is at the very heart of the Japanese bureaucratic managerial system.

But if this is so, why does it follow that graduates from Todai and schools that are close to it in stature are especially important? "The dominance of the graduates of a few leading universities in the highest levels of the major companies in Japan is overwhelming. For better or for worse, a graduate of one of the leading universities who is hired by one of a *sogo shosha's* [corporate] clients is very likely to rise further and faster than most employees. . . . The young core [*sogo shosha*] staff member [dealing with these clients] can therefore quickly get a fairly rough idea of who is likely ultimately to wield more power at the client firm in later years, merely by learning who the graduates of the elite schools are. . . . If the two happened to attend the same university, they far more readily form a lasting and valuable tie."

Once a manager has formed such ties, such "members of his outside network have their own networks in their own firms, which are more vertical, composed of superiors and subordinates. Therefore a manager can gain access to vertical networks within his client companies through his ties to contemporaries, who can use their own networks on his behalf."[12]

This is the sinew of *keiretsu* interaction, taking place at levels both high and low. The *sogo shosha* are leaders—pathfinders of new business—for not only themselves but the *keiretsu* they belong to. But most large corporations work internally the same way. Externally, adding the relevant, appropriate government bureaus to the phrase "client firms" expands the scope of networking, and the place of elite graduates in it, to very nearly its full natural borders. Everywhere, from grade school to the boardroom, the Japanese elite spells, knows, and relies on educational background with a capital E.

The results may have been cozy for an economy forced to compete internally so as to build up the strength to compete in global markets. At the same time, Japanese executives have avoided wherever possible the building of relationships with foreign executives, who are as far removed from the "old school" of mutual reliance, common university ties, and proven loyalties as it is possible to be. An executive who embraces a personal partnership with a foreign businessperson runs the risk to his career that the foreigner will prove unresponsive to the subtle bonds of personal obligation, uncooperative, and even unreliable.

"The overall trend [in enterprises] is toward bureaucratic, consensus-oriented leadership," wrote Jiro Tokuyama, a Todai grad and former Defense Agency and JETRO executive. "Competent, but hardly outstanding. [There have been exceptions, but] especially in industries insulated from free competition by government regulation, it is hard to find executives with strategic global vision, firm principles, and high ethical standards. The scandals that have shaken the real estate, securities, and banking industries in recent months have revealed the shameful extent of mutual backscratching among Japan's corporate executives, and given one cause to doubt whether the supervisory government agencies have any concept of the paramount importance of fair competition in a free society."[13]

3. Politicians

"The American President," said Chalmers Johnson, probably America's finest Japanologist, in a recent interview, "on the day he's elected, can name to high public office between three and four thousand officials. The Japanese prime minister, on the day he comes into office, can name only 20 or 21 ministers and Directors General of agencies. The bureaucracy under these politicians remains constant from one administration to the next. This is one of the great sources of Japanese strength in economic planning."[14]

There is no question that the "institutional memory" that this lifelong career employment in the top bureaucracies ensures for Japan's administrators has given the country a great advantage in dealing with nations like the United States, where policy experts come and go and where the bureaucrats represent a living encrustation of generations of new, old, failed, switched, faltered, revamped, redirected, and moribund policy, overlaid back-and-forth across one another as alternative administrations and Congresses of Democrats and Republicans have replaced one another with nearly as many shifts in policy as personnel.

But that is not the only reason that the Japanese bureaucracy is so much stronger than the elected representatives of the people: the National Diet and the cabinet selected from its members. Rather, it is that the politicians have long allowed the ministries to research, lobby, and draft almost all legislation that the Diet passes—leaving the Diet members mere lobbyists in the crudest sense for their own constituents, be they farmers, steelworkers, or white-collar middle managers. Although every ministry has a parliamentary vice-minister as well as a cabinet minister, these posts change hands with a revolving-door speed that leaves one breathless, as prime ministers have been forced to shuffle the relentlessly competing pressures and ambitions of faction leaders and would-be leaders. The men really in charge are the administrative deputy-ministers, the career bureaucrats, who go so far as to orchestrate not only the answers but the questions both government and opposition hurl at each other in Diet plenary sessions.

The U.S. Congress, a virtual industry unto itself, has been criticized in recent years for employing around 25,000 staffers as direct and indirect support to members of the House and Senate. Diet members, on other hand, are each allowed two state-paid office secretaries and more recently were granted one more secretary for policy affairs, to handle the total of their legislative business. Almost no Diet member can survive the rigors of his duties and his dealings with his constituents without a large private staff, paid from his own pocket.[15]

The influence of the bureaucrats, moreover, reaches even into the day-to-day operational affairs of the cabinet. "The Prime Minister's backup staff," explains Kenzo Uchida, a former prominent journalist and now a professor at Tokai University, "consists of five organs within the Cabinet secretariat under the Chief Cabinet Secretary: the Councilors' Office on Internal Affairs, The Councilors' Office on External Affairs, the Security Affairs Office, the Information Research Office, and the Public Relations Office. These are staffed by *high level bureaucrats on loan from related ministries*" [emphasis added].

"Although the general public may not be aware of it," adds Masaru Gotoda, a senior member of the Diet and former Chief Cabinet Secretary, "one of the most pivotal jobs in the day-to-day operation of government is that of Administrative Deputy Chief Cabinet Secretary. This person handles the crucial task of coordination and liaison among the top ministry bureaucrats, the vice-ministers. These deputy chief cabinet secretaries have almost always been officials from one of the agencies created out of the old Home Ministry.

"There's no question the Prime Minister needs better support [from aides chosen from outside the ministries]. But an elaborate advisory apparatus would weaken the ministries' influence. That's as it should be, but the bureaucrats won't yield an inch of their precious turf. In effect, they determine government policy instead of working to carry it out. The tail wags the dog. You can't accomplish a thing without the cooperation of the bureau-cracy."[16]

Just one illustration serves to show not only the attitude but the intransi-gence of these administrative barons: When Prime Minister Tomiichi Murayama, intent on leading his party into the thicket of deregulation by calling a meeting to consider disbanding ninety-four extra-ministerial agen-cies controlled by various ministries, the meeting was boycotted by the bureaucrats.

The politicians, meanwhile, are constantly caught up in a spiral of fund-raising, often by illegitimate means, that the very longevity of the conserva-tive party in power in Japan has helped to create: Constituencies until very recently have been multiple-representative districts, and so candidates with similar neighborhood credentials, whether conservatives who have long represented old farming districts or liberals who have long represented city neighborhoods, battle each other for victory not on the basis of policy opposition but on the basis of money each spreads throughout the same district to influence votes. This is all done in a very Japanese way—with traditional cash gifts offered at the funerals of constituent families, or "study trips" to hot-spring spas for constituents to take mini-vacations at the expense of their elected representatives. But however the money goes, it flows and flows. " 'I need two hundred million yen (two million dollars) in January and February,' " the *Asahi Evening News* quotes a young incumbent from northern Japan about to run for re-election in 1990 as saying. " 'The amount is smaller than what my rivals are spending.'

"Where does such money go? The lawmaker's spending items include these: ten million yen ($100,000) to maintain four campaign offices in his constituency; twenty million yen ($200,000) to get two hundred telephones installed and pay the charges accruing from them; fifteen million yen ($150,000) to get campaign literature printed and mailed; twenty million yen ($200,000) in personnel expenses for a hundred and twenty campaign-ers; thirty million yen ($300,000) to hold campaign rallies to be attended by two thousand people.

"The Diet member needs help from aligned local assemblymen who in turn need money to cultivate support on his behalf. Handouts of this nature and what he calls 'unmentionable expenditures' account for large propor-tions of the remaining sum of more than one hundred million yen ($10 million)."[17]

Though the Japanese electorate often cries "Shame!" at these figures and the kind of thinly disguised financial shenanigans that produce them from donations that may be largely illicit, there is a great deal of cynicism opera-tive among voters as well as candidates. Everyone knows this is what Diet

members have done for fifty years to win elections; everyone in a conservative constituency expects to benefit from the money and from the lobbying
efforts the victor will exert on his constituency's behalf once he reaches the
corridors of power. But the greater hypocrisy is in expecting that politicians
will not be driven to distraction by the need to raise these funds, their need
for more money to keep up good relations that "cultivate support" throughout their terms, and their lack of time and research capacity to spend on
legislation.

Indeed so closely interwoven with this system have many constituencies
become that they have made it very difficult for any new candidates to raise
serious challenges to sitting Diet members during elections: Change is too
expensive. So much has been invested to get a Diet member to Tokyo that
no one wants to risk donations on a candidacy meant to defeat him. Thus it
has reached the point even of dynasties. In the general election of July
1986, over 60 percent of the new candidates who entered the lower house of
the Diet (where most of the power resides) were succeeding a close relative
who had died or retired from office immediately preceding the election.
Thus does "support" sustain politicians, with their reciprocal obligation
being to go on supporting the parochial interests of the constituencies—not
those of the country at large.[18]

Nor has democratic control of political power fared much better at the
local level. Japan's three-thousand-plus towns and villages, all of which
have elected mayors and councils, are so deeply dependent on Tokyo's
central control of their governments that they cannot vote their own local
taxes or bond issuances without permission from the bureaucrats in the
capital. And much more than local finance is controlled from administrators
on high. As an example cited by Richard J. Samuels in a study of local
government in Japan, "The Construction Ministry's prior approval is required for a) all prefectural roads wider than sixteen meters, b) all city
roads, c) parks larger than four hectares, and d) eight different sorts of
land-use designations in urban plans, ranging from housing sites to manufacturing zones. The transport minister's prior approval [meanwhile] is required for a) the creation of new, or changes in existing, bus routes and bus
stops, and b) the granting of taxi licenses among a variety of other things
such as port and harbor planning."[19]

Moreover, as Samuels points out, it is not enough that the localities,
ranging from Hokkaido to Okinawa, be overseen from Tokyo. Through a
procedure known as *katsuai* (transfer), career bureaucrats from the Home
Affairs Ministry itself are constantly dispatched to actually serve as local
administrative officials. "At any given time well over one-half, and closer
to two-thirds of the elite [administrators] of the Home Affairs Ministry are

not in the Home Affairs Ministry per se. Under this *katsuai* arrangement, they are officially [serving as] prefectural and municipal officials. . . . On the average, more than 65 percent of the prefectures have a Ministry of Home Affairs *katsuai* placement in one of their top administrative posts. . . . The Ministry of Home Affairs, in spite of Local Autonomy Law guarantees of the independent authority of local chief executives, enjoys what amounts to a *carte blanche* in the appointment of those prefectural officials most directly responsible for the oversight of local public policy."

It is perhaps little wonder, then, that local politics as well has been infected with the "money" germ of the Diet politicians. These transferees build up local networks of contacts and even supporters, and after retirement often decide to run for local elective office. "In April 1979," writes Samuels, "over 40 percent of Japan's prefectural governors came to be ex–Home Affairs Ministry or ex–Home Ministry (the name of the prewar Ministry) officials." Perhaps it is no wonder that, as the *Asahi Evening News* reported, between 1991 and mid-1994, in 504 contests for local mayors or for ward chiefs in Tokyo, an incredible 25 percent of all candidates ran completely unopposed.[20]

The impact of money politics, brought on by the bureaucracy's almost complete vitiation of electoral authority over government, and the consequent pitching of candidates against one another on purely personal, nonpolicy grounds even in Japan's distant localities, struck this writer most directly after an interview with a local council member, in a town far from Tokyo. As the hours-long interview stretched into the evening, my interpreter and I were invited to dinner at the council member's home. Not wanting to impose, we demurred, and our interview subject instead drove us to the rail station for our return to Tokyo. At the moment of parting we were presented with an unmarked envelope "for a snack on your way home." We guessed that it contained cash. Nonetheless, it was in line with the gracious tradition of Japanese hospitality. At any rate, it was not campaign season, and a foreign writer could hardly be expected to influence any local debate or political contest in this neighborhood. It would be impolite not to accept it; I thought the envelope might contain perhaps thirty dollars.

We were both flabbergasted to discover, when we opened it on board the train, that it held two hundred dollars.

The Pathways of Power

A middle manager of one of Japan's three largest trading corporations had just returned to his office in a driving rain, but he was quietly angry about more than the weather. "It's the pork again," he said, rummaging through a pile of telexes that had accumulated in his in-box. "And it's the damned ministry."

The ministry was that of agriculture, forestry, and fisheries, and the pork was the meat products, mostly processed items like canned hams and sausages that his company imports from Scandinavia and elsewhere. The manager had just been "invited" to a meeting at the ministry, where he had been spoken to carefully but clearly by a bureaucrat about the difficulties assailing the Japanese livestock industry because of this season's oversupply of hogs hitting the market.

"He never told me, or asked me, to lower our import levels," said the manager, whose department supplies imported as well as domestic meats to food processors, supermarkets, wholesalers, and restaurant chains all over the country. "But that's what he wants. To ease the excess on the market and make it easier on the farmers to get better prices for their hogs." But, I asked, if there was neither regulation nor directive—why comply? The manager made an extra effort to be patient with the unsophisticated foreigner. "It's because of the beef!" Beef imports at that time were carefully controlled by the Livestock Industry Promotion Council, a government bureau set up to do nothing more than protect livestock producers by keeping cheap meat imports—especially beef—out of Japan through a system that rationed importing permits among all competing wholesalers and trading companies. An importer might not, he suggested, be pleased if a bureaucrat in the ministry happened to inform a bureaucrat on the council that his particular company was not cooperating with the "suggestion" that pork imports be lowered.

But what could the beef–pork connection be? "If we don't cooperate by lowering our bulk pork imports, at the next round of import licensing for beef, the council will find it somehow expedient to lower our import quota below what we need to supply our customers' beef orders." Japanese trading companies large and small, like all Japanese wholesalers, live and die on the strength of long-term contracts that link the producer, in Japan or abroad, with the customer. If a middleman fails to deliver the goods specified in the contract, customers will quickly begin to look elsewhere, to more reliable suppliers. And they won't come back.

The message delivered at the ministry meeting, then, was an unwritten, unspoken, and implicit threat—though beef had never once been mentioned by the polite bureaucrats. Cooperate, or we'll conspire to wreak havoc with your multimillion-dollar beef market. The fact that this *sogo shosha* manager read the message perfectly was proof enough he knew the technique to be routine. It would be inconvenient, juggling his purchasing and shipping schedules in Scandinavia. But then he knew that, by doing so, his company could expect reciprocal help from the ministry the next time that there were crop failures that affected, say, Japan's schedule of imports in the grain market.

That is a fine example of one of the several ways that informal authority governs Japan—micromanaging markets and industry right down to the sausage. The Japanese call it *gyosei shido* (administrative guidance), and it has been used to fix everything from gigantic industrial cartels, to protective shields against imports and foreign capital, to the prices of airline tickets. The three principal methods that make this informal networking of power so potent and make it rely so much upon the system of personal networking that grows from the Todai system are the exchanges of personnel within and among bureaucracies and enterprises and the face-to-face flows of information and intentions exchanged among good ol' boys, all parts of *Gyosei Shido;* the literal "descent from heaven" (*amakudari*) of retired bureaucrats into industry, and governmental and quasi-governmental associations and bureaus; and outright regulation.

Gyosei Shido

Adopted as a cabinet policy amid what was then Japan's worst postwar recession in the mid-1960s (driven to some extent by overinvestment in production capacity), "administrative guidance," writes Chalmers Johnson in his definitive *MITI and the Japanese Miracle,* "has done more than any other Japanese practice to spread the belief around the world that the Japanese government-business relationship is based upon some underlying, possibly culturally derived, national mores that have no parallels in other countries." But "there is nothing very mysterious about administrative guidance. It refers to the authority of the government, contained in the laws establishing the various ministries, to issue directives, requests, warnings, suggestions and encouragements to the enterprises of clients within a particular ministry's jurisdiction. . . . Although it is not based on any explicit law . . . its power comes from government-business relationships established since the 1930s, respect for the bureaucracy, the ministries' claim that they speak for the national interest, and various informal pressures that the ministries can bring to bear. The old Japanese proverb used to describe this threat of governmental retaliation is "To take revenge on Edo by striking at Nagasaki," meaning that the bureaucracy has [many] means to get even with a businessman who refuses to listen to its administrative guidance."[21]

This modern incarnation of an old principle made its first order of business the establishment of legalized, rationalization cartels to save certain industries from ruin in the recession of the 1960s by adjudicating, amid "discussion" with their representatives, the allotment of production capacity, capital, and so on into these capacity-reduction cartels. Between 1965 and 1994, the Japan Economic Institute listed the annual totals of "Depression, Rationalization, Import, Export, Small and Medium Firm-Related, Environment and Sanitation Act, and Other" cartels created as legally exempt from the Antimonopoly Law: They range from a high of 1,079 cartels in 1966 to 67 in 1994.[22]

Gyosei shido has long outlived many of these cartels in industrial sectors that hardly need government protection today in the world's second-largest economy. But, as Johnson points out in his book, the habit of commanding obedience to central authority, cartel or no, has long outlasted quasi-formal and alegal industrial restructurings. "Generally speaking, few objections are possible when administrative guidance is couched in terms of the national interest. The press likes to cite the case of the city bank executive who called on the Ministry of Finance to protest that his bank could not absorb the full quota of government bonds assigned to [be purchased by] it by administrative guidance. A Banking Bureau official replied, 'So you think your bank can survive even after Japan collapses? Go back and tell your president exactly what I said.' "

Today, the superefficient sectors of globally competitive Japanese industry generally find administrative guidance per se—such as the tradeoff between pork and beef—a nagging and intrusive hindrance, while the sectors of Japan's economy that are vastly less productive than the foreign or domestic competitors (such as the Japanese distribution industry, for example, which employs a tenth of the working population, and is less than half as efficient as that in the other advanced nations) that might overwhelm them without close government protection, have little to complain of. Yet even among the giants—say, the Japanese banks that at the height of the bubble economy commanded 20 percent of the global financing market—there are times when government "guidance" is comforting enough. For instance, at present although their portfolios of bad debts from the collapsed bubble are said to run into the hundreds of billions of dollars, the Finance Ministry still protects them through various maneuverings from having to disclose fully to the public and the capital markets just how bad the internal damage really is. Bureaucrats, as usual, do not wish to give up the power of *gyosei shido,* whether exercised openly or in secret. And even industries of the most giant sizes are occasionally reminded of how expedient it is to have it to fall back upon, when times turn unexpectedly hard. After all, no business executive can really be blamed by his shareholders, no matter how bad his results are, when he was just following the government's orders.

Amakudari

A comparison of the power of the banks versus that of the Finance Ministry (and the Bank of Japan) is of special interest in an examination of the second system of networking, *amakudari*, because this amazing system of second-stage power networking, which spreads farthest and most power-fully throughout the structure of Japanese government, is by far most visible in the financial industries of the nation. In fact, about one in every seventeen board-level executives in the nation's banking and securities industries has retired from the Ministry of Finance (MoF) or the Bank of Japan (BoJ), a total of 153 bank executives and 17 brokerage executives with high positions.[23] The president of the Tokyo Stock Exchange, the governor of the Export-Import Bank, and the governor of the National Finance Corporation are all former deputy ministers of finance as of this writing. So is the president of the Bank of Yokohama, as well as the governor of the Bank of Japan himself, after taking time off following his ministry career to serve as chairman of the Sakura (formerly Mitsui and Taiyo Kobe) Bank.[24] As of 1993, the chairman of the Fair Trade Commission, the president of the Overseas Economic Cooperation Fund, and the governor of the Japan Development Bank are also all former deputy ministers of finance.[25] Also in 1993, 26 percent of the presidents of Japan's 150 private banks had come either from the MoF or the BoJ. That does not, of course, count the many MoF officials retired from lower posts, sitting on bank or brokerage boards, or officering important trade associations around Tokyo.

Even an acquaintance of mine, who runs a small economic research institute in the city, was advised by the auditor from his nearby branch of the Tax Agency that "things would probably go smoothly" in filing future company returns if his enterprise were to put on annual retainer an "adviser" who was a retired bureaucrat from the same tax office.

It is no exaggeration to say that the practice of *amakudari* is pernicious. In it, Todai system bureaucrats who are pushed out the retirement door at around age fifty-five because they did not win the competition for higher ministry or agency posts and could not stay on in the same "class" as their more successful colleagues, are "parachuted" into corporate or agency jobs in many cases tailored for them by their very ministries. The legalities force most of these retirees to wait for two years before accepting employment in an enterprise formerly connected to their government jurisdiction, but for top-ranking bureaucrats even this restriction can be waived by their ministries.

Amakudari affects all inter-enterprise and government–corporate relations in Japan. The National Personnel Authority announced that 208 senior bureaucrats had parachuted into the private sector related to their ministries' purviews in 1993 alone; men such as the former director-general of the National Tax Administration, who became president of the former government monopoly, Japan Tobacco Inc.—the third such director-general to take that specific job since the monopoly's privatization in 1985.[26] But this does not even count those who skydived into public corporations, or other private firms unrelated to their ministry jobs, or who took two years off and then went back into the job market.

Indeed wherever money is made from government contracts or through government contacts, parachutists fill the atmosphere. In 1992, seventy-four companies handling 93 percent of the value of public orders placed by the Kanto Regional Agricultural Association were discovered to have in their employ 434 retired Ministry of Agriculture, Forestry, and Fisheries officials.[27] Former bureaucrats of the Health and Welfare Ministry headed 90 percent of the nation's six hundred small-business association pension funds in 1993. "Many of the associations that wanted to set up funds were strong-armed into appointing the former bureaucrats because they knew if they didn't, the ministry was unlikely to accept their applications to establish the funds," an *Asahi Evening News* investigation revealed.[28]

In 1993, the Japan Civil Engineering Contractors' Association confirmed that sixty retirees from the Construction Ministry were directors of thirty-eight construction firms that were members.[29] Sixteen retirees of the Post and Telecommunications Ministry held down jobs ranging from president to director at seven of the nation's largest telecommunications firms.[30] And even local officials leap into the act with silk 'chutes spread: *Asahi Evening News* discovered that Tokyo city officials of director-general rank or higher are "guaranteed" employment after retirement at one of the seventy auxiliary metropolitan government agencies,[31] and even an association of former civil engineering officials of Shizuoka prefecture—out in "the provinces"—was found to have placed about 70 percent of its membership in the construction industry.[32]

Those who do not go directly into industry have found places to while away their time in public corporations. In 1992 the Federation of Government Special Corporation Employees reported in a survey that sixty-one of these organizations had drawn almost 80 percent of their executives from among retired government officials.[33]

These postretirement jobs are lucrative indeed for their holders: "If a bureaucrat ends his career as the director general of a bureau," reports *Nikkei Weekly,* "his lifetime wage is estimated at 3.4 million dollars. If he succeeds [after his 'retirement'] in getting an *amakudari* position in a prestigious public corporation, his lifetime wage jumps to 4.48 million dollars, mainly because of high retirement payments from the corporation."[34] It is not clear just how much private-sector jobs fatten the purses of retired bureaucrats, but because many are forced to leave their main career posts at a young fifty-five years of age, there are many cases of retired bureaucrats, called "migratory birds," who take two or even three of these truncated post-retirement careers in succession.

This is not a system of bribery. In the workings of the Japanese economy, information is the life-giving, pure water of contracts and strategies. It is the "face" of these retired bureaucrats that corporations are buying: the connections they retain with younger, or older, officials within the same ministries that regulate their new employers. It is they who keep in closest touch at all important levels within the bureaucracy, to find out which way the policy, budgetary, and contractual winds are blowing; what the hard realities that shape "administrative guidance" (*gyosei shido*) are—or could be adjusted informally to become.

Bureaucrats put in long hours at low pay during their ministry days, and the parachute that lands them in green pastures is usually considered nothing more than a fair chance for them to make up what they would have gained as executives wielding comparable power in private industry if they had chosen a business career instead. In the circles where it is practiced— and where it smooths the path to useful administrative guidance—it is considered a fair trade.

Even in the two hundred-plus *shingikai,* or advisory councils to the ministries that study and deliver policy opinions on everything from taxes to the environment, the old boy network preserves an atmosphere of harmony and helpfulness. A December 1994 article in *Tokyo Time Out* reported that "according to a recent survey of one hundred and ninety-five *shingikai* by *Nikkei Business,* 42 percent of the chairmen were ex-bureaucrats."

It is in this arena of the semi-official, in fact, where the advisory ties of *amakudari* and those of industry find another bridge to cross: There are ninety-two public corporations, employing over half a million people, where everything from the cost of wheat to the provision of credit insurance for small businesses is decided. But beneath them there exist many subordinate agencies and organs where thousands more *amakudari* and government industrial representatives meet and mix. "So many special corporations," in fact, according to *Tokyo Business Today,* "that no official tally exists."[35] Social critic Sakuzo Yoshikawa was willing to hazard a guess at twenty-four thousand in an essay in 1994 in *Gendai* magazine, suggesting that their usefulness paralleled the economic-efficiency logic of at least one of the ministries itself: the Ministry of Agriculture, Forestry, and Fisheries, which, responsible for some 2 percent of the nation's productivity, he claimed, itself employed some fifty-three thousand persons—four times as large a staff as that of the Ministry of International Trade and Industry.[36]

More conservative sources give the number as 6,799 "public profit corporations."[37] Whatever their number, the names do not roll flowingly off the tongue—the Japan Raw Silk and Sugar Price Stabilization Agency, the Maritime Credit Corporation, the Railway Development Fund, the Coal Mine Damage Corporation, the Social Development Research Institute, the Japan External Trade Organization, the Institute of Developing Economies, and the Mutual Fund for Official Casualties and Retirement of Volunteer Firemen. But the government of Tomiichi Murayama, which before leaving office early in 1996 tried heroically to condense at least some of the larger ones, claimed that rationalization in the financial and postal sectors alone could save the nation ¥24 trillion ($240 billion).[38] The bureaucrats, as of early 1994, were not persuaded. Perhaps that is because they do not agree with the assessment of the writers of the *Tokyo Business Today* report, that "It is high time a big broom—or perhaps a shovel—was finally taken to these Augean stables of corruption and waste."

Equally likely, it is because they so usefully serve the purpose of networking: using *jinmyaku,* or webs of personal relationships dating back not only to previous careers but to previous cliques of schoolmates or simply of shared alma mater, to pass vital information to all concerned parties, in an economy where corporations otherwise compete so fiercely that they have little chance to communicate, and thereby to coordinate their pricing strategies and their proposals to divide up certain key markets and save themselves the cost of a great deal of price competition.

There are many other, formal ways in which the exchange of personnel and information goes on every day in Japanese business and industry. At the highest levels of the private sector, the six giant *keiretsu,* the leaders of all firms within each group—the presidents—meet jointly at least once a month (four times a year, in the case of the Dai-Ichi Kangyo *keiretsu*) for an exchange of views on the business outlook, the various industrial landscapes, joint projects and mutual business interchange, and the directions of government policy. At the mid- and lower-level management strata, a very common tool of personnel policy is "secondment," in which, for example, Ministry of Finance bureaucrats might be detached for a time to work inside brokerages or key banks, learning the system and the personalities firsthand. The Home Affairs Ministry and its unambiguous interweaving of personnel with local government staff were discussed above; *keiretsu* groupings do the same thing with their middle and upper managers, posting anyone from development engineers to accounting specialists with allied firms, for periods ranging from weeks to months to even years.

Taken together, then, thousands upon thousands of people, from both the government and industry sides, meet and talk within these nexuses daily, far below the summits of the ministries and the watchful eyes of *gyosei shido,* yet still trading intelligence, and trading personal support, and trading goods and services—just as the younger elite managers of the trading companies learn to use the personal networks of their clients and partners within those manager's own organizations, as described above by Lifson and Yoshino. The semi-public companies and trade associations are, after all, merely one more dimension of Japan's national interests secured by the cash necessary to support both the people, and the activities, that make informal government so easy, and so effective.

It should be clear by now that Japan's staggering economic successes, and the speed with which they have been achieved, are no accident of the free-swinging competitions of the marketplace—at least, not any more than of the sub-rosa deal-makings with administrators, cartel partners, and present and potential competitors. If really getting things done for your section, department, or company means not only building a better mousetrap and exporting it at the world's lowest price, but getting the good ol' boys to help put together compromises and pricing cartels and inject information and influence where it is crucially necessary, then these are places to meet—and more important eventually become—one of them.

Regulations

For a nation in which so much of the authority interchange is informal, a vast amount has been said and written about the famous Japanese regulations. Most especially, comments have been made in the context of what Americans and others claim are regulations that serve as trade barriers making it very difficult, if not impossible, to do business in Japan (and, of course, in the context of much public breast-beating among the Japanese public and power establishment themselves, about what a curse they are to modernizing Japan's economy and government). The actual number of regulations on Japan's government books is slowly increasing, not decreasing. The bureaucracies have some 10,942 rules and laws on those books (as of 1993), regulating everything from the operating hours of automatic teller machines to which prefectures (just one) are allowed to license bicycles-built-for-two, to the business hours and practices of barbershops.

That constitutes only the rules that are written down: " 'The Transport Ministry alone has around ten thousand regulations,' including rules not actually on paper, grouses Masao Ogura, senior adviser at Yamato Transport Company, Japan's leading parcel delivery service."[39] The rules are indeed there, and they are indeed used—or manipulated—to keep foreigners out of certain protected markets, at certain crucial junctures. One example was the New Kansai International Airport, completed in 1994 by a public-private corporation capitalized partly by government and partly by enterprise. The venture was hailed at the time of its inception as a new example of the government's willingness to work formally with the business world to accomplish public works that would yield distinct monetary profits. Yet, months later, when the Americans demanded the same access for U.S. construction firms to bid contracts in that massive project to build a manmade island in Osaka Bay that their competitor Japanese contractors enjoy in open bidding on U.S. construction projects *in America,* the same corporation declared it was a solely private enterprise and was under no public-procurements obligation to let any contracts to foreigners. Only after a tremendous diplomatic wrangle between the two national governments were foreign firms grudgingly given small, "set-aside" percentages of the project.

But the issue of regulation, at least as far as foreigners understand it, is a red herring. The regulations, in all their rich written detail, are indeed there, as signposts more of the government's ultimate authority, which must be taken into account, than as a means of ruling Japan. After all, as Philip K. Howard has reminded fellow Americans in his book *The Death of Common Sense: How Law Is Suffocating America,* U.S. federal statutes and formal rules "now total about 100 million words"; the *Federal Register* of new and proposed regulations expanded from "15,000 pages in the final year of John F. Kennedy's presidency to over 70,000 in the last year of George Bush's."[40]

No, regulations in Japan just make a handy tar-baby for Japanese and foreigners alike who need to be slowed from their purposes of averting Japanese bureaucratic control over actions and access. It is a famous axiom of those who wrestle with trade problems that "in the United States, everything is allowed unless specifically prohibited, while in Japan, everything is prohibited unless specifically allowed."[41] Japanese agreements and pronouncements—"in principle"—that Japan really ought to be deregulated are made to give the illusion not only of willingness to cooperate but of real forward motion toward that end. It remains largely an illusion: "Even if all of the one thousand and ninety-one items in the [government's current proposed deregulation] package were implemented immediately," wrote veteran Tokyo correspondent Lew Simons in the spring of 1995—and many are not scheduled to reach fruition until the year 2000—"there are still ten thousand other areas of trade requiring some form of government approval or permission. Beyond that, thousands of other areas are restricted by unwritten rules."[42] The regulatory reforms Japan actually makes are naturally those that are to its own advantage: In the absence of official protest made directly by Washington, virtually no changes are made in the barriers to automotive-parts imports, where, with the vastly cheapened dollar exchange rate, Americans are truly competitive. And promises to loosen rules to permit both Japanese and foreigners to open large, discount superstores in Japan are issued unencumbered with specified target dates or details of the actual changes to be made.[43]

What really determines official prohibition or dispensation is the informal —and often informally obtained—consent of the bureaucrats, in concert with the large-enterprise executives that make up the core of Japan's economy. Regulations can be written and torn up overnight in this scheme of government, as it suits the real purposes of groups of administrators to attain their intended ends. Battling them in fine, formal American lawyerly style is no more productive today than tilting at windmills, unless and until the personal groundwork for permissions, purposes, and strategies has been laid beforehand, on a face-to-face meeting ground.

Inside, and Out

"One American insider remarked that in the waning days of the Miyazawa Administration, Foreign Ministry officials had begged the U.S. government to ease up on trade pressure, arguing that otherwise it might inadvertently contribute to the LDP's [the ruling Liberal Democratic Party's] downfall. And then [after that downfall] under Hosokawa, these same Foreign Ministry officials pleaded with the U.S. government for some slack, this time arguing that pressure on trade issues might bring the LDP back!"[44]

"Recently," observes economist Leon Hollerman, "under the pressure of the protectionist tide that is seeping through Europe and America, Japan's task of managing its dependence on the world economy has raised new anxieties."[45] It is precisely this anxiety that has produced the kind of mumbo-jumbo in the previous paragraph that has come to substitute for reasoned, sustained, and pragmatic foreign policies on Japan's diplomatic front—invariably intertwined with its economic front, as the nation has come to be identified, and to identify itself, as a sort of disembodied economic entity floating among nations, seeking always the security guarantee of open markets. Everyone knows that MITI now has more influence on Japan's external policies than does the Foreign Ministry.

"The policy of liberalization has been a divisive force in Japan for various reasons," continues Hollerman, pointing out the difficulties this quintessentially involuted, self-centered power structure has produced. "It creates dissonance between cultural norms and institutional arrangements." (In fact, this writer would conclude, the obvious dissonances that emerge as more trade pressures are placed on Japan are just what has made it seem to outsiders trying to understand the country that Japan and its economy *are* in fact a "culture.") "The entry of foreigners and foreign investment into Japan induces a form of dualism in a traditionally xenophobic society. Liberalization threatens the traditional role of bureaucracy as leader and planner . . . [and] threatens the traditional principle of an assumed identity between national interests and the interests of the firm, or between macro and micro interests. It brings the conflict between Japan's domestic and international policies, as well as between economic and political goals, into the open.

"On the international policy plane," he continues, "Japan's chief preoccupation during the interregnum of the 1980s concerned the nature of its relations with the United States. In the latter 1980s, the question of whether Japan should behave as a 'small' nation or as a 'big' nation [on the world stage] was no longer at issue. United States demands were sharply directed at Japan as a major industrial power. In the short run, Japan brooded about the optimal degree of acquiescence to U.S. demands. In the long run . . . the problem concerned how it could best fulfill its objective of reducing the degree of its dependence on the United States as a market. . . . In the meanwhile, the pragmatic issue concerned how Japan could manipulate foreign pressures in such a way as to make them serve its own objectives and fulfill its own national interests."

Far lower on the list, in other words, was the bureaucracies' and the politicians' priority on how to preserve, strengthen, and add to international institutions of cooperation in the economic or security spheres, the two very foundations upon which the United States had sacrificed so much blood and treasure and upon which so much of Japan's house of prosperity had been built. It took America's direct promotion of NAFTA to galvanize serious action on Japan's part to support the idea of the Asia-Pacific Economic Cooperation (APEC) forum.

Hollerman, who spent five years as an international trade economist on MacArthur's Occupation staff in Japan, finished his book, an analysis on the impact of postwar demands from abroad for liberalization in Japan's financial polices, in 1988. Where do we stand now?

At first glance, amid the rubble of recession produced by the horrendous collapse of the bubble economy—a phenomenon triggered by the Ministry of Finance and the Bank of Japan through horrific overlending and overmonetarization policies in the mid-1980s. This has been the impression so warmly received overseas, where advanced-nation audiences had grown distinctly uncomfortable at the roaring pace of growth and international financial power in Japan during the bubble years. The economists of the United States, as Chalmers Johnson has noted, "endlessly publish articles about how Japan is falling apart; this is the fourth time in my adult life that the English-language business press has published the obituary of this nation."

Yet, Johnson pointed out in a speech to the Foreign Correspondents' Club of Japan seven years later, this outcome has been manifestly exaggerated: Japan still runs record trade surpluses with America, even with the yen (at this writing) at less than 90 to one dollar.[46] "Already this decade," pointed out economist Kenneth Courtis, Deutsche Bank capital markets analyst for Asia, just three months before Johnson's speech, "Japan has run an accumulated surplus of some four hundred and thirty billion dollars. That is greater than the surplus for the entire decade of the 1980s. By the end of this year, the accumulated surplus will be in excess of half a trillion dollars, and it will double again over the remaining five years of this decade."[47] Whether those forecasts are accurate or not Japan is not yet broke, nor is it likely soon to be: $430 billion is not that far from the total government debt that the U.S. Congress was scrambling madly in 1995 to cut from its budget over the coming five years.

Discussion of these figures have a place in our delineation of the networks of Japanese power, in part because they show that, despite the fallacies of its "omniscience," and the fact that competition of ministries, bureaucracies, businesses, and politicians can make possible such horrendous collisions of mismanagement as the bubble economy, the successes of the system are so large, and its authority so entrenched that even its gravest errors do not dilute its legitimacy in the Japanese public's eye. Mostly, however, they are relevant because they demonstrate concretely how little we understand what this culture of political leadership has accomplished for Japan—and what it has done to us.

The situation of this leadership and its aggregate goals, Johnson told the press, "is that Japanese nationalism is expressed almost entirely through economic claims and achievements." Americans remain "baffled by the Japanese economic and technological challenge," says Johnson, "because [they refuse to admit that] the Japanese economy is guided by a state strategy."

But how *does* strategic state direction coincide effectively with the centrifugal displacement of political power and competition throughout such a huge elite establishment? As discussed above, every Japanese is made to feel that he or she has a stake in the success of this system. "There are many different strategies that grow out of Japan's economic nationalism," said Johnson in the same speech. "These include industrial policy itself, economic intelligence-collecting, both domestically and internationally, foreign aid tied to sales by Japanese companies, concessionary sales of technology to key agencies in order to secure foreign markets (for example Fujitsu's virtual gifts of computers to South Korean banks and government agencies), promotion and protection of general trading companies that have the capacity to tie together many companies into package deals, including the Baoshan Steelworks in China as an example, the strategic use of joint ventures and co-production schemes to extract proprietary knowledge from foreign enterprises, the rigging of stockholders' rights to prevent the foreign takeovers of domestic companies, and so forth. These are all the common, day-to-day realities of business in Tokyo."

They also automatically engage the vast networks of managerial elites, from assistant section chiefs in banks and engineering companies to vice-ministers at the MoF, MITI, and other ministries, to achieve what they do as an ongoing matter of national policy direction: Thus do all the identical pieces fit together into the rational, strong form of the geodesic dome of "Japan, Inc." Thus, while elites all know that they share in the power of leading Japan and compete personally for more of that power, none of them feels any individual responsibility for national consequences (and all in fact are comfortable operating without any single, national center of accountability): Whatever they do to serve the interests of their groups is, by definition, also in the best interests of the nation. "Japanese economic strategy," Johnson continued, "requires that the public interest be elevated over the private interest, and it de-legitimizes the pursuit of private motives openly acknowledged. The Japanese economic strategy is comparable to the American pursuit of a military strategy"—that is, toward goals so implicitly understood, accepted, and internalized as not even to rise to the level of public debate. "I mean that the Japanese pursue economic activities primarily in order to achieve independence and leverage over potential adversaries." How close we stand to the category of "potential adversaries" could already be seen in early 1994, when Prime Minister Hosokawa, meeting President Clinton in Washington, for the first time represented a Japan that flatly refused to accede to specific American requests for liberalization in its national trade stance.

It is the failure of the American economics and political establishment to understand how different this "raison d'état, prevailing over the economic individual in Japan," for reasons that grew out of (as did Todai itself) the imperatives of the country's modernization at the start of the Meiji period, that has placed the two nations "on a collision course."

The dangers arising are not wholly the fault of Japan. Persistent American failure to negotiate real reductions in trade imbalances shows that "We must recognize that in dealing with Japan, the United States is virtually flying blind. There is no apparatus in place to provide middle managers throughout the American government with the kinds of information they need on Japan. Throughout that government today, such expertise is conspicuous by its absence. Equally important, if the U.S. government ever does wake up, and wants to staff its departments and agencies with knowledgeable personnel, it will discover they are few and far between. This is because of the failure of American universities to internationalize and to begin to respond to the new agenda after the cold war.

"There is today no single American university"—no Harvard, no Stanford, no Princeton, no Georgetown—"with a fully adequate program in Japanese studies, backed by a library oriented toward current affairs.

"The first thing to be done is to strengthen and reorient our national analytic capacity to understand and react to Japanese achievements. This includes recognition that the world center of gravity in manufacturing has migrated to east Asia, where learning from Japan and competition with Japan are simultaneously being pursued. . . . Japan and other high-growth economies of east Asia have demonstrated that the state can be a critically important contributor to the success of market economies. These contributions included the things that Adam Smith specified—education, investment in infrastructure, incentives to save. But they also include public measures to provide Japanese citizens with good jobs in high-tech industries. That is, the Japanese government's criterion of what it's doing is simplicity itself: the number of high valued-added jobs held by Japanese citizens. That's a criterion a government can work with," Johnson concluded. "I don't know what criterion of effectiveness there is in the American government today."

Certainly there is not, and most likely never will be, anything like the Todai system.

Notes

1. "How Bureaucrats 'Fix' the Numbers," *Nikkei Weekly,* January 17, 1994.
2. Leon Hollerman, *Japan, Disincorporated* (Stanford: Hoover Institution, 1988).
3. Michael Gerlach, *Alliance Capitalism: The Social Organization of Japanese Business* (Berkeley: University of California Press, 1992).
4. Ibid.
5. Ibid.
6. Interview with the author, February 11, 1994.
7. Gerlach, *Alliance Capitalism.*
8. M.Y. Yoshino and Thomas B. Lifson, *The Invisible Link: Japan's* sogo shosha *and Organization of Trade* (Cambridge, MA: MIT Press, 1986).
9. Ibid.
10. Ibid.
11. Ibid.
12. Ibid.
13. "The Leaderless State," *Japan Echo,* no. 4 (1991).
14. Interviewed in the newsletter *Critical Intelligence* (August 1994).
15. "Doubts Linger Over Tax-funded Diet Secretaries," *Asahi Evening News,* March 14, 1994.

16. "A Peek Down the Corridors of Power," *Japan Echo,* no. 4 (1991).

17. "Massive LDP Campaign Spending," *Asahi Evening News,* January 18, 1990.

18. "Powerful Families Hand Down Diet Seats," *Japan Times,* February 2, 1990.

19. Richard J. Samuels, *The Politics of Regional Policy in Japan* (Princeton: Princeton University Press, 1983).

20. "Many Elections Go to Anyone Who Runs," *Asahi Evening News,* August 22, 1994.

21. Chalmers Johnson, *MITI and the Japanese Miracle* (Stanford: Stanford University Press, 1982).

22. "Competitive Conditions and Competition Policy in the Japanese Economy," Japan Economic Institute Report No. 9A, March 10, 1995.

23. "One in 20 Bank, Brokerage Execs from MOF or BOJ," *Asahi Evening News,* September 14, 1991.

24. "Glut of Ex-Finance Ministry Officials in Top Bank Posts Not a Healthy Trend," *Nikkei Weekly,* May 23, 1994.

25. "Power Stays with 'Old Boys' of Finance Bureaucracy's Top Slot," *Nikkei Weekly,* March 28, 1994.

26. "Top Tax Man Lands Tobacco Job," *Asahi Evening News,* May 26, 1994.

27. "Ex-bureaucrats Land Jobs in the Private Sector," *Asahi Evening News,* August 10, 1993.

28. "Ex-Bureaucrats' Pension Fund Sop," *Asahi Evening News,* November 27, 1993.

29. "Ministry Sets Terms of Ex-officials' Jobs," *Asahi Evening News,* November 13, 1993.

30. "DDI Head Puts Business Before Telecom Vision," *Nikkei Weekly,* December 27, 1993.

31. "Tokyo Bureaucrats Assured Soft Jobs," *Asahi Evening News,* December 20, 1993.

32. "Prefectures Rethinking Relations with Industry," *Asahi Evening News,* October 12, 1993.

33. "State-tied Firms Offer Nest to Retiring Officials," *Japan Times,* April 19, 1992.

34. *Nikkei Weekly,* March 28, 1994.

35. "When in Doubt, Cut It Out: Trimming Useless Organs of the Bureaucracy," *Tokyo Business Today* (June 1994).

36. *Asahi Evening News,* extracting an essay from *Gendai Monthly*, April 2, 1994.

37. "Take Administrative Reform Seriously, Cabinet Is Urged," *Japan Times,* December 17, 1994.

38. "Privatization Benefits to State Seen," *Japan Times,* February 2, 1995.

39. "The 10,942 Rules of Doing Business," *Nikkei Weekly,* January 18, 1993.

40. Reviewed in *The New Yorker,* March 13, 1995.

41. Henry Marini, quoted by Clyde Prestowitz in *Trading Places: How America Allowed Japan to Take the Lead* (New York: Basic Books, 1988), p. 80.

42. "Japan to Relax Trade Rules," *San José Mercury News,* March 31, 1995.

43. "Deregulation: The New Transpacific Battleground," Japan Economic Institute Report No. 10B, March 17, 1995.

44. Steven K. Vogel, "American Press Illusions About Japanese Politics," Japan Policy Research Institute Critique, February 1995.

45. Hollerman, *Japan Disincorporated.*

46. Speech at the Tokyo Foreign Correspondents' Club, October 26, 1994.

47. "Markets Look to Naples for Answers," *Nikkei Weekly,* July 4, 1994.

11

Fifty Ways to Lever the Governed

Even for a modern Japanese, role behavior becomes a means of self-realization. He learns to dedicate himself to the role prescribed for him by his culture and finds it difficult to think of himself apart from it.

—George A. DeVos and Hiroshi Wagatsuma,
"Socialization for Achievement" (1973)

It is an even graver issue to confront when scholars at the university undertake, as they must, to construct and propose models of the good society as alternatives to the present, or at any rate as improvements to the present. . . . The idea of the university, moreover, defines the intellectual ambience of the high school no less substantially.

—Jaroslav Pelikan, President, American Academy of Arts and
Sciences, "The Idea of the University," 1992

One evening I was having a drink with a Japanese editor, a long-time friend, when I mentioned some crisis of the day in terms of whether it was possible for the Japanese to reach a "consensus" for this or that remedy. *Consensus* is not only a term but a concept that virtually every foreign journalist and many scholars reach for to describe how decisions for institutional action are made in Japan—whether over a business contract or over sending military forces on UN peacekeeping missions.

My friend was reflective for a moment. "A 'consensus,'" he mused. "You know, it's funny. We Japanese hardly ever use the word that way among ourselves."

Exactly. The true "consensus" concerning Japan is only among foreigners. It is that Japanese act on almost every important issue by some unique, egalitarian social process of consensus formation. A process that levels the authoritarian platform of the superior, while elevating the self-effacing subordination of the junior, to a common ground where all members, be it of a corporate section or the national population, are heard *and their views are incorporated in the decision.* Though almost any Japanese knows well his or her chain of social, professional, or administrative command, at home, on the job, or in the community, and knows how its top-down, male-centered authority actually works, even many of *them* will explain their society's workings to outsiders in terms of the importance of "consensus." The phenomenon is what Karel Van Wolferen refers to as "what the Japanese believe that they believe"—and its hardy diffusion throughout the generations is, of course, due to the universality of the way the unified Japanese educational system socializes the Japanese: Do whatever the group does.

That has, perhaps, served Japan positively as social myth through all these years of recovery and industrial development. If nothing else, it shields the real lines of authority described in these chapters from outside influence—even from the idea that *attempts* at outside influence would be seemly in such a hallowed social tradition. Either consensus or lack of it, after all, can conveniently forestall all appeals for cooperation from those who are outside the group, or who don't know the game—which certainly includes foreigners.

But there is an insidious side to "consensus," for it is in fact a lie. Sometimes it is a nicely window-dressed, even a convincing lie, as any outsider will attest who has been obliged to sit through endless group meetings in Japan where discussion never seems to reach a point of agreement, disagreement, or in fact any point at all. What appears to be a ponderous effort to include everyone's views is, really, no more than a careful dissembling, meant to apportion responsibility among many instead of fixing it on the supervisor, in case the agreement finally reached turns out to be wrong. But that does not alter a whit the fact that nothing will ultimately be adopted that runs counter to the principle wishes of the senior leader of the group.

Nevertheless, the consensus myth does serve to explain a troubling doubt we feel when we consider how the elites manage to extend their authority so monolithically through whatever groups they are in charge of: units of the society, of business, of the government, of the universities. These groups indeed compete, sometimes brutally, and must have unified tactics. But the larger question still seems disturbing: Are 124 million people, college graduates or high-school dropouts, divided into whatever size of units for whatever purposes, really so unindividuated as to ultimately agree on everything?

Of course not. Subservience is assured—and the elite exercise command —in ways different from those in the West, that's all. These are ways that the national educational structure, influenced from the Todai system above in just the manner that Pelikan suggests, teaches people to obey. The schools have far more influence here than the Japanese will admit. This chapter explores the many ways that elites, once placed in position at all levels, use the leverages of the Todai-predicated system, in its broadest sense, to run all of Japan—including the leaders as well as the followers. In the process, we will see again why, as Van Wolferen and many others have suggested, no single source of national accountability exists in Japan; how so many, but no *one*, can be in charge here.

It is not only the diplomas of Todai, Kyodai, Keio, Waseda, and Hitotsubashi on which are written the success in one's life. In his study of a representative Tokyo suburban neighborhood, which he names "Miyamoto-cho," Theodore C. Bestor describes in detail just how vital, to individuals and families, school linkages that go clear back to elementary school are in the social infrastructure of the community. Not only do new families integrate themselves into their neighbors' lives and activities through the attendance of their children at the local elementary school, but,

> Classmates may remain intimate friends all their lives, even when their statuses [afterward] diverge sharply. Dr. Nishino, a physician who now lives elsewhere in the ward, stays in close touch with his elementary school friend, Mr. Arakawa, a baker who with his son runs a tiny shop near the railroad tracks. The two talk on the phone several times a week, visit each other's very different homes often, exchange gifts and favors, and speak to each other using childhood forms of address. . . . There may be good instrumental reasons for each to keep up the connection; still, childhood ties enable them to continue an intimate relationship that transcends the differences in their adult social and economic statuses. Even if such ties do not always develop into warm bonds of adult friendship, the childhood relationship can remain strong enough to be called upon in certain circumstances, particularly among classmates who continue to live in the area, as many graduates of the elementary school do.
>
> Even less intimate ties endure, and for many residents school ties form a significant frame of social reference that extends throughout Miyamoto-cho and the surrounding areas. For example, residents often casually identify adult acquaintances as their younger brother's classmate, or the mother of their daughter's former classmate, or someone two years behind their wife's sister at school. This ability to so classify innumerable other residents and thus identify some connection to oneself is an important social resource, useful in many ways. It can be the basis for creating a new relationship or reclaiming an old one, for example. Residents often explained to me their patronage of a given shop or business (or others' patronage of their own) as due in part to old school ties. Tsurumi-sensei [Teacher Tsurumi], the politician, who is not a native of the area himself, uses his connection to the school—his wife and children graduated from it, and he is a past president of the PTA—to garner support through these networks of *tsukiai* [friendship] and to bolster his status as the candidate of the local community. Even in matters of social control, old school ties have force.
>
> Relationships between *kohai* [juniors] and *senpai* [seniors]—between a subordinate and a superior, based on seniority within an educational institu-

tion or a bureaucratic organization—characterize Japanese social life in many domains: higher education, companies, government bureaucracies, political parties, and artistic groups, among others. Typically a *kohai* may rely on his or her *senpai* for advice and aid; in turn a *senpai* should be able to count on the *kohai*'s loyalty and respect. Such ties—based on elementary school classes—function at the level of neighborhood social relationships, too, and even well into adult life *senpai* retain some degree of moral authority over their *kohai*.[1]

Not only the university but even the grade school, then, reaches down into the very neighborhoods of the blue-collar workers and white-collar salarymen, to create a social seniority system that has direct connections to advantage and competition in everyday life. As in the ministries and the *keiretsu* corporations, success can depend on who you went to school with, and how much attention you pay to the informal systems of rank and authority that school created for you merely because you are Japanese.

This condition of life is also often the reason political arrangements seem to pass for culture, when we look at Japanese power structures from the outside—or conversely, why culture seems interchangeable with political arrangements. It is almost as if every grouping of people in Japan resembles what in our instincts would be the cliché called a small Southern town run by good ol' boys.

What can be seen from this, and from what follows, is that the mechanisms and structures through which the elite command the social and economic systems around them are in fact nearly seamless, stretching from the family through the neighborhood to the job to social institutions to the government. As seen above, for example, the elite corporate employment system commands a loyalty from those in the family, through its male workers, that is almost absolute: The lifetime employment system is not merely an economic security net but a system of almost complete economic coercion to those within it. Despite a great deal of contemporary talk about younger Japanese bureaucrats and employees preferring more time off and placing greater value on their family lives than do their seniors, a junior elite is extremely careful not to "blot his copy book" anywhere along the course of his career, because he is stuck in that career. This message of loyalty can be drilled in quite strictly, and from the earliest possible moment: Not only do companies themselves give induction classes for new recruits that isolate them at training centers or in Buddhist monasteries, but Japan's army, the Ground Self-Defense Forces, gave special quasi-military "drill camps" at its bases, arranged and paid for by employers, to an astonishing 123,000 *corporate* recruits in fiscal 1994.[2] (Even Japan's preciously famous Takarazuka All-Female Musical Revue Troupe introduces its inductees annually to the levels of discipline required for success, by inviting Japanese soldiers to give its young ladies "basic training" in proper carriage, posture and bowing.)[3]

The disciplinary results work out along the lines Robert E. Cole suggests in his article "Work and Leisure in Japan": "A willingness to take [one's] full vacation days is seen by the company as an act of disloyalty. Employee loyalty is a key ingredient of an employee's annual performance assessment. The higher the number of vacation days [one] uses, the greater the tendency to see one as disloyal and the lower will be one's annual performance appraisal."[4] The same thing could be said about willingness to stay on for the overtime hours requisite in so many companies. In fact, work-hour demands place such an obtrusive burden on Japanese workers, simply in terms of overtime hours demanded, that one of the most recent public worries to surface in the country has been *karoshi*—death by overwork. One group of families of victims claims that almost ten thousand Japanese die each year from the physical strains of working so many hours,[5] though all such connections are admittedly hard to prove and the government has recognized only a very tiny fraction of that number as official victims, for purposes of granting official workers' compensation to their families.

Whatever, then, may be the level of silent resentment among the younger generation, as male workers near the stage of their first round of competition for promotion into the junior managerial ranks, the preference for more time spent with the family and less with the company does quietly evaporate. The reverse side of the coin of lifetime employment is that one is stuck with one's employer for life. If a *kaisha* (company) man quits, he can expect to find alternative employment only at a much lower level of salary, with far fewer guarantees, in a company of much less prestigious stature— or occasionally with a foreign employer, which is usually considered much the same thing. In many cases, middle-level employees and higher cannot quit, simply because the company in effect holds the mortgage on their homes.

Everyone attending a "consensus-finding meeting" at the office is aware of all this. If the boss is seriously offended by a contrary opinion stated too directly or an attitude that is less than enthusiastic, one has indeed seriously blotted one's career "copy book": That boss and his wrath are inescapable for the employee, young or old.

It is often said, particularly beginning with the recession of the 1990s, that the Japanese lifetime employment system is too inflexible, too costly, and on its way out. In any company that counts, that is hardly likely. Of Japan's approximately 31 million male workers today, there are roughly 5 million career employees—about a sixth of the total—retained under a formal lifetime employment system, and many more who are either retained under an informal version of the same system, or who hope and plan to stay with the same employer their whole careers. A 1993 Ministry of Labor survey showed that in companies of more one thousand workers, more than 96 percent of all male employees who were between ages thirty and thirty-four in 1986 were still working for the same companies in 1991.[6] Even in early 1994, in the depths of recession, a poll of personnel managers of large, listed companies found that nearly 90 percent felt, either completely or with some mild reservations, that the lifetime employment system would continue to operate in their own firms on into the future—even though almost 40 percent of their employer firms already had excess employees on the payroll at the time.[7]

In fact the pressure that lifetime employment puts on employees is even stronger now because Japanese firms in general have an excess of managers that numbers into the hundreds of thousands and are constantly reviewing ways to farm out the more expensive ones—those past forty—to subsidiary, joint-venture, supplier, or even unconnected companies. The pressure and competition to remain on the right side of one's superiors and one's company policies is very tough for these men because transfer amounts to demotion—and sometimes to pay cuts—and the chances of being recalled to the alma mater *honsha* (main company) at the next business upturn are likely to be virtually nil.

Reinforcing this "clinging to a life raft" psychology at the other end of the scale is the constant drumbeat of coverage given to the competitive aspects of education by the Japanese media. That is especially true in the mid-1990s, when the vast number of large corporations hit by the need to restructure and reduce personnel expenses were doing so by cutting the number of college- and high school-graduate recruits inducted annually, leaving all those but the graduates of the very top schools frantic to locate a starting rung on the career ladder. It is common to ride Tokyo's commuter trains and subway cars and see flyers hawking weekly and monthly magazines in massive numbers, headlining stories about the crisis in hiring cutbacks of graduates. These stories take on banner dimensions around the time that lists of successful college-entrance exam candidates are posted by the schools. Rare is the magazine or newspaper that does not carry photos or stories or both about at least some aspects of this year's contest to attain the brass ring of freshman status at Todai or elsewhere near the top of the ladder. Anxieties of high-school, junior-high-school, even grade-school students and their parents are kept at a fever pitch over what is, after all, access to the lifetime employment system. No one finds much encouragement in all this to voice rebellious opinions.

Another arena in which the elites collectively exercise their power over groups under the guise of consensus is to be found in the confusion in Japan, in so many administrative sectors, between what is public and what is private.

Chapter 10 discussed *amakudari*, the practice through which retired government bureaucrats parachute into board-level, advisory, or other powerful executive positions within the industries they formerly regulated. Also described earlier were sectoral industrial-government organizations that staff their executive ranks from both the private and public sectors. But it goes further than that. The private–public lines are damagingly blurred in the practice of *allowing professional groups to set, and sometimes to administer, government policy themselves.*

As Aurelia George explains: "The Japanese bureaucracy enlists the active cooperation of interest groups in the pursuit of government policy objectives by *formally incorporating* them [emphasis added] into the processes of policy formulation, decision making and administration." In this Japanese form of subjectivized cooperative government, legal statute "assign[s] administrative and policy roles to interest groups [themselves]. . . . Organizations such as *Nokyo* [the national union of farm cooperatives], The National Fisheries Co-Operative Federation, The National Chamber of Commerce and Industry, The National Federation of Commerce and Industry Associations, and The National Central Association of Medium and Small Enterprise Organizations all operate under their own laws and perform state-recognized roles as part of their day-to-day functioning. In most cases legal provisions also allow for an officially sanctioned interest articulation function, which permits organizations to make proposals to administrative authorities [on behalf of their group memberships]."

These groups, though composed entirely of private members, often function themselves as administrative arms of the bureaucracy, "and are accorded a legitimate role in processes of policy formulation affecting their respective areas. They are," then, George points out, "legally authorized interest groups with a foot squarely in both the public and private sectors."[8]

This is somewhat more than what Americans would think of as lobbying. In the United States, it would be roughly comparable to industry representatives, called before congressional hearings to give opinions on proposed legislation, stepping into the cloak room among the members of Congress to discuss policy formation with them as junior partners. Further, once policy is set into law or regulation, it would be as if these group leaders acted with the authority of government officers in actually enforcing and administering them. Helping draw up the rules they wish to be governed by, those regulated at the same time become the regulators; it becomes impossible to separate their private interests from the public's interests.

It cannot be surprising, then, that the true power-holders, not Diet members in the case of Japan but the bureaucrats, who thus allow the delegation of their own authority, at the same time stress so heavily the necessity for the compelling Japanese "consensus": "You may make your own rules only so long as they conform with our policies" is what they tell these intricate amalgams of formal and informal, public and private authority. There will be consensus—with the government—or there will be ejection from the councils of power. To maintain position in an economy that pretends to be a society itself, one must choose between the carrot that is consensus and the stick that is exile.

Rewriting History

Absolute faith in the beneficent nature of elite authority is easy to understand among those enfranchised to share some of it basically on behalf of their own interests, such as corporate managers or the interest groups described above. Yet there are those, the vast majority of citizens, far from the circles of institutional power, whom the elites must also reach through persuasion or indoctrination, with the idea that all authority is exercised for their own best interests. For this national audience, besides the great socializing influence of the educational and Todai systems, there are three principle tools: the rewriting of history to fit conceptions of Japan-as-a-culture, the use of (sometimes rather blunt) social censorship and controls, and the use of pure social mythologies. They share similarities, yet essentially each has a different way of indoctrinating the Japanese people: not only of selling them on the righteousness of "consensus," but making them believe that their very survival depends on it.

Mistakes, when we make them, are never comfortable to think about. Japan, largely through its educational system, has devised a method for avoiding this discomfort by sweeping its worst national errors under the national rug. In the most outstanding and most shameful example, public school textbooks are censored in Japan, with the principle goal of distorting, minimizing, or screening off altogether the history of Japan's fifteen-year war in Asia and its aftermath, an aftermath that echoes to this day.

True enough, all grade-school textbooks in the world are edited, by their publishers if no one else, and are screened—by local school boards, or schools themselves, if by no one else. And it is probably safe to say that in most communities, the interests of national pride, popular ethics, or even patriotic, religious, or regional values are standards to which authors are encouraged to adhere—or at least to pay some attention. But Japan's centrally directed censorship, operated through Ministry of Education itself, has been especially egregious in contributing to the erasure of almost all history of the war itself, including the most salient details of Japan's responsibility, from the official canon of the national record.

The citizens of Hiroshima have built in their city an enormous peace park, complete with a graphic museum, commemorating the horrific atomic bombing by the United States in 1945. Almost completely missing there, and elsewhere, is any evidence that Japan had prosecuted an illegal and rapacious war of conquest first on the Asian continent, and later in Southeast Asia and the Pacific Islands, beginning in 1931 with the invasion of Manchuria. According to official Japanese memory, the Great Pacific War began at Pearl Harbor—a war that Japan was forced to fight by the intransigence of the Western powers—and ended more or less with the atomic explosion at Hiroshima.

As American correspondent Lew Simons has put it succinctly, "The authorized version [of publicly taught wartime history] skips, for example, the ten million Chinese killed by the Japanese army—one hundred thousand to three hundred thousand deaths and twenty thousand rapes in the city of Nanjing alone; the two million Vietnamese who starved to death under Japanese occupation; the thousands of Allied POWs who died in germ warfare experiments; the thousands of Okinawans forced by Japanese troops to commit suicide in the name of Emperor Hirohito when it became obvious that the United States would capture the island";[9] and the some two hundred thousand "comfort women," most of them Korean teenagers abducted forcibly from schools to serve as official army prostitutes in both front-line and rear areas across Asia.

Indeed the "comfort women" issue, the most recent chapter of Japan's dark military past in Asia to surface (it is estimated to have resulted in the deaths of 70 percent of those two hundred thousand women), has triggered yet another round of controversy in a long-standing demand by China, Korea (which was actually annexed to Japan between 1915 and 1945, and for whose present partitioning Japan bears no little blame), and other Asian nations that Japan apologize and admit what it did in the war. For almost two decades, these countries have insisted not only that the historical record be corrected in Japanese textbooks (in cases, for example, where bureaucrats censored out the term *invaded* and replaced it with *advanced*) but that Japanese officials ranging from the Emperor to the prime minister to Cabinet members acknowledge and apologize for Japanese atrocities and aggression that stretched over a war of fifteen years.

Still, it seems, the Japanese cannot bring themselves to do this. Two cabinet ministers have recently been forced to step down, in fact, for insisting that the war was not really one of aggression. Other ministers have danced semantically around the wording of acknowledgments of Japan's actions in Asia. The Supreme Court has ruled that Education Ministry direct censorship of textbooks in these and other matters is entirely legal. Moreover, very high-ranking politicians continue to infuriate Japan's neighbors with their nationalistic ambivalence. In late 1994 Minister of International Trade and Industry Ryutaro Hashimoto (who became prime minister in 1996), for instance, insisted in the Diet that whether Japan waged wars of invasion on the continent is really a matter of subtle definition,[10] and as late as February 1995, Prime Minister Tomiichi Murayama backed away—within the space of twenty-four hours—from an admission that Japan did bear some responsibility for the division of Korea, to adopt the position that it bore no responsibility at all. At the same time "half [his coalition] Liberal Democratic Party legislators [on] the same day indicated they do not wish to apologize to Asian nations for Japan's actions during that war."[11]

This is not only a matter of refusal to admit before the nation's young the culpability of Japanese leaders and the horror they wrought. It is both heartbreaking and politically dangerous.

In his travel journal Japanese filmmaker Shinpei Ishii, born in Dalian—occupied Chinese territory then—has written of his recent return to the Manchurian frontier area with a group of Japanese senior citizens who were commemorating their last days in school in that region as "settlers" when the war ended, and who just barely survived the vicissitudes of the Russian recapture of Japanese-held Manchurian territories:

> On May 30 (1945), the very day that the middle school students arrived in Dongning, the [Japanese Army] Imperial Headquarters issued an order to the Kwantung Army [occupying Manchuria and charged with governing the puppet state and protecting its millions of Japanese "settlers" there] known as "A Strategic Plan Against the Soviets in the Korea-Manchuria Region." The plan called for "abandoning defenses in three-fourths of the entire Manchuria region." The middle-school students [then in their young teens] were in fact sent to the abandoned region as decoys. Furthermore, two hundred and ninety thousand [Japanese] women and children lived in this "abandoned region" at the time. They were also left behind as part of the Kwantung Army's smokescreen strategy and were given no warning of the impending Soviet offensive. The death count reached eighty thousand. Many survivors, as a last-ditch effort to save their children's lives, left them behind in the hope that they would be taken in by the local [Chinese] populace. This resulted in today's eight thousand Japanese war orphans who were raised in China [and who still venture to Japan today, in search of their lost families].[12]

This heart-rending account, which shows not only the "patriotic" Kwantung Army in less than a glorious light, but what modern Japan's forefathers did to their own children, is the type of history that does not make it past the censor's cut at the Education Ministry's textbook screening. (Doubtless, a part of the reason is that the Imperial High Command in October 1943, when Japan's troop losses began to mount, turned to conscripting in Tokyo some 130,000 college students down to the age of nineteen, about 20,000 of whom never came home.) Not only does it hide a shameful truth from the Japanese youth of today, but its lack of disclosure leaves the aging survivors feeling as if a part of their own past has been torn off and trampled by the current Japanese establishment, which seems to feel that only the nation-building triumphs of the Meiji era and the industrial triumphs of postwar Japan constitute a sufficient history of the nation's twentieth-century travails.

Not everyone has forgotten the war, of course. Fortunately, parts of it such as this journal (published in the intellectual periodical *Chuo Koron* in 1991) continue to make their way into the media. In another journal, one history professor candidly comes to grips with the murky question of the Showa Emperor's real culpability for the war, in the eyes of the Japanese intellectuals: The Americans may have exonerated Hirohito, but "As commander-in-chief of the army and the navy, Emperor Showa held the position of highest-ranking leader in the execution of the war. This position was not just formalistic because he did actually offer advice on specific battles and strategies at crucial phases of the Fifteen-Year War, especially the Pacific War [after Pearl Harbor]. As is clearly demonstrated in historian Yamada Akira's book *Showa Tenno no Senso Shido* (Emperor Showa's War Leadership, 1990) the emperor involved himself deeply in the leadership of the war and the choice of tactics through *gokamon* (seeking counsel) and *o-kotoba* (remarks) directed at the military high command. There were more than a few cases in which these imperial remarks had a decisive influence on operational strategy and specific tactics. Unlike the Manchurian Incident (which began the war in China) and the Sino-Japanese War, the Pacific War began as the result of a decision made at the highest level of state and given the final sanction of the emperor. That can only mean that Emperor Showa's responsibility for the outbreak of the war in the Pacific was serious. And based on Yamada's evidence we must conclude that he was also deeply responsible as far as the execution of the war was concerned as well. . . .

"I have made such a point of the war responsibility of the Emperor Showa because there is still strong social pressure in Japan sustaining the taboo against candid discussion of the subject. I am concerned about some elements of society that do not hesitate to use violence in attempts to suppress freedom of speech, as evidenced by the January 18, 1990, incident in which a rightist shot and wounded the mayor of Nagasaki [which was also

A-bombed at war's end], Motojima Hitoshi, for his statement in the city assembly that some responsibility for the war rested with the emperor."[13]

While there are some brave souls who venture what could even be the risk of physical injury—or death—to speak the truth about the war, the broad, reverberating silence throughout the society on the totality of Japan's wartime behavior and its responsibilities has had effects so damaging as to be inestimable.

First, a failure to teach and study the war as Japan took part in it is a failure to study the modern history of Asia itself. Huge gaps in the knowledge of neighboring countries, and the factors influencing their contemporary relations with and policy on Japan, grow in the minds of students. When Japan annexed Korea as a prefecture, it forced all Koreans to adopt Japanese names and to speak only the Japanese language; it has been said that by the time of the early postwar period, not a single Korean family had not been affected, tragically or at least severely, by what the Japanese did. Yet young Japanese cannot understand why the Koreans appear to hold such harsh grudges against their country. They cannot understand the history of Japan's own colonialism in Indochina, in Malaya, in Singapore, in Hong Kong, in Thailand, or its record of mass brutality in invading China. Thus they cannot truly understand those neighbors' histories and feelings.

Second, Japan cannot begin to muster the ideas and the initiative it needs now, commensurate with its gigantic economic status in Asia, to renew balanced, egalitarian, untroubled relationships at all levels, from social to diplomatic, with its Asian neighbors. As Ivan Hall has put it, "Japan's recurrent pan-Asianist paradigm, simply expressed, is that of two posts and a lintel. On one side a solidified Asia, much put upon and brimming with resentment; on the other an equally monistic but predatory West; and between the two a cultural gap spanned only by Japan, which towers above the Orient and serves as its cultural spokesman to the Occident."[14]

This concept—that only Japan can "speak" to the West for Asia, is fantasy at a dangerously advanced level. It is based on an ingrained self-conceptualization of ethnic, cultural, and national superiority over all of Asia that the Japanese cannot rid themselves of until they began to speak and hear the truth about, and seriously ponder, their own past and their own culpabilities in Asia. As World War II recedes into history, they want less and less to be bothered with these things; indeed their leaders have made it easier for them to consider their own nation a "victim" of the war. And so the risk of serious collision with a rising China and a rising Korea, not to mention the rest of Asia, increases.

Third, this manipulation of history has diluted the very value of truth itself in the Japanese scheme of things. For example, when the story of the two hundred thousand "comfort women" began to emerge, Japanese officialdom was at great pains to present itself as blameless, insisting at first that the women were recruited and supplied and managed by procurers. A stream of official documents, however, continued to be unearthed proving beyond a shadow of a doubt that the imperial forces themselves managed the "comfort women" and the use of their services during the war. As the government was forced at each step to admit more and more of its complicity, the surviving women themselves came to Tokyo, demanding to tell their tragic stories and asking for compensation. While official apologies have at last been offered, the government has tried to evade their claims by offering instead the expenditure of a billion dollars on "youth exchange" programs with Asian nations, vocational training sponsorship, and so on—anything but direct payments of compensation to the women themselves. That is because Japan fears that still larger corners of the carpet will be rolled back, revealing the massive use of Korean slave labor, the losses suffered by Asian holders of wartime Japanese scrip, what really happened in the POW camps and in the germ- and chemical-warfare labs, and on and on. No one in government wants to contemplate the responsibility of compensating those survivors as well, preferring to claim that the signing of peace treaties and the payment of national reparations have long since "settled" all such responsibilities.

These malleabilities in facing the responsibilities of the past have opened the door to new myths just as pernicious. There is a constant, though small, undercurrent in Japan of anti-Semitism, which has boiled to the surface with the publication and open marketing of books claiming the existence of Jewish conspiracies to rule the world and to destroy Japan. As recently as early 1995, a respected publisher of intellectual periodicals was forced to close down a popular magazine after it published a story claiming the Holocaust never happened.[15] One Japanese author even published a book blaming the Kobe earthquake of early 1995 on the Jews, whom he suggests planted nuclear explosives surreptitiously beneath the city.[16] No one knows what impression these lies leave on the public psyche of Japan, and the Foreign Ministry has at last felt sufficiently pressured by international opinion to denounce this new "fad" of anti-Semitism. But then, how much can the Japanese be blamed for not knowing precisely what to make of information presented as historical "truth," in the shadow of their own dysfunctional national memory?

Social Censorship and Control

There are other forms of censorship and outright control used to keep the society, as well as the body politic, in line with elite purposes in Japan.

• The prescription upon request of birth control pills remains forbidden by law in Japan to this day. Ostensibly, the reason is that the pills' safety has not been "sufficiently tested," as if the millions of women who now routinely take them in other nations are consciously endangering their own health. The real reason is that conservative elements within the bureaucracy and the parties fear that pills will give women a social emancipation that Japanese society is not prepared to afford them.

• Family registers are kept by local governments on every Japanese citizen, recording births and deaths, heads of households, marriages, adoptions, and residential registrations. These records list the illegitimacy of children born before marriage, even when they are raised by their natural parents, if the marriage registration date falls after the child's birthday. This stigma attaches to these children—documented by the government—all their lives; the information could be used privately by prospective employers to withhold jobs. And children who simply remain unregistered in the official system are not given passports by the national government.

• The same registers do not allow spouses to keep their own family names at marriage: Legally, both must choose one of the spouse's surnames and use it alone for all purposes in the worlds of employment, taxation, licensing, and anything else of an official or quasi-official nature.

• Divorced women (and only women) are required to wait until six months after the recording of divorce before they may remarry; this is ostensibly so that the fatherhood of any succeeding children will be unambiguous.

• The Japanese are told repeatedly that they are a nonlitigious people, unlike quarrelsome Westerners. And that is probably true—because the government restricts carefully the number of lawyers who are admitted to the bar, with an entrance exam so onerous that the average success rate is but 2 percent per year. Japan has just fifteen thousand practicing lawyers, compared with America's eight hundred thousand,[17] and whole townships in Japan are without the services of any attorneys. It takes on average several years to prosecute virtually any civil case; that is by design of the Justice Ministry system, which tries hard to discourage litigation in all cases ranging from domestic to corporate law. It would be almost, though not quite, true to say that if you want to sue in Japan, you can't: "Scholars have pointed out that lack of competition among lawyers has estranged citizens from seeking legal advice and the situation is responsible for the lack of public interest toward the judicial system and the use of trials in Japan," as the *Asahi Evening News* summarizes it.[18]

• Indeed some retributions of a punitive nature are imposed without the legal establishment's involvement at all. When media kingpin Haruki

Kadokawa was arrested unexpectedly on cocaine charges, a twenty-million-dollar film that his company had just launched through a nine-million-dollar promotion campaign throughout the nation was voluntarily withdrawn by it and by its distribution partner, the Shochiku Company, because of "moral embarrassment" over Kadokawa's predicament.[19]

• Japanese cannot even trust their doctors to give them the truth on life-or-death health situations. The tradition in Japan is not to inform a patient that he has a potentially lethal illness, so that the patient "will not give up hope." "Even today," reports *Nikkei Weekly*, "health authorities estimate that less than 20 percent of patients with cancer are told the truth about their condition. A survey by the Ministry of Health and Welfare found that just under 20 percent of those aged between forty and sixty-four who died of cancer between March and April 1992 had [ever] been informed of their ailment."[20] A national poll revealed in 1992 that more than one out of eight respondents claimed their doctors had them given insufficient explanations of both their ailments and the prescribed treatments.[21]

• Another, less obvious aspect of public health through which the elite leadership structures sanctions and controls its power relationships is, interestingly, alcohol abuse. Whereas illicit drugs are still by and large under control, alcoholism is the great and largely unrecognized social problem in Japan. In 1987, 14 percent of Japan's 1.4 million hospital in-patients were being treated for alcohol-related illnesses. But this is likely only the iceberg's tip. A massive study of the health-check reports on 1.78 million Japanese working adults in 1993 showed that a full 25 percent suffered some kind of liver ailment.[22] Another survey from 1992 showed that 70 percent of employed respondents drank more than five days a week.[23] Per-capita consumption of alcohol ranked just below that in the United States in 1993, yet cirrhosis deaths per one hundred thousand men were a third higher.[24] Why this murderous pace of consumption? Because, found DeVos and Wagatsuma, "It is not considered outside the boundaries of the acceptable male social role to become drunk so long as there is no interference with one's work pattern."[25] The locus of elite culpability is that intersection where, in fact, the economic structure of Japan *promotes* drinking among male colleagues and business associates, as a way of lubricating the social strains and tensions that might otherwise occur in this densely interwoven social fabric. Corporate Japan spends over six trillion yen each year on "entertaining," which is a direct subsidy of the drinking, golf, etc. parties held internally and externally by its employees: That figure works out to 197 million dollars a day in "entertainment," on the company tab.[26] "Much information that a man imparts while drunk is supposed to be forgotten by the recipient," goes the theory, "so that the informer is in no way punished."

Obviously drinking is an approved escape for the pressures of competition and disagreement that build in the "consensus-forming process." "Individuals who drink over a quart of cheap sake every day are rarely considered 'sick' in any way."[27] Obviously, alcohol consumption, if not alcoholism itself, has been socialized as an effective control mechanism, passed off as a part of Japanese culture, by the elite establishment that keeps the system running smoothly. (So, by the way, we might almost say—and just as ominously—of smoking. Reports show that more than 60 percent of adult males in Japan are smokers.[28] And in 1993, lung cancer rose for the first time in Japan to be the leading cause of cancer deaths in males.[29])

Social Mythology

In their comparative study of Japan, the United States, and Sweden, *Elites and the Idea of Equality,* Sidney Verba et al. produced the remarkable finding that all Japanese power groups in the surveyed spectrum, ranging from politicians to bureaucrats to business executives to economic and social interest groups, placed the public media at the top of the list of the groups they believed held the *most* influence in the country—more than bureaucrats, politicians, and business executives themselves. (The only group that demurred was of course "media," which modestly ranked itself number two.)[30] While the other two nations placed media high on the list, "the Japanese place them in a more unambiguously top position than elsewhere."

There are 52 million newspapers sold daily in Japan and thousands of weekly or monthly magazines, and over 80 percent of all Japanese homes have two or more televisions. While it is not strange, then, that the Japanese would interpret the influence of media reportage and opinions as quite strong, it is startling that they would hold journalism above the great bureaucracies, the most powerful politicians and the vast *keiretsu* industries— the iron triangle of elite national leadership—in terms of power to affect events. There is a reason for this, of course. In a society sectored into so many exclusive groups horizontally, most communication on events and public affairs as a matter of course permeates the society vertically—from the top down. Japan's biggest newspapers publish millions of copies each day (the largest claims a circulation of close to 14 million copies) and distribute throughout the nation. In big cities, subscribers receive not only a morning edition of their paper but an evening one as well.

But this alone is not as startling as their homogeneity. Most of the papers report the same things in the same way, and even hold editorial opinions very close to one another's. There is a wide range of commentary available in print and broadcast, and even a strong trend to criticize politicians, administrators, and industry. But the criticism itself has behind it a uniformity that gives it real power as social mythology. Editors and producers see themselves as guardians of the national interest, and when promoting views and interpretations tend to put a distinctly "Japan-versus-the-world" spin on their reasonings. Whereas they are often seen by Japanese readers as critics, in fact, they are actually very tame, even complicit, compared to the interests of the power elites, and even act in concert to secretly promote goals of the government. One obvious recent example—over which there was no end of breast-beating and second-guessing after the event had safely passed and journalists were free to discuss it—was the media's total acquiescence in a self-imposed, eleven-month "blackout" on the Crown Prince's search for a prospective bride, the better not to frighten off any candidates with the glare of paparazzi flashguns and social-column hysteria. The blackout was undertaken at the request of the Imperial Household Agency, and in fact it held up so well that it was broken only when a foreign newspaper, the *Washington Post,* printed the story that the Prince's suit had been accepted by Masako Owada, who is now the Crown Princess.

That may seem harmless enough on the surface. Yet something of a more sinister cast occurred in the spring of 1993, when MITI's Agency of Natural Resources and Energy asked five of the nation's largest dailies to carry paid advertising supporting the harmlessness and the necessity of Japan's use of plutonium (an issue of great contention in Japan), in the form of reportorial stories and *without revealing* any sponsorship—in other words, as straight news. Three of the papers actually complied and carried the material, supplied by an ad agency, as news stories.[31]

Indeed, the news media are co-opted into supporting elite interpretations of stories at the very source of the news. There is in Japan a structure known as the "press clubs." There are about four hundred of them, each containing a group of journalists assigned to cover the club's beat. That beat could be the prime minister himself, or any of the ministries, or certain of the largest banks, or many other institutions and blue-chip corporations of the elite establishment. Only reporters accredited to the club are allowed access to information from the sources within that beat. So, rather than working as independent correspondents scouring for information, in other words, reporters are all spoon-fed the same information at the same time. Over time, they tend to become attached to their subjects almost as much as if they were adjunct members themselves. The actors reported on by each club—ministers and vice-ministers, captains of industry, party politicians, and so on—promote a cozy relationship of familiarity with the reporters, letting them know that, in exchange for tips on certain breaking stories, the journalists are expected to honor requests not to release certain other information when the actors do not want all the facts known. Some cabinet ministers, for example, conduct "midnight briefings" when they return home to a crowd of waiting club reporters late at night, dispensing inside information as background with the understanding it will not be reported, or will be reported only in a favorable light. Ministers, in fact, often take reporters so far into their confidence as to ask their advice.

A retired *Asahi Shimbun* journalist recalled an interview with a transportation minister that he once had in the postwar period: "At the time, the government was considering licensing independent taxi drivers, instead of forcing them all to work for cab companies. He asked me, 'Mister K, you have been to the United States as a student; what do you think about this—is it a good idea?' And I said 'It's a good idea, let's promote it, because we need the competition.' So he said 'I will do it—please support me [in your paper].' And I did."[32] That this sort of thing still goes on today is demonstrated by the fact that some one hundred and fifty journalists currently sit on the various ministry *shingikai*, or closed advisory panels that work out policy recommendations on an infinite range of interests, at the invitation of bureaucrats themselves.[33] Media representatives, indeed, make up 9 percent of the representation on the twenty most important of these councils.[34] There is in fact a sort of alliance, charges Van Wolferen, between the journalists of the *Nihon Keizai Shimbun*, Japan's *Wall Street Journal,* and the Ministry of Finance, "solidified by a seniority and promotion structure inside the newspaper (itself), which is to a large extent shaped by the closeness of relations between individual editors or writers and Ministry officials."[35] *Nikkei* career journalists who want to get ahead, Van Wolferen is saying, have had to make themselves and their columns useful to the ministry bureaucrats to do that.

What this means is not that the media or reporters in Japan are censored as such, or that they are openly tools of certain elite agencies, groups, or individuals hoodwinking the public. First, it means that they, like so many other public-interest organs in Japan, *self-censor* themselves: Yet another center of power is co-opted into the system itself, to voluntarily serve "the public good" as elites perceive it. The uniform sameness of reporting and editorial opinion, from medium to medium, can be befuddlingly homogenized. In Van Wolferen's words, "In the first morning edition of the five major national dailies, the choice of news and the tenor of editorial comment may vary somewhat. But by the last morning edition—read in the large cities—there is a homogeneous approach to all but certain routine controversies. Editors furiously read each other's early editions, and keep adjusting their own."[36] In some instances, I have been told, editors are reluctant to print a real scoop simply because the information from their own reporters within the relevant press club does not tally with that sent out to *their* employers by the other reporters in the club. It is not unusual for club members to fix embargoes and work out common angles among themselves, before ever filing their stories.

Second, it means that this group of media elites, seen by all elements of the elite structure, and relatively speaking, all citizens, feels that it, too, is a leader in Japan and must be willing not merely to report the news but spin it in ways favorable to the sources, the elite leadership of the country's institutions. A good example of how this spinning works in preserving certain useful social mythologies to guide the thinking of Japanese citizens in paths constructive to the needs of some bureaucrats can be found in the reporting on Japan's suicide statistics. Recently the annual total of suicides of senior citizens, released to the press each spring by the National Police, has been rising. News media report the figures, and commentators and editorial writers decry the harsh social neglect of the society that drives its old people to these extremes, implying, if not stating outright, that Japanese need to be more loyal to the traditional three-generation structure of families, so that seniors have a comfortable home and family surroundings in which to spend their last years and upon which to rely for care and support. This is not a new issue in Japan, where the number of seniors is growing and elements of the bureaucracy are worried about how the government will afford to care for the elderly if families will not keep them at home. But, with regard to the ever-increasing percentage of senior citizens in the population, suicides per capita are in fact *declining* in this demographic sector. Moreover, some sociological evidence shows clearly that the situation in which seniors are most likely to be driven to suicide is not where they live alone or with each other, but in those same three-generation families, where the pressures of little space and a housewife forced to care for elders seems too often to cause intolerable personal conflicts.[37]

Another example of social mythologies propagated in the media comes from Ikuya Sato, a professor of cultural anthropology who did a book-length study of Japan's "new" generations of delinquents, the *boso-zoku*, or motorcycle gangs that disturbed the peace on highways and in the minds of good citizens in the 1980s.

> In media reports as well as in the public mind, miscellaneous crimes including theft, glue sniffing, drug abuse, battery, rape and murder were attributed to *boso-zoku*. *Boso-zoku* were also said to be the first reserve for *yakuza* (the Japanese mob). An article in a national paper even attributed one-fourth of all criminal offenses committed in a year to *boso-zoku* and concluded that the offenses by *boso-zoku* made the "record of juvenile delinquency in the past

year (1980) the worst in history." Strangely enough, the *boso-zoku* was also often characterized as a pitiable victim who suffered from chronic frustration and an inferiority complex. In such a pathetic characterization, the "real" origin of the evil forces was attributed to adverse social conditions such as meritocratic society and "academic-pedigree-oriented society." In short, while motorcycle gang activity might be play for most Japanese youngsters on the street, it meant a grave threat to the social order or a manifestation of social maladies for the general public.

The diabolical and pathetic characterizations of the *boso-zoku* were, in many cases, achieved by arbitrary and all-inclusive use of the term *boso-zoku*. The nebulous use of the term also led to unfounded inferences from official reports and statistics. The official documents themselves were often constructed in misleading ways. It seems to me that the media reports and official documents reveal much more about moral confusion in Japanese society than about the social background of motorcycle-gang activity.[38]

What the media seemed to be doing, in other words, was compiling a laundry list of growing social ills that troubled the national consciousness and loading a huge part of them arbitrarily on the baggage racks of a new scapegoat, the youthful motorcycle gang rider. More recently there have been perhaps even more driving reasons for this confusion, in which "the ubiquitous presence of factors leading to crime and to confusion of traditional moral values [lends] a sense of urgency to the search for the "real" cause" of crime, for an identifiable villain who was the master of all the evil forces," as Sato puts it: Violent crime, while beginning from a far lower numerical base, has been rising for years at a faster pace than in the United States;[39] so have divorces.[40] As people are mass-murdered in subway terrorist attacks, and the nation's top police administrator is gunned down in front of his own home, it is harder for the people to believe that Japan is a law-abiding paradise of public safety, especially when they see figures like the 1993 Osaka Prefectural Police Estimate that one out of every three hundred men in the prefecture between ages twenty and seventy belongs to a gang![41]

A joint study conducted by the Mansfield Center for Pacific Affairs on media balance in coverage by three leading Japanese and five American newspapers of contentious bilateral trade issues in the 1988–90 period showed a third example relevant to Japan's view of itself in the outer world in its final report: "By and large, both American and Japanese coverage of the three issues [chosen] tended to be balanced, only about one fourth of the reports being scored as one-sided on our measures. However, there is a difference in how this balance is achieved—the Americans by reporting the positions of both sides, the Japanese by ignoring them. . . . Japanese reports clearly supported Japan, tending to justify their country and to blame the

United States. However, American reports did not show a parallel tendency to justify the United States and to blame Japan. Instead, blame tended to be placed on the United States, though not as strongly as in the Japanese press."[42]

It could be that reportage of this stripe is the reason why, as the Japan Economic Institute reported in March 1995, "fewer than one in four Japanese polled in 1993 believed that the United States was a fair trader, *down from one in three in 1991*" [emphasis added].[43] This was in the face of record and ever-growing Japanese trade surpluses, of $50 billion to $60 billion per year recorded with the United States in the early 1990s. The social mythologies being perpetrated here seem helpful, at least, to those elites in charge of sheltering Japan's markets from open global competition.

The self-appointed role of nationalistic guidance in the press is damaging enough to Japan's efforts to find an identity and a balance of true interests for itself among its neighbors and the global community in the new, post–cold war era. But it is even more hurtful in the shadow it unintentionally creates when foreign reporters, who are forbidden from joining almost all press clubs, turn to the Japanese media themselves as sources for the material they gather to write their own stories. It is not that they are lazy, it is simply that this reliance in many ways cannot be helped, especially for a single correspondent, perhaps new to the country, trying to "cover it all" for his newspaper or broadcast employer back home.

And the press is not the only agency that helps create or perpetuate social mythologies that support the purposes of the elites. In one way or another, vast numbers of institutions beyond both press and classroom do that. The conservative Japanese bureaucratic establishment around the imperial family, the Imperial Household Agency, for example, wishes to preserve its own myths concerning the inviolate descent of the imperial family from native Yamato stock since time immemorial. It forfends any challenge to its pure-blood-line myths by forbidding any independent archaeologists to excavate what it says are 187 tombs of Emperors and Empresses under its jurisdiction. "In no other country," says a frustrated Japanese scholar bluntly, "does the government fabricate history like this."[44]

Class

An economy masquerading as a society; a bureaucracy masquerading as a culture. The aim of this chapter is, through examining the elites' intellectual control strategies, to understand *how* the Japanese elites maintain these impressive, utterly subjectified systems of popular compliance (or as they would say, consensus) so successfully: not to suggest that 124 million citizens are all being hoodwinked, but that nearly all of them have been indoctrinated, co-opted both with and against their wills into the economic system, and convinced that it is in their own best material as well as ethical interests to embrace these mythologies publicly—and, in the vast majority of cases, privately as well.

Perceptively, DeVos has remarked that "I maintain one can demonstrate that, viewed historically [i.e., in the context of premodern Japanese tradition], particularized traditional Japanese social values (as they were inculcated within the context of family life) were to no small extent responsible for a prevailing type of personal motivation, expressed both in the implementation of government policy and in social relationships centered around work, that made possible the rapid industrial modernization of Japan."[45] This is a formal way of simply saying that the Meiji founders of the modern state took the Confucian order of values as they found them in the family and built upon them the individual's modern dedication to work and to state. One has but to read or hear all the allusions to modern Japanese corporate groupings as "families," both in personal and institutional senses, to hear echoes of the installation of this modern industrial overlay on old Japan.

The faith in the spiritual fathers of the Japanese was tested, and might even have been torn, by the results of the war, which left thousands of people starving to death in city streets. Then, as the national energies of rebuilding refocused this internalized work ethic of the Japanese, it took advantage of an important legacy of MacArthur—the erasure of the entire old class system in Japan, from peerage to peasant, in favor of classless "democracy"—to create the new and very potent mythology that *all* Japanese are official members of but one class, the new, economic middle class. And this remains the *most* potent weapon in the hands of elites today, for holding the populace to the national course of ever-continuing economic expansion and answerability to the economic command structure. The Japanese more or less accept the idea that they *are* all in the middle class; that they all enjoy equal opportunity and fair sharing of the nation's resources in a social setting that is ultimately egalitarian and just. "Egalitarianism, lifetime employment, never-ending economic progress and trust in technology are the articles of faith upon which the confidence of the Japanese in their society was founded," is the way *Nikkei Weekly* columnist Masahiko Ishizuka put it recently.[46] "These things boil down to a single word: security."

Of course, this is false. The very workings of the universities themselves show it. Few people study once they are admitted to even the best schools because they are considered to have already passed the gateway to elite status. And lifetime employment itself is nothing hallowed, only a shrewd reinvention of labor policy in the postwar period. But because of the ethnic similarities of the major part of the Yamato inhabitants of Japan, and the insular nature of the social controls that have all long been placed on the Japanese (by bureaucracies masquerading as culture), this uni-class concept has been an easy idea to propagate. Yet, like all national myths, it has its vulnerabilities in an era of jet travel, global economics, and digital communications.

"The Japanese society is genuinely a class-based one," says Hitotsubashi Professor of Sociology Dr. Masao Watanabe, who is applying research from both England and his own country to prove his point. "In an economic sense as well as the political sense." Education, the use of varying degrees of polite and informal language, and especially the concern with marriage within one's own class stratus all prove the point that is "the most hated notion among Japanese social scientists"—that Japan is indeed divided into classes, and those stratifications grow farther apart with each passing year.

"Japanese themselves simply dislike the notion of class; that's why they never understand social issues in class terms. The most important issue [of proof] which comes to mind is that free competition for entering the higher-status universities is actually purely nominal. Every participant [in the winnowing program of the examinations] thinks himself to be fairly treated. And from the starting point, they [do seem to] share the same common conditions. But if you look at the outcome, competition has never taken place in balance, openly. So, I can show from child-rearing to junior high school, senior high school, university, every differentiation of academic achievement was closely related to the social background, the family background. There are many more reports [now] that Japanese higher-prestige universities are occupied by students with particular social and particular family backgrounds. Let me take the example of just Tokyo University: their own survey data clearly shows almost all the students are from the managerial class. And the annual average of the family income of those students clearly shows itself to be in the nation's upper 10 percent.

"But the most important point is that even with such a harsh, or hidden, reality they [student candidates and their families] still tend to see themselves as *fairly* treated. There is a widespread, false notion, I must say, that the competition is open and free. And the unfairness of such differentials in their own backgrounds, to start with, never reaches the minds of any of the participants. My own students, when I lecture on class, are very excited. They were never taught to think in such a way. Their commonly shared experience is that they were indoctrinated and discouraged to think about things in this way—I mean that to them, thinking about class is very risky and dangerous. No one ever mentioned such an idea to them before."

Yet, says Watanabe, "unconsciously, they actually behave in a way appropriate to the class background they come from. They would never think, for example, of having a serious romance with a coffee-shop waitress." While most Japanese believe that the shift from arranged marriage to love matches, where partners choose each other, has obviated one of the oldest class barriers in Japan, he believes that this is a smokescreen that, once viewed from behind, shows class division in marriage to be as stringent as ever. "Choosing a partner matched to your status, to your academic achievements, to your possible job and *its* status, that's the most crucial factor in realistic terms."

Is it the parents that insist on this? "No. The most important factor nowadays is not the parents at all. The company [employer] is the most crucial. In Japan, on every occasion of a marriage ceremony, several of the high-ranking supervisors of the groom are always invited to come to the celebrations, and give congratulatory speeches. With such circumstances, how the company approves of this newly starting couple presents, psychologically, a great degree of pressure. The greatest influence to the individual, of course, is his or her own choice. But without any awareness of the particular pressure, they realistically are driven in particular ways. That is one of the most deliberately sophisticated structures of the class society; so what is seemingly most distant from any class element, the choice of marriage partner, *is* a disguising feature of class." Watanabe notes that women too, concerned with the future career prospects of their marital choices, actually select husbands from the highest-status groups possible. "The heavy pressure for wives is very serious." Why? "Because the husband's future will affect the chances of the children on the educational ladder. The wives know that. As long as the people still believe in education as the main course for promotion and social mobility, the whole situation remains one that disguises the evidence of class."

While Watanabe's statistics verify that mobility is yearly becoming more rigid in Japan, both journalists and social scientists find the concept of a class-bound Japan anathema. There are political classes, there are income and career-based classes, there are land-owning classes, there are elite classes—and yet this remains "the most hated notion among Japanese social scientists." In putting themselves in unconscious service to the elite imperative of homogeneity among all parts of the economic society, these academic elites have, Watanabe accuses, attempted to reflect the obvious changes that the data show by semantically confusing the concept of class with "stratus." "By doing so, they take every opportunity to postulate Japanese society as an open society where the notion of class has no relevance, no input at all. They try to postulate that industrialization of the Japanese economy makes everyone the same—destroys class. But ironically, from the 1970s on they suddenly began to find clear evidence that the Japanese society was not an open society at all. And so they lost confidence in their own research."

Watanabe, on the other hand, has lost no confidence whatever. He continues to publish his evidence on his own campus and declares openly that "my first and foremost aim is to postulate Japan as a true class society. Probably, the reaction of my colleagues is to generally ignore me. I think I'd be considered an eccentric among the social scientists of the top Japanese universities. Yet after the bursting of the so-called bubble economy, the realities are getting much more harsh. So some of the comments even in the popular journals are clearly showing that there is something wrong with such a theory, that Japan is an open society with no classes at all."[47]

But other sociologists, at least those less bound to the Japanese mythology, may be coming around to the same conclusions. Watanabe points to the work of Hiroshi Ishida, who, in a comparison study of Japan, the United States, and Britain, found that "scholarly work in Japan often demonstrates evidence of a constant effect of social background on college attendance across different cohorts. . . . The advantages and disadvantages associated with social background are not necessarily only economic in nature. 'Social capital'—the social circumstances surrounding childhood development—is as important a factor as economic capital in influencing educational achievement. [Watanabe has data demonstrating that, for example, the influence of a Japanese mother's own educational background begins to affect her child's chances of success even from the child's *preschool* age.] Differences in the 'amount' of social capital come mainly from variations in three major life circumstances: urban and farm background, number of siblings, and the father's occupational status."

And most shockingly, "In all three societies, [lifetime] income attainment is more likely to be affected by social background characteristics than by education, and the attainment of current occupational status in Japan is also influenced more by social background than by education."[48] Since "occupational status" in the artificial economic society is the only status that Japan recognizes among individuals, Ishida is coming close to the great, dirty secret of Japan today: Where you wind up in the hierarchy of elites does not really depend on which university you got into—it is how your class background, with all its money, parental ambitions, and connections, facilitated your acceptance into that university.

This explains why so many of the elite students in the humanities at prestige universities do not bother to study. "A university that does not offer good employment opportunities for its graduates would quickly lose its credibility and prestige, no matter how good the academic training it provides. Thus universities accept, as it were, a sense of patronage for their students, implicitly recognizing an obligation to provide them with jobs."[49]

This is the most carefully, almost desperately nurtured mythology that the elites perpetrate on Japan, with the aid of the educational system and the media—because it alone is the glue that holds the entire society together. If, to begin with, you have no suspicions and no evidence that you are unfairly disadvantaged, and if you believe that you are in the same social and national boat as everyone else, then you will not rebel; you will not strike or protest the imprisonment of lifetime employment or the unjustness of the seniority promotion system; you will not become upset that your wife and daughter are treated with egregious economic unfairness; you will not even insist on taking your vacation days, because you know that giving them up is "something we Japanese do." You can hear accusations that you are housed in rabbit hutches—and actually take a perverse pride in it: You are *morally stronger* than other cultures. Thus most Japanese, perhaps, would vehemently deny the connections of class to the elite stairway upward: It invalidates those "arguments of faith" of which columnist Ishizuka spoke.

Nevertheless, to insist that the social calculations here really do work by a different form of mathematics accepted by all affected by it, demands proof at the other end. We might start looking for it with David Slater, a University of Chicago graduate, in Japan on a Japan Foundation Grant to study education at the bottom of the ladder, teaching and researching in Japan's *kogyo koko* (industrial-arts high schools). This is where the kids with no college future, no "social capital," come. What the teachers try to do here is simply to motivate young males to whom school, and perhaps life itself, have no distinct goals merely to earn a diploma. It is where the lower classes are ground through the educational system, at almost any cost. Here is where people are *not* middle class.

"The lower class here is not something that jumps out at you and says, you know, we are of a different breed, we are of a different background," says Slater. "So what I'm looking for in them is, in just what way *do* they see themselves as different?"

In many ways, apparently. In fact, Slater paints a picture of what could almost be called a special educational society, where students may or may not show up for class—or may walk out in the middle of one; where aspirations among sixteen- and even seventeen-year-olds run to simply getting that certificate, so that they will not have to deliver pizzas or mop 7–Eleven store floors as part-timers for the rest of their lives. They're not trying to prove anything about who they are; they are just trying to hang on.

With that level of aspiration, the situation is very different from the picture most outsiders hold of Japan's glitteringly successful education system.

"The teachers work with these kids; they know themselves to be the gatekeepers," says Slater, echoing even here at the bottom of the ladder the same self-arrogations that the country's highest-ranking pedagogues, at the top end, hold as their sacred duty. "[They are just] trying to get the kids through the gate and into society. I was just talking to a teacher today about it. These kids' lives are so chaotic that a lot of the time, they're just trying to get them through the day. You know, like 'What's been going on with you? Where did you get those black-and-blue marks?' Your responsibility as a teacher is to find a way to get them to pass. They don't do any homework. They barely know anything of the content matter that's being taught here. The [teachers'] only real responsibility is to get them through, graduate the child. Because they know that in Japan, if you don't have that diploma, you're screwed.

"The lower-class students' teachers are much more likely to make home visits. . . . As soon as you walk into a house, you see what they read, you see what they eat, you see how they keep their house, you see [whether or not] the mother works. You understand. Basically every one of my students at this technical high school [has a father in a] blue-collar job, and 70 percent of the mothers are working. You have divorce rates of 30 to 40 percent, phenomenally high for Japan. And the teachers will gloss this situation as poor upbringing, not lower class.

"These young kids are looking at: What do you want to be when you grow up? 'Well, I would really like to be a rock star. I have my guitar hero.' Or 'I'd like to be an athlete.' It's all sumo and baseball and race-car drivers; things from the *manga* [comic books]. Even among some of the third-year (high school) students, it's still, 'Well, I'd like to be rock star.'

"There's no violence, no antisocialism. But there is some anger toward their parents, usually their mothers. Like, why isn't mom here, hanging around more? I don't really get to talk to her, so I don't really know. She doesn't know anything about my school.

"At graduation, out of forty students, there were thirty people in the audience. And most of them were in couples. So you're looking at about half the students' parents not showing up even for graduation. And graduation's a big deal in Japan."

Teachers tend to feel the same way about absent mothers. "Instead of saying, 'Of course the family structures reproduce themselves over generations,' they say, 'Well, this particular kid happened to have a mother who didn't raise him correctly. That's why he didn't do better; that's why he's at this low-level school.' It's only the mothers. If the father deserts the family, that's not even the issue. The issue is if the mother dares to work."[50]

And so the teachers here too really do know now, though they do not admit it, what no one in Japan wants to face: There are classes, lower classes; there are advantages and disadvantages growing from the home that determine the entire life courses of these young people. Most of them are finally dragged through to graduation, thanks to those teachers, even if they wind up finishing at night school. The important thing is to get through that gate.

Where they go after that, no one is really sure. Or even cares. They've just taken their places in the economic society, that's all.

Watanabe would understand instantly the lack of antisocialism or of class resentment that Slater sees. The class barriers remain well disguised, thanks to the social mythologies perpetrated by everyone from the prime minister's office down to the teachers of these confused young people, who would rather blame a pressed mother trying desperately to support her family than the society that left her in the lurch. "In America, in a public high school, you're sitting there among public high school kids who are going nowhere in life and know it. And they see a Harvard kid walk by, and there'd be an immediate 'screw that guy' kind of response: an envy. But among the Japanese kids, it's harder for them to read those class markers of other students, who are on the fast track. It's not 'I could have been him,' or 'Why him and not me?'—it's just that 'He's different from me.' Even the recognition that we're looking at supreme privilege is not real clear to them," Slater says.

Lay blame for that, too, on the designs of the economic society. In 1991, the average CEO of a big corporation in America earned eighty-five times the income of a typical factory worker; in Japan, the spread was seventeen times.[51] There is no immediate classifiable difference in the material prospects of the two youths of such a level as to *cause* envy. While the "supreme privilege" student will enjoy just that in his career, and likely a great deal of power and perhaps a handsome *amakudari* parachute income at the end of it, the lines are kept blurred near where they start: College graduates' beginning pay, even for the most elite career tracks, is not much more than that for high-school graduates.

This too goes a long way to disguise differences between the classes. Some would point out, as noted at the beginning of this chapter, that a class structure so anonymous as to leave individuals feeling that not they, but a fixed, unalterable system is responsible for their *ultimate* fates, is a structure that obviates any need—just as it does among elites—for anyone, anywhere, to take responsibility for the larger directions of society. But its ultimate effect, for those on the career ladder, is perhaps most important: It sets the stage for personal competition in corporations, bureaucracies, and other organizations on the basis not of income or material reward but of *position*—power, influence, connections, and personal prestige. The employer does not *have* to pay large amounts of money to reward or motivate his best achievers because title and responsibility are the rewards everyone craves.

This channels career competition in ways very beneficial to the employer, of course. But aside from making any organization and the real powers behind its "consensus" opaque to outsiders like Westerners, it also eliminates to a large degree something Japan increasingly needs: imaginative, break-the-mold creativity and entrepreneurial initiative. Very few individuals, on a high rung or low, in whatever class, find any incentive in kicking over the traces, rebelling against tradition, or breaking away from the pack.

Notes

1. Theodore C. Bestor, *Neighborhood Tokyo* (Stanford: Stanford University Press, 1989).
2. "Banker's Boot Camp: A Taste of Army Life," *Nikkei Weekly*, May 9, 1994.
3. "Onward and Upward With the Arts: Selling Dreams," *The New Yorker*, September 28, 1992.
4. "Work and Leisure in Japan," *California Management Review* (spring 1992).
5. "Overwork Said to Kill 10,000 a Year," *Japan Times*, September 19, 1992.
6. "Japanese Anxiety Over 'Giant Sucking Sounds': Hollowing Out and Other Changes Affecting Japanese Employment," Japan Economic Institute Report No. 39A, October 22, 1993.
7. "Lifetime Employment Gets Firm Support," *Japan Times*, January 21, 1994.
8. Aurelia George, "Japanese Interest Group Behaviour: An Institutional Approach," in *Dynamic and Immobilist Politics in Japan*, ed. J.A.A. Stockwin et al. (Honolulu: University of Hawaii Press, 1988).
9. "Sex Slaves, Not Japan, Were Victims," *San José Mercury News*, May 2, 1993.
10. "Hashimoto Remark Draws More Fire," *Japan Times*, October 27, 1994.
11. "A Backing Away from War Responsibilities," *Asahi Evening News*, February 1, 1995.
12. Shinpei Ishii, magazine article, "A Return to Wartime Manchuria: The Travel Journal of a Postwar Japanese," *Chuo Koron*, September 1991.
13. Kentaro Awaya, "Emperor Showa's Accountability for the War," *Japan Quarterly* (October–December 1991).
14. "Japan's Asia Card," *The National Interest* (winter 1994–1995).
15. "Publisher Folds Magazine That Denied the Holocaust," *Asahi Evening News*, January 31, 1995.
16. Koishi Izumi, "The Secret of the Jewish Religion That Moves the World" (Dai-Ichi: Kikaku Shuppan, 1995).
17. "Judicial World Not so Merry for More Lawyers," *Asahi Evening News*, November 16, 1994.
18. Ibid.
19. "Director's Arrest on Drug Charge Cans Cute Dinosaur Movie," *Nikkei Weekly*, September 6, 1993.
20. "Hospices Offer Dignified Approach for Terminal Cancer Patients," *Nikkei Weekly*, May 31, 1993.

21. "Poll: 26 Percent Dissatisfied with Doctors," *Daily Yomiuri,* October 19, 1992.

22. "Drinker Recalls His Life on the Rocks," *Japan Times,* November 17, 1994.

23. *Daily Yomiuri,* "Report: 1 in 4 Middle-Aged Workers Mentally Unhealthy," May 17,1992.

24. "The Tipplers and the Temperate: Drinking Around the World," *San José Mercury News,* January 1, 1995.

25. George A. De Vos, ed., *Socialization for Achievement* (Berkeley: University of California Press, 1973).

26. "The Two Costs of Drinking in Japan," *Japan Times,* December 27, 1992.

27. George A. DeVos with Hiroshi Wagatsuma, "Status and Role Behavior in Changing Japan: Psychocultural Continuities," in *Socialization for Achievement,* ed. DeVos et al. (Berkeley: University of California Press, 1973).

28. "Almost Two Out of Three Men Smoke, White Paper States," *Japan Times,* May 29, 1993.

29. "Lung Cancer Hits No. 1," *Asahi Evening News,* January 23, 1994.

30. Sidney Verba et al., *Elites and the Idea of Equality* (Cambridge, MA: Harvard University Press, 1987).

31. "Papers Carry Plutonium Ad without Revealing Advertiser," *Asahi Evening News,* April 6, 1993.

32. Interview with the author, autumn 1992.

33. "Media Role in Government Advisory Councils Questioned," *Asahi Evening News,* August 16, 1994.

34. "Shingikai Shenanigans," *Tokyo Time Out* (December 1994).

35. Karel van Wolferen commentary, *Sapio,* 1994.

36. Interview with the author, spring 1992.

37. William Wetherall, interview with the author, July 30, 1993.

38. Ikuya Sato, *Kamikaze Biker: Parody and Anomy in Affluent Japan* (Chicago: University of Chicago Press, 1991).

39. "Crimes Are Fewer, but Fiercer," *Nikkei Weekly,* August 15, 1994; " 'Explosion' in Crime Powerful—But False," *San José Mercury News,* October 24, 1993.

40. "Birth Rate Hits Bottom; Divorces Rise to New High," *Japan Times,* January 1, 1994.

41. "Doing More to Stop the Gangs," *Japan Times,* August 2, 1993.

42. "News with a View: Comparing Notes on Japan-U.S. Coverage," *Japan Times,* March 3, 1993.

43. "American Attitudes Toward Japan: Is Malaise Setting In?" Japan Economic Institute Report No. 10A, March 17, 1995.

44. "How Old Is the Imperial Family?" *Time,* June 7, 1993.

45. George A. DeVos, "Achievement Orientation, Social Self-Identity, and Japanese Economic Growth," in *Socialization for Achievement,* ed. DeVos et al.

46. "Japan's Security Blanket Fraying at the Edges," *Nikkei Weekly,* April 10, 1995.

47. Interviews with the author, spring 1993.

48. Hiroshi Ishida, *Social Mobility in Contemporary Japan* (Stanford: Stanford University Press, 1993).

49. Florian Coulmas, "Responsibility Allocation and Networks in Japanese Society," *Japan Quarterly* (April–June 1993).

50. Interview with the author, May 1993.

51. "The Flap Over Executive Pay," *Business Week,* May 6, 1991.

12

Reform: No Exit

The ideal Japanese life is one from which uncertainty has been removed as early as possible—by getting into the right school, by joining the right corporation, by doing the expected thing.

—James Fallows, *Looking at the Sun* (1994)

For several decades now there has been a hue and cry for "an education that stresses individuality" in Japan, and a glance at the uniformity of Japanese education certainly makes one feel that more of the individual should be stressed. A reform of curriculum and university entrance examinations under the name of "individualized education," if not handled with care, however, can bring a lowering of Japan's own "cultural literacy."

—Nagayo Homma, former dean,
College of Arts and Sciences, University of Tokyo

There's no mystery about the misery that the Todai system, embedded in Japan's "cultural literacy," causes. And indeed a continual refrain of demand for "reform," as noted above, echoes up and down the Japanese archipelago constantly—one might say almost ritualistically. For the sake of selecting the fewer than two hundred graduates who each year progress from the elite springboard of Todai Law into the top government–ministry jobs, and for the sake of cementing a few thousand more useful, acquiescent college graduates each year into the machinery of national economic aggrandizement, all of Japanese higher education, all of Japanese secondary and basic education, and almost all of Japanese family life is made to suffer. People, the press points out tirelessly, are mad as hell—but will they take it anymore?

Of course they will. Because it *is,* as seen in the first chapter, the expected thing. The system will remain the status quo not only because the platitudes of the press are meant to be simply anodyne, but because the people *that the system itself produced* are in charge of it and need it to continue for their own reasons. Although many university professors, including Todai professors, have spoken out, even resigned, in disgust, and despite "major decisions to reform" at the level of the Education Ministry, the system has itself become one more self-steering bureaucracy within the country's framework of administrative bureaucracies—and no one dares or even knows how to stop it.

Even many of its beneficiaries resent the system. A survey of University of Tokyo students published in *Aera* magazine in 1992 revealed that 56 percent of all freshmen and sophomores were either partly or completely dissatisfied with the curriculum they faced. Complaints have poured in even from the specialist faculties teaching the junior and senior years, many of whose professors believe that liberal-arts and humanities students are beginning their majors unprepared to do university-level work. Industries and parents have joined the clamor for repair.

These protests, too, flow into the popular refrain rising here and there among the great Japanese middle class: Even parents who have seen their children's way through Todai and into elite careers privately complain about the system that got them there. The Ministry of Education, understanding the palliative effects of resistance that allows itself only to emerge privately, informally, verbally, or in the insipid realm of popular-press editorializings, had remained largely deaf to this dissatisfaction for decades. But, beginning in the mid-1980s, it did confront something far more serious then societal griping and sniping: complaints from the elite corporate levels themselves that the "product" universities and colleges were turning out for them was unsatisfactory and unprofessional.

This was the first sign that the successful assembly line of Japan's educational system, turning out standardized "parts" to fit the complex machinery of economic expansion, was beginning to reach the limits of its instrumentality. Better levels of learning—or at least, more sincere levels of professional motivation—were found to be lacking in the "quality checks," the employment interviews, that the corporate recruiters run each year on their new inductee-graduates. Having pulled itself even with the advanced world, Japan's establishment found itself in new need of original thinkers and truly creative scientific minds, something the system was ill-equipped to produce.

Most important, within the government and the industries in general there was a growing awareness that Japan was facing increased levels of real competition, both at home and abroad, that in the future would allow less time and investment lost for "basic training" given by employers to new recruits, to make up for what they were not getting at college. The standard complaint heard on the Todai campus was that juniors with two years of English-language studies could not read and explain an editorial from the pages of the *New York Times*.

Realizing at last that universities were falling dangerously behind not only in this respect but in the pure research produced at the graduate-school level—the kind of research Japan needed to do on its own, now that it had "caught up" with the West—Monbusho in 1992 responded finally with its version of reform. It changed the law governing national universities, dropping core curriculum requirements the ministry itself had long imposed and leaving each school free to restructure its educational priorities on its own. This amounted to acknowledgment that the Todai system, for the first time since the end of the war, was under serious attack. Todai itself, for example, formed a panel of professors to effect what one of them told me was "the first really big reform of curriculum in the past forty years." It focused almost exclusively on general education, and its decisions took effect in April 1993.

How far-reaching has change been? On most private-school campuses, which have always set their clocks according to Monbusho standard time, it created little more than mass perplexity. One memo I have seen, addressed from a private-college president to all faculty members, admits to open confusion about what to do and implies that the school would mainly have to wait and see what other schools do—and then do something "independently, in keeping with our own traditions." One of the teachers at that school told me frankly that, though some of his colleagues had suggested a few tentative ideas, none of them really had any idea what all this new freedom was supposed to mean. In the national universities, moreover, aside from some increased accent on the study of international relations (very little of it having to do with "multiculturalism"), not much more clarity has emerged about where to go next. In fact at Todai, "change" sounds more like reform aimed at the teachers themselves; no student representatives were included, nor were their opinions officially solicited, as faculty members alone discussed and decided what should be done.

"We are trying to give more standardized, stricter classes to humanities and social-science students," explains Professor Susumu Yamakage, who teaches political science at the Komaba campus. In exchange, "They are now freer to choose their subjects." Efforts are being made to cut some class sizes, though this will be difficult without expansion of the faculty. And "we have introduced two new, compulsory, seminar-style courses. One is to give all freshmen an idea of what is required for college-level studies; the other is to give more exposure to the use of computers and information-processing to our humanities and social-sciences students.

"And finally, we are trying to change the English-language curriculum. This is the most drastic change."[1] The university, it seems, will use more audiovisual technologies and more teaching assistants to improve basic communications skills; whether or not close analytical, not to say heuristic, readings of the *New York Times* op-ed section will be part of the syllabus is not known.

Spread all across the nation's 490 public and private universities—with each school free to redesign its own curriculum—can these reforms have any genuine impact?

"At the strongest schools, where the general-education [*kyoyo*] teachers are already fully qualified academically, the core curriculum will probably eventually disappear into a full, four-year elective curriculum," says Yoshiya Abe.[2] But in the other schools, where removing compulsory classes from the freshman and sophomore requirements will frankly threaten the jobs of the lower-level teachers, "they would probably band together to protect themselves. At best, the general-education curriculum may only shrink in these schools from two to one-and-a-half years, depending on the outcome of faculty struggles on each campus."

The short answer is, then: not for the better, and probably for the worse. It is sad to contemplate, for example, what effect the disappearance or shrinking of a core curriculum will actually have on the "liberal education" of new adults. With competition increasing in Japan's job market, there is a good chance that many students—especially those in engineering and the sciences, who are already trying to cram five or six years of learning into four because of the underdevelopment of graduate education—will simply focus their new elective-course choices on their technical majors, to give themselves more time to keep pace with the grueling undergrad work demands. This will more than likely have an effect opposite to liberalizing their exposure to the humanities on a college campus, by default instead terminating much of it at the level of the didactic drilling of the high schools, whose texts are directly censored by the Education Ministry.

Yamakage—one of those "reformed" at Todai—isn't buying it. "They [the ministry] want to destroy—actually they *did* destroy—the importance of liberal or general education at the introductory level. Many universities now are trying to scrap-and-build this [whole] level of education."

In fact the reforms may really be not so much what Monbusho has advertised them as to the public, efforts to "liberalize" college education, as to intensify its training-oriented academic regimens. Strong parallel attempts, it is worth noting, are also being made to expand graduate schools, especially for the engineering and science disciplines in the national universities that have big departments in these areas. In 1992 and 1993, as it became apparent that private industries were cutting back on their R&D in-house budgets because of the extreme pressures of the recession, the national budget for R&D expenditures in universities has tried to pick up some of the slack, expanding an average of more than 7 percent in each year. Due to Japan's prolonged recession, this figure is not likely to expand by much in the near future. And while moves are afoot to engage university academics in helping the government to decide from the start where to set funding priorities among the sciences, it is also true that by fiscal year 1994 the ratio of all professional researchers on Japan's university campuses, compared with those in industry and research institutes, had actually fallen by 5 percent below a decade earlier. Research personnel on campuses have increased in numbers, but at a slower rate than anywhere else.

For their part, Abe points out, corporations are beginning to evince a greater willingness to take engineers and technical graduates with more than a baccalaureate, which has allowed for an expanded enrollment in the select universities' science and engineering grad schools. Students there now have some assurance that they can take that extra year or two required for an advanced degree and still find jobs waiting after graduation. Abe estimates that fully half of Todai's engineering grads now want to go on for master's degrees. Whether they will or not remains to be seen.

In fact Yamakage thinks that the natural sciences and engineering faculties at Todai actually may have been the ones to start the university reform ball rolling, years before the ministry did. They long "had a design to shift the University of Tokyo from a college-style university, or an undergraduate-based university, to a graduate-based university," he says. (In Todai itself now, about a quarter of all 20,000 students are in graduate school; though in four-year schools nationwide, the figure is over 5 percent.) The reason was that the departure of the best and brightest for jobs in industry after only four years was robbing the school of an opportunity to further build its own research capabilities and add to the future stream of its once-considerable scientific achievements.

The most salient fact about the reforms, however, is not really that they are going on, but that they are because the government said they must. The university community is still not genuinely free in Japan to pursue its own destiny, its own calling. In answer to the directives of the Ministry of Education, which is playing an almost Svengali-like role, behind the scenes, in these "independent decisions" the schools are allegedly free to make, they are trying hard to comply with the directive for change, without in most cases changing anything much at all. They really do not know how to do anything else.

"There are people who claim that the universities are changing," a retired ranking Monbusho bureaucrat who dealt heavily with university affairs told me in an interesting interview, "and the ministry encourages that. But, you have to look at reality." And what is "reality"? "Most professors do not really know Monbusho and the situation inside it, not at all," he says. "To the public or to the parliament, Monbusho says that the situation in higher education is not bad. But to those who are involved in the field, Monbusho says, 'You have to change; you must lead society to a new world.' But, since initiative is supposed to come from the college presidents or teachers themselves, Monbusho cannot say in public what changes ought to be made. There is a status quo, in other words: [whatever Monbusho may say] those who have serious [formal] power to make the decisions are on the campuses and in mid-career. For these people, that status quo is the best. Why make changes that might sacrifice their own futures? Monbusho knows this. And so it ends up representing both sides. It represents the faculty's status quo to the public, and at the same time reflects the voice of the general public's urgings to change." It claims, in other words, that change can and should come only from within the schools—while implying at the same time that on its own authority it is insisting the schools institute change, and that these changes are being made.

"Let me give you the exact situation between the ministry and the universities from my experience [to show how complicated this can get]. I was once appointed to the job of ministry section chief [*kacho*] for matters involving foreign university students. The biggest part of my responsibility was to place foreign students in exchange programs in the universities. But when I first took over, I was told by my staff 'Don't be too pleased to be appointed as the *kacho*—this *kacho* is different from other *kacho*s. In this section, we have to bow to the universities to get them to accept foreign scholars as students.' Now, Monbusho wants very much to find room for foreign students in the universities, going back many years now. But the universities did not want them. I was actually put in a position, at first, of having to visit each university three times in a year just to get it to accept some foreign students. That is quite unusual.

"Very quickly, I realized that even university presidents had little influence over their professors in promoting this matter. Many of the student applicants spoke insufficient Japanese, and there was a strong feeling that all university classes in Japan should be conducted in Japanese, no matter what. So obviously it was going to be very hard to find foreign students who could even qualify, in the eyes of the schools.

"For the first year, I was very agreeable with everyone, just building up my good relations with them. Then I advanced an idea: How about taking some in-service trainees, Southeast Asian scholars, in a nondegree program in the graduate schools, and helping them to study—in English? One university president I knew, who used to work in Monbusho himself, was cooperative; he went through his roster of professors and found several who could teach various subjects in English. And he said, 'I can do that.' But, in the Japanese scheme of things, it doesn't help much if only one university is trying to do something new. So I had to find two. Now, I knew another university that was quite competitive with his. I went there and met the key man, who happened to be a Christian, and I said 'so-and-so university is doing this, you know.' And he said, 'Oh, I like that idea very much. But I don't have so many professors in administration who are that good in English.' But, I reminded him, in his particular school he did have many science departments, and the better science professors are usually pretty good in English because of the international nature of their research. So I said, 'Why not ask the science professors if they would give lectures in English to foreign science majors?' And so we got that program started.

"Then, in the same year, I received a surprise proposal from a Todai engineering professor, who actually came to ask whether Monbusho would *prohibit* them from teaching in English at the Todai graduate engineering school! I said, of course not, that's all within your own realm of authority. He was surprised, because his colleagues had told him Monbusho would forbid such a thing. But I warned him that, before starting, he might have trouble getting his colleagues to agree. He was certain they would all be enthusiastic—but a week later he was back, dejected, telling me his faculty meeting had said 'no English.' I told him not to be disappointed, but to go and tell his department colleagues that he was proposing not that the faculty sanction such a program, but that he be allowed, with volunteers among his professors, to merely experiment with the program. 'That way you won't be asking for the professors' approval—you'll be informing them of what you intend to do on your own.' He did that, and he got their backing to start his program independently, and it still goes on to this day. So then we had a third university with foreign students.

"The upshot was that we always had to take that form to get our job done—to pretend that it was the university itself that wished to invite foreign students, and to pretend that Monbusho had been persuaded by such a sincere request to 'allow' the university to go ahead; that we would 'approve' it."[3] The professors, he believes, never really caught on to the fact that the change was what Monbusho itself had been pushing for. Had they known it, they would all have echoed the Todai engineer's colleagues' suspicions of "government interference" and would have delighted in turning the Monbusho down.

As of the mid-1990s, postsecondary foreign students studying in Japanese schools (not all of them in universities) totaled nearly 54,000, with close to 10 percent receiving at least partial Japanese government scholarship assistance. It took a long time—my informant's efforts began in the mid-1970s—but with Monbusho willing to say both "yes" and "no" and making each answer sound sincere to those who most wished to hear it, and with a huge boost from former Prime Minister Yasuhiro Nakasone, who announced a formal goal to bring a hundred thousand foreign students to Japan, progress has been, somehow, pushed through at least on this front. But it remains true that a large part of the reason that basic change comes so slowly and with such difficulty is that it is not supposed to come from Monbusho at all—yet, it will not come from the colleges at all, unless Monbusho finds a way to push it through *in response to policy imperatives from its own clients.* Amidst these topsy-turvy protestations of mutual recrimination, in which each side blames the other for failing to exercise its leadership, Todai's Professor Yamakage, asked why the ministry looms like Darth Vader incarnate on the campuses themselves, merely shrugs; he has a much simpler answer. "Professors are not trustworthy, at least from the ministry's side."

From the professors' perspective, it might be pointed out, Monbusho currently seems hardly trustworthy itself. "Independent" changes will be tolerated only as far as the ministry agrees they are useful. A stroke of the budget pen can erase even the most progressive ideas, along with the status and even the futures of their proponents, they all know. Thus again, and just as in all of Japan, almost all motivation for real change ends up buried in bureaucratic struggles over power.

But there is something still more desperate in the insistence behind this issue of control, and Ivan Hall, in his article in the *National Interest* comes closest to it: "What makes Japan fundamentally different [as a society] is that its racially based national consciousness and exclusivity, far from being the objects of [domestic] attack, disdain and efforts at amelioration, are openly sanctioned by the intellectual establishment, public consensus, and government policy."[4]

Those are harsh words to level, particularly at the academic constituent of the "intellectual establishment," which surely has one of the highest responsibilities for unseating this dangerous a degree of national introversion. But that's his point: Government policy does not want it unseated, in the academy or elsewhere. Hall's three "sanctions" form a nexus—of government, of education, and of public opinion—that prevents the cultural and intellectual internationalization Japan supposedly urges upon itself.

To weaken one leg of the tripod would weaken the other two. To truly free the academy, which could take at least a generation, would be to brook, inevitably, the rise of open censure from one of the society's most respected tiers of social and intellectual influence. Eventually, this would undermine public opinion, frustrate government policy, and erode the government's control over its vast, homogeneous socializing mechanism, the national educational system.

That is why, in the spring of 1993, Japan saw its Supreme Court defeat the generation-long legal challenge to such control of a single, brave college professor, by refusing to remove powers of outright censorship of grade- and high-school textbooks from the hands of the ministry.

"We Japanese are raised up," says Professor Mikio Arai, a retired NHK journalist and now a teacher at Toyo Women's College, "so that when we grow up and enter college and university, mainly it is to learn 'how to deal with' [matters]. That is the main thrust of Japanese society and Japanese education: Not what to be, or how things should be. But how to *do*; how to *comply*."[5]

We are brought almost full circle, then from kindergarten through college, again to the real status quo: social control.

The daughter of an elite family, she was a serious student and certainly had never thought of herself as a rebel. But this was 1969, and campuses all across the country were ablaze with rebellion. Student radicals had paralyzed the University of Tokyo and seized Yasuda Hall, Todai's main administration building. Police had been called onto the campus to lay siege to them in the dark, hulking tower. There was an uneasy standoff—the calm before the first storm in its century-long history in which civil authorities would, at the school's own behest, use outright violence to settle Todai's affairs. The whole nation watched, stunned.

"I had joined a few of the demonstrations that spring on campus, but basically I was against the way the radicals had paralyzed the campus for months, disrupting everyone's education," the woman remembers now. "I agreed with some of their causes, but I never cared all that passionately about the movement itself. But when the police were called onto the campus, and we saw them threatening to storm the tower and drag everybody away to jail, I began to get very angry."

The radicals inside the tower called for help to barricade themselves in the building, and everyone knew both sides were committing themselves to a final battle. And she came down on the side of the radicals. "I had a driver's license, and my friend—a music student—knew a campus back road that led to the tower's rear entrance." The two women rented a truck. They drove to a lumber yard and filled it with timbers. On top of the wood, they piled concealing loaves of bread. Using the back road, they threaded through police lines—risking instant arrest—to smuggle the barricade timbers as "food" to the students cordoned inside Yasuda Hall. "I didn't think much about getting caught," she says now. "It was just something we had to do."

No more than a day or two later, sitting with the family at dinner, her father, who knew nothing about any of this, suddenly began to speak of the turmoil at Todai. She had seldom talked with him about the months of campus disturbances and disruptions that filled the newspapers daily and had said little to expose her sympathies with the Left.

The company of riot police would, her father was saying deliberately, be unleashed to end the siege by storming Yasuda Hall tomorrow morning. Not only would all students caught in the battle be headed for jail and for trial, but the resulting blots on their records could blacklist them for life from elite employment. He never once implied that she might have any connections with the radicals or be thinking of going there herself. But his tone was unmistakable.

The daughter excused herself from the table, went to the telephone and began calling as many student friends as she could reach whom she thought might be planning to join the tower vigil next day. She warned them not to.

None doubted her sudden prediction because all knew that this class-mate's father was none other than a high-ranking official of the university itself; one of the very men whose responsibility it was to give the final order to the police.

And the next day it all happened, just as he said it would.[6]

The lesson here is neither irony nor the communications breach between generations in Japanese families. The important point in an assessment of reform—or the actual need for it—against the accomplishments of history is that, despite the constant pressure for and image of conformity, the Japanese do have passions and deeply individual personalities, and do occasionally rebel against authority if pushed too far. However invisible to outsiders, there is conflict, competition, love and hatred and lust, connecting and separating individuals every bit as strongly as in the most extroverted of Western societies. Japanese can be as bold and opinionated and gregarious, and even as emotionally demonstrative, as any Westerners. All the while living together in reasonable peace, in the most intimate relationships, just as Westerners do. They are just forced to be more careful about it.

It surprises many to discover that the Japanese, typically stereotyped as gray, undistinguished masses of social followers, are in fact people of great passion, even fanatical romantics—"the Italians of the Orient," as a friend of mine once put it. Their highly eclectic tastes in modern architecture are one highly visible giveaway. Design inspiration for their public buildings ranges from Frank Lloyd Wright to Univac. Homes to be seen on a single block in a well-to-do suburb vary in stylistic themes from Swiss restaurants to Persian ziggurats to the Versailles Palace.

Japanese office workers and grandmothers study, practice, and perform song and dance, ranging from *buyo* to the tango to modern ballroom. They take flower-arranging and tea-ceremony and public-speaking courses by the hundreds of thousands. They have also highly developed, and well-patronized, popular theaters in romantic opera, including classical Japanese, classical Western, and contemporary of both. They have a long literature and folk tradition of epic heroes and tragic outcomes, both on the historic scale and the personal.

They have their own perennially popular version of country music: ballads with endless litanies of broken loves, lost chances, the loneliness of empty roads and ceaseless wanderings leading ever farther from happiness. They have a dismayingly powerful inclination for, and fascination with, double love suicides, which naturally receive great prominence in the popular press. And they are famously fascinated with things and ideas foreign to their own culture, of course, whether they be French fashions or fast-food pizzas or bungee-jumping from hot-air balloons. Westerners miss much of the individual in the Japanese precisely because the Japanese are encouraged to conceal it. Among humans who are socialized from the earliest age, at home and in school, to live all their lives within a relatively permanent circle of mutual human sensitivity and to subordinate (or at least delay) personal gratification to the feelings and goals of the group, it is only natural to find that men and women have long since trimmed the "rough edges" of individual behavior, forced to hide their anger, disapproval, or passion, for the sake of the group.

For the sake of fairness we are obliged to remember this much about the Japanese as we judge the intents and exigencies of their reform of such elite institutions as their universities; not only because it explains why these institutions are failing the nation, because they do not correspond to what is truly liberal in the Japanese nature, but because we should recognize how much their measurements use different yardsticks from ours. Westerners come from a cultural mold of Greco-Roman, Judaeo-Christian social and intellectual traditions of individualism. We have long-established mechanisms of Socratic dialogue, Aristotelian rationalism, legalistic argument underpinning our civilizations and behaviors. When we ask a question, we expect an answer. It is hard for us to see that another culture may have been based upon precisely opposite traditions: to avoid verbalizing the obvious, to avert stated confrontation, to allow the simple passage of time and development of events—rather than debate—to suggest mutually acceptable ways around controversy.

Western governments, intellectuals, and media today all demand that the Japanese explain their values, their aspirations, and the way they see themselves relating to the rest of the world, in exactly that medium in which disagreement and conflict are most likely to come to a head most quickly: verbal debate. This is the medium, and the political outcome, their culture and their schools teach almost all Japanese to approach with the greatest of reticence. That is why they seem so subdued.

The Todai system where so much of this teaching finds its origins begins to fail precisely here, to founder upon its own successes. The Japanese no longer live in a national cocoon. As they themselves unswervingly emphasize in their vision of international economics and in their commercial advertising, they are now a "global" nation, for better or for worse.

Those public virtues that work best in the Japanese national interest—social and cultural insularity, self-control and self-abnegation, the dynamic cooperation of the in-group, and the dynamic of organized competition that results between out-groups—do not apply to a nation that has forced itself to "go global" politically, socially, academically. Japanese leadership has for too long embraced the obviously incorrect position that economics as a form of human interface exists apart from passion, on a high and antiseptic plane of systemic rationalism. Perhaps it was the Westerners, with their great libraries of social theories (à la Marx or Adam Smith), who first persuaded the Japanese to hold that view. But they cannot acquit themselves by claiming that they never really understood that economics is an intensely political form of intercourse because, as seen here, it is certainly that just as much within Japan as anywhere outside it.

Civilizations do not change their ideas and values to suit their neighbors and trading partners, of course. Japanese universities can teach foreign studies and foreign languages, but they cannot start turning out Japanese versions of Americans, Englishmen, or Australians, no matter how great the demand for them abroad. Yet there is a great deal of socially crucial disequilibrium within Japan itself, with which the educational system has refused to cope. Instead it has relied on that most dishonorable and dangerous of defense mechanisms: refusing to admit, for the most part, that the problem exists.

The university is not exactly bursting its bounds trying to contain this problem. Yet one Western intellectual, Karel Van Wolferen, who keeps in somewhat regular communication with parts of the humanities and social sciences academic communities through his frequent invitations to speak in Japan on the problems of Japanese politics and civilization on campus, has noticed that there are stirrings beneath the great facade of dissimulation: "[My] audiences differ. Sometimes you think, God, this really is a very good audience, very good questions. Some schools are more enthusiastic, but it probably also depends on professors who happen to be there. . . .

"Foment wouldn't be the right word, [but] you can detect an eagerness, a hankering after more than they are getting. And I think that they appreciate if you address questions that they have in their minds. I think there is a natural impulse to want to be effective in helping to shape one's environment," allows the Dutch writer, who says he always speaks to full lecture theaters when he goes to universities. "That's a very human trait. It's not just simply absent in the Japanese, even though they have been brought up as it were to accept passively whatever comes and to say *'shikatta ga nai'* (nothing can be done) at every juncture. They can't eliminate that human hankering to do something and so they think about things, and they do not normally get it through their courses, and so when I come and speak, and actually say that they are citizens and therefore can consider themselves as political entities even though all their activities may not result in anything noticeable, while having exercised their rights and duties as citizens, that being concerned about the political realities, that that in itself is rewarding, you get response. Again and again I'm struck by the seriousness of some of them, their questions and their whole demeanor."

It is not the citizens who are adrift. It is their leaders.

In the rustic winemaking village of Katsunuma, which lies below the Japanese Alps, one can travel a narrow lane through the vineyards of history to reach a hilltop, a geographic centerpiece crowned with the little town's proudest monument to itself: a modern community center that includes an authentic European wine cave, a French-style restaurant, and a sparkling new municipal recital hall. The wines are passable and the food is actually good. But the hall is a marvel: Two stories high, with parquet floors and acoustically baffled walls, it was built to incorporate the most refined auditory design concepts of the 1990s, and it is said to be an especially good venue for the performance of classical chamber music. Unfortunately, not many Katsunumans know whether it is or not. The village has no chamber ensemble, and the hall is booked mostly for local wedding parties.

Thus it is throughout much of *official* Japan today. Gorgeous public performance halls and theaters are erected from national and municipal budgets, in cities and in mere towns, for orchestras and opera troupes that do not exist and for which *no* budget has been provided; splendid art museums are constructed to house collections that no one has assembled, for masterworks that will be purchased, from whatever is available in the international and national art markets, as an afterthought. Twenty-three hundred musical performance halls and theaters have been erected by municipalities across the land. Each is used, on average, only forty-five days out of the year. Back in Tokyo, a half-billion-dollar performance arts center, dubbed the Second National Theater, is rising near the new metropolitan center of Shinjuku—with no orchestra selected to use it as a home, and no permanent full-time opera or ballet troupe even in existence in the country.[7] Thus while the popular culture is bursting with a new cosmopolitanism, there is something strangely empty at the center of official Japan these days, a shell of almost hubristic form and architectural pretension that has only an artistic and intellectual vacuum at its heart. In a country where some 25 million Japanese study as hobbies the classic forms of calligraphy, dance, *haiku* poetry, and even Western-style operatic song; in a nation that has produced prodigies of individual talent in music, painting, ceramics, literature, it is as if Japan itself has no soul. In place of one, it officially wishes these architectural symbols of intent to be seen by outsiders as achievement.

It is important to ask why, because this vacuum that lies at the heart of Japan's stubborn governmental insularity is the fault of the university, too. The answer is that culture, on an institutional level, is in the hands of bureaucrats: from Todai and other Big Five graduates who staff the Agency of Cultural Affairs, to town-hall functionaries who graduated from local colleges and were suddenly handed the cultural-affairs portfolio after ten years of dutiful work in the accounting section. There is then yet further significance to this common thread of a Japan that, as someone has put it, "is in this world, but not of it." The control of culture, as designed and presented in tutelary fashion by the various levels of government, is no accident: It is seen as important to the national character itself. "We have suffered so much from this myth of one nation-one culture business," says Michihiro Watanabe, a former senior official of the Agency for Cultural Affairs (under the Ministry of Education) and now a visiting professor at UCLA. "That 'duty-bound, hard-working, unified and non-materialistic Japanese' really is a myth introduced by the Meiji government. Before that, Japan was divided into three hundred and some feudal fiefdoms, and each competed culturally as well as politically, to an extent, with a certain independence. But the Meiji government's policies of national unity in all things have actually continued until as late as the mid-1980s."

And its sturdy vehicle has been the Todai system. Acknowledging that the educational system lies at the heart of this creation and maintenance of an artificially homogeneous culture, Watanabe denies that universities in Japan have even really been universities, in the Western sense, since their founding. "The Meiji government used all of these educational systems to carry out their policy of modernizing Japan. The university, supposed to cultivate or civilize Japan in a Western way, instead of pursuing truth or scientific discovery, from the beginning imposed upon people certain out-side values and outside ideas. Unless they change from their very basis, then, they cannot meet the aspirations of people. And no, I don't think they are changing—or at least not much. They are indeed stagnant, and that is really a problem."[8] Watanabe is striving to interest Japanese universities in arts curricula at the graduate level, so that more young, professional manag-ers and curators can be cultivated, but acknowledges that he has not met much enthusiasm. Instead he has had to settle for formulating brief "train-ing classes," given to bureaucrats from every sort of municipal and town-ship echelon who find themselves unexpectedly placed in charge of cultural affairs and budgets in their own bailiwicks.

The creation of full-fledged degree programs in the university would in any case be only a partial answer, as what Watanabe must aim at from the outset is promoting native Japanese cultures to native Japanese people: teaching them their own folk and art histories, as it were. The real job of the university, if not of the cultural bureaucracy, ranges much farther even than that, of course—to teach its students the cultures, the arts, the politics and the societies of the world as well—and it is in large measure failing that already. Here again, we can learn by asking "Why?"

We have already seen what a closed community the Japanese campus is. Ambassador Walter Mondale, early in 1995, deplored in a speech to the Japan–America Society the fact that only 1,700 American students were studying in Japan, a nation of 124 million, while 47,000 Japanese students were at the same time pursuing studies in America.[9] There were just two American undergraduates among the entire student-body of Todai in 1993–94 academic year, for example.

On the surface of it, this point might seem explicable by the language gap: One could hardly expect, as the former Monbusho official explained above, Japanese colleges and universities to offer a wide range of instruc-tion, let alone degree programs, in a foreign language when only one per-cent of the population is non-Japanese and most of those non–English speaking. And with the exception of Japan specialists, few American stu-dents in the United States are truly encouraged to master enough Japanese to survive on a Japanese campus. But that is not all there is to it: Various U.S. institutions, such as Temple University, offer partial or full degree programs inside Japan. But they are refused accreditation by the Ministry of Education, no matter what the content of the curriculum, and so their own American students cannot transfer credits to Japanese schools even when they become language-proficient. And their *American* degrees are not offic-ially recognized in Japan at all. Among the requirements for accreditation of a private institute of higher learning, for example, is that a school, even a foreign-owned school, must own the land it operates on, a huge burden even since land prices have declined from the peak years of the bubble economy.

(Among the 53,787 foreign students from all nations studying at both the graduate and undergraduate levels in Japanese universities and colleges in 1994, by comparison, 92 percent are from Asia, and some 80 percent from China, Korea, Taiwan, and Hong Kong—places where the Chinese script that forms the basis of the Japanese written language is at least familiar, and, of course, places where familiarity with the Japanese language, society, and management as well as technology could reasonably leave a student with expectations of securing employment as the Japanese economic sphere spreads and strengthens rapidly throughout Asia. As one magazine article put it, "Confident that Japanese economic might guarantees them solid career prospects, they use their time in Japan to develop expertise, personal contacts, and the language ability that can be acquired only by two or more years of immersion in Japanese life."[10])

But even setting aside that point, where the Japanese universities continue to fall down in failing to present their students with an opportunity to broaden their scope of thinking beyond Japan and its nationalist interpretations is in the failure to add foreign scholars to the faculty community. Among the 104,000 full-time staff at Japanese public and private universities in 1992 were only 2,345 regular and contract foreign staff, according to the *Asahi Shimbun*,[11] all on terms of renewable contracts, not the tenure track, with many in fact living with nothing but year-to-year employment agreements and a huge percentage involved in teaching only foreign languages, principally English. The condition that Japan's ninety-nine national universities impose on tenured professors—that they all be civil servants—forbids these schools from granting true lifetime employment to any foreign teacher. (Of course, Japanese as well as many other foreign nationals enjoy tenure in American universities; many have filled positions of great prestige, including one who has won a Nobel Prize while at MIT and another who has been a dean at Princeton.) While many foreign teachers in Japan have remained at their schools for decades on renewed contracts, they still serve at the campus president's pleasure. (And in many cases at the government's pleasure as well, as was made obvious by the back-channel circulation of an advisory to the national schools by the Education Ministry in 1992, suggesting that senior foreign staff, supposedly because of the high cost of their employment, should be eased out and replaced with younger, less-costly instructors—a condition brought to the U.S. ambassador's attention by Ivan Hall and others.)

The United States for its part has pushed at what pressure points it can, officially and unofficially, to draw Japan's attention to the fact that America would like to see a healthy, constructive broadening of academic as well as cultural dialogue taking place between the two nations, within Japan.

The reaction, much as in negotiations over troublesome, flash-point trade issues, has been largely reserved. One senior U.S. official dealing with educational and cultural relations with Japan was shocked when, in early 1995, he presented for discussion a carefully diplomatic list of unofficial suggestions, authored collectively by American and Japanese academic experts, to the official Japanese delegation to the U.S.–Japan Conference on Cultural and Educational Interchange; he got the distinct impression that the Japanese side was prepared to formally withdraw from the conference altogether rather than even discuss them. (Since that time, however, he says the Japanese have relaxed their stance, "the reaction has turned around," and progress has been made on discussion of such hard points as visa qualifications and the possible instruction of classes in English on some Japanese campuses.)

Private schools in Japan may hire faculty at their own discretion. But the point here is not a "trade imbalance" in professors (Hall has told me he estimates some 7,000 Japanese professors now teach in the United States): The point is that not nearly enough foreign instructors of any nationality are found on *any* Japanese campuses to qualify the schools sufficiently as cosmopolitan universities. As Hall summarizes what he calls this brand of "academic apartheid": "As far as its prestigious national universities are concerned, Japan isn't opening up as advertised—it's closing down."

In America's case, reciprocally, this inability to gain access to the academic community in Japan and all the sources in the broader society that are in turn open to it has, as James Fallows points out, its own deleterious effect. Fallows quotes a U.S. scholar, a Japan specialist at Berkeley, who was actually upbraided by an industry executive when he visited Tokyo for having written critically about Japanese manufacturing transplants—*in America*. It is not that American academics cannot survive crude attempts at censorship of this kind. The real problem that results, said the business professor, "is perhaps how we Japan scholars unconsciously [begin to] censor ourselves to avoid embarrassing our hosts or to avoid endangering our sources of future data. . . . We tend not to write what we think might embarrass our Japanese hosts."[12] Except for those doing "approved" research or, in case of the sciences, needed research, the Japanese academic establishment remains a largely closed circle, an empty performance hall, even to those scholars trying to learn and teach from thousands of miles away.

In the end, what blocks reform the most is that every Japanese parent knows his or her child's life will be blueprinted largely by success in school. Any real reform of the system would focus on that fact, not on what happens inside classrooms. Because successful civilizations seldom voluntarily reform themselves organically on the strength of public debate, but rather on the issue of who holds power and how intent they are on maintaining it, the larger reality of the system is not likely to be swept away, no matter how many credit hours are required or removed from the catalogue. Indeed, an important function of the system is to atomize families into competitive units, vis-à-vis one another. Mothers and fathers may well wish to see the system's load lightened for their children. But few wish to be the first to experiment with their own child's future in any new system being "tested out." While the changes and ultimately their children could fail, all the other children who soldier on through the "old" system will be guaranteed of its rewards. Many of the children freed from some of their Saturday classes by Japan's stately, onward-grinding progress to a five-day schoolweek, for example, are simply choosing to use the extra time to take more classes in *juku,* the cram schools.

Little wonder, then, that what is encompassed in Japan by the term *education* is seen as so all-embracingly crucial to one's fate and one's ultimate chances for the future. It is something that every Japanese is taught to believe holds the key to his or her professional and marital success, comfort, status, and even self-worth in Japanese society. It actually does only to those who are intent on entering the elite; as seen here, however, in a certain sense almost everyone in Japan is actually ranked by his or her distance from Todai.

Not everyone, though, shows signs of willingness to remain in perpetual thrall to this national imperative. There is another constituency to the national educational system whose members are growing restless. The Japanese who are truly beginning to see less and less merit in the system are the same ones on whom the system actually falls hardest: not students, but their mothers. "Japanese mothers feel that they are responsible for their children's future," as one international education scholar reminds us.[13] As seen in this book, springing from this obligation is the belief that it, "coupled with the importance of the child's success for the mother's own identity, is the basic source of the child's success in school."

But it is publicly obvious that the reason the mother's identity is coupled so firmly with the child's success is because the socioeconomic system of contemporary Japan wants it that way. It structures a school system, an establishment set of values, and a business culture that keeps the father away from home and away from the school system that is so important to the child, so much of the time. Almost all responsibility for the social success of young children in lower grades, and the academic success of older children in more competitive grades, does indeed appear to fall on the mother. She becomes not only her child's prime socializer but the educational system's chief source of authority for compliance with its rigors; its chief bridge to the child. She is clearly, even stridently, urged to abandon all career aspirations and devote herself foremost to her child. "For without such mothering, it is understood within the Japanese cultural unconscious that both the future of children *and the survival of the nation* are imperiled" (emphasis added).[14] Reform aside, mothers remain the support troops in the war for Japan's economic prosperity.

Never mind that the original reasons seemed logical enough. The great domestic movement of the postwar period, of young people away from their homes in small towns, cities, and villages, where they often grew up within extended families of grandparents, aunts, and uncles, to cities—where they married, established nuclear households among strangers, and the mothers began raising their children alone—is what placed virtually all weight of the socialization of children on their mothers' backs. We have by now seen the evidence of how this has been used to capture social control of the entire family. The pressures the society and the school exert, naturally, remain for young mothers to leave the work force at the first pregnancy and devote all their energies to child rearing.

An increasingly large number of them refuse, or cannot afford, to do it. No matter. What has not been reformed is Japan's economic culture and formal power structures, which remain rigidly male-dominated. It is why the paternalism of the corporate employment system still grants special salary allowances for marriage and number of children born and special allowances for male employees establishing new households. For nearly forty years it was "the system." Women could do little about it; for a woman to remain unmarried and without children could evoke peer contempt, and even something akin to social ostracism. Women were afraid not to do their national duty.

Now that appears as though it might be starting to change, as more and more professional women have realized at last that male attitudes and the pressures of this "system" simply cannot be modified in any other way than ignoring them, and rejecting them.

Today it is these single professional women who, in greater and greater numbers, are refusing to become mothers and who are quietly, but convincingly, "dropping out" of the Todai system. They are either not marrying or are only marrying much later. More than 40 percent of all Japanese women between ages twenty-five and twenty-nine today have never married.[15] True, they still hope to marry and have children, and the majority will still leave their jobs at the first pregnancy. But the net of their decision is that women of child-bearing age are now producing just one and a half offspring each—the lowest national level of reproduction in recorded Japanese history. If the trend continues, the population of Japan will fall by 25 percent with each generation. The next century could end with only half as many Japanese alive as there are today.

This development has naturally set off alarms among government, bureaucratic, and industrial leadership. There are broad discussions of changing tax and labor law, and corporate salary systems, to give Japanese couples financial incentives to have more children. While financial considerations limit the size of Japanese families today, it is difficult not to suspect that the real issue is not money but, rather, the conditions of employment for Japan's single most important cadre of civil servants, its young mothers. And so reforms that begin here, which could really change things throughout the national educational system, *ipso facto* really could also threaten the stability of the national order of authority.

B ut the last link of this circle of "reform" must be the college student, who is trained to be compliant, cooperative, and responsive, and raised always to ask "how to comply" with what the educational system wants; he is a scholastic soldier, fresh from a Spartan lifetime of eighty-hour weeks of classes, tutorials, and cram courses. Yet also, as Van Wolferen has said, the student has "a natural impulse to want to be effective in helping to shape one's [civic] environment."

The student is thus perhaps the weakest link—or maybe the strongest. "They fulfilled these roles, they went through these procedures, they became that person the [future career] role demands," says Harry Wray, a Japanese educational historian and now a professor of economics at Nanzan University. "In a Confucian society role is a very important kind of thing; you have a duty in that role, and if everybody fits into that niche, society will operate smoothly."[16]

But is it really only the case that a Confucian sense of "duty" victimizes these young people, exempting them from any expectation that they, too, bear a momentous responsibility to their society for reform? On the face of it, I find that hard to accept. True, the pressures of family, school, and society seem overwhelming. But still this is a *winnowing* process, designed in the end to select for admission those who are the "best and brightest"—not only the most compliant, but the most intellectually competent. And to those who are in such measure competent, it cannot forever elude them that what they are ultimately engaged in here is a race for power. In the end, the reform of Japan's civic society will depend on how they feel about that race and that power.

It is not merely the power of title or income, in the sense that that may drive those who enter a university seeking only professional goals; nor is it the power of wisdom, which is by unspoken consensus assigned almost no validity at all by either students or teachers at the university. But it is public power, political power, the power of control over state, institution, and ultimately society. The reason it becomes available *only* with passage through the academic sieve is that Japan itself has actually become an illegitimate, if not truly alegal, state. The powers of the constitution, vesting sovereignty in the people and the power of rule in their elected representatives, have been hijacked in Japan. They have been expropriated from the people and parties by the bureaucracies, first of the government and second of the major and even minor business *keiretsu*. And what is all the struggle of the Todai system about, if not for places in these same bureaucracies? As Van Wolferen has said of universities and this power in a different context, "Since Japan's elections of recent decades have not had any influence on the nation's policies, and since the judiciary system [itself a product of the bureaucracy] does not supply any external check on Japanese government institutions, Todai is, by default and aside from the imperial household, the single most important legitimating agency of the Japanese political system."[17]

"Legitimating" is the key word here, for it is the motive power of the whole educational system that all Japanese, including the students, recognize. The path to power does not lie in democracy, as is clear by the time the students face the entrance exams. It does not lie in working within the framework of a party, or a citizens' movement, or even within the boundaries of a civil society. Power, illegitimately, is taken right along with the entrance exams by those who pass them. Far more than the dispenser of credentials, the university, whether it be Todai, Kyodai, Keio, Waseda, Hitotsubashi, or schools of lesser rank, is the straight and the sole road to legitimating the individual's grasping a share of direct political authority over society. No student with the intelligence to get through the exams can fail to understand that, and this is what makes his or her race so desperate.

In this sense the university has become, and remains despite all talk and all effort toward "reform," illegitimate itself. It offers to its student a passage to an illicit national power that will come with no real public accountability attached to it. Bureaucrats can make policy for administrative government, and strategy for capitalist enterprise, and cooperation for the mutual success of both. But they do not take responsibility, except in the narrowest sense, for the fate of the nation—only for that of their own spheres of power and interest. That threatens Japan; it does not (as is most often thought) guarantee its success. A nation without an accountable center of political power is not a real nation. For one thing, it has no valid foreign policy-making structure, responsive to the vast array of necessities and responsibilities of *all* parts of a state that is now ranked second in strength in the world. It can and does continue only toward the overweening goal, first set in the postwar years of reconstruction, to continue along the successful track of economic super-production and marketplace victory.

For another, it has no responsiveness to those in whom sovereignty resides: the people who *are* the nation. The bureaucracies are self-serving machines, struggling on many fronts with one another, interested only in their own success and self-preservation. The nation continues on the world stage leaderless. And of course any such state bereft of leadership cannot help but see itself as a "victim," taken advantage of, in *every international adversity* it encounters. It has no other choice, really, but to insist that responsibility or blame falls mostly on the other side whenever it encounters international dispute, especially when it suffers public criticism or cost to any national interest, because there is no leadership institution within it who can take the weight of Japan's own responsibility on its shoulders, and answer for it. And the party who is blamed cannot respond to this complaint, because for the same reason there is no one legitimately accountable for the national interest among any of the Japanese power holders with whom it tries to settle conflict. The foreign power is always bound to be a convenient scapegoat for the indecisiveness that cloaks the vacuum at Japan's political center.

This accounts more than a little for the unwillingness of the university to permit much of any "internationalism" of curriculum or of intercultural perspective in its training of future leaders. How much simpler it is to explain their society as "unique" to all Japanese elites, rather than as politically compromised.

It follows that, because of both the successes and the failures of the Todai system, every nation dealing with Japan on matters of national interest is at risk on two counts: First because it can make deals only with those who have no legitimate power to speak for the whole nation in the first place; that is, with those ministers and cabinet authorities from whom legitimate power has been stolen. And wherever a deal can be struck with the consent of those bureaucrats who really do hold the specific, relevant power, the agreement is ultimately unenforceable. The nation's executive cannot guarantee all of the bureaucracy will conform to it, and the bureaucracy will not hold itself accountable to outsiders, be they Japanese politicians or foreign diplomats or businessmen, in any matter in which its own interests are felt to be at stake. This is what accounts for the failure of so many loosely given promises of Japanese prime and cabinet ministers to resolve legitimate complaints from trading partners and diplomatic allies.

The bureaucrats of ministry and *keiretsu* simply refuse to comply.

Second, since no one can answer for the whole nation, any bureaucratic party that suffers a loss from a concession granted by a competing bureaucracy will feel no compulsion to abide by it; rather, it will ignore or defy it. This means really that every deal made with Japan is an alegal deal, and any nation dealing with as powerful a state as Japan on such terms is at risk itself.

As long as the university remains unreformed, the nation itself will lie in peril under the university's informal authority to recruit and legitimate Japan's leaders. In terms of assigning the power to govern, it is plain, Todai is the nation, and the nation is Todai. No bureaucratic institution would seek to reform that degree of power right out of its own hands. Only when the nation has first reformed itself, into a legitimate state, can it reform its universities. Only then will the world be safe from Japan, and for Japan.

Notes

1. Interview with the author, February 1993.
2. Interview with the author, February 3, 1993.
3. Interview with the author, April 1994.
4. Ivan P. Hall, "Samurai Legacies, American Illusions," in *The National Interest,* no. 28 (summer 1992).
5. Interview with the author, July 1992.
6. Interview with the author, June 28, 1986.
7. "Opera Plan Seen as Showy Shell, No Core," *Japan Times,* December 31, 1992.
8. Interview with the author, January 1995.
9. "Mondale Asks Schools Shift," *Japan Times,* January 16, 1995.
10. "Closing the Student Import Gap," *Intersect Japan* (August 1995).
11. "Second-Class Citizens in the Academic World," *Asahi Evening News,* May 26, 1993.
12. James Fallows, *Looking at the Sun: The Rise of the New East Asian Economic and Political System* (New York: Pantheon Books, 1994).
13. Merry White, *The Japanese Educational Challenge: A Commitment to Children* (Tokyo: Kodansha International, 1987).
14. Ibid.
15. "Population Growth Hitting Postwar Low as Number of Elderly Rises," *Japan Times,* November 30, 1991.
16. Interview with the author, May 1992.
17. Speech delivered to students and faculty at the University of Tokyo, June 1995.

Index

Robert L. Cutts, a free-lance journalist resident in Asia for twenty-five years, has been a daily newspaper reporter and editor in Tokyo, a war correspondent in Vietnam, and a news bureau chief in Seoul. He has written extensively on Japanese society, economics and business, publishing in magazines such as the *Harvard Business Review, California Management Review*, the Japan Air Lines' inflight *Winds*, the *American Chamber of Commerce Journal*, and *Intersect*. He has also done special-research essays and writings for the Asia Society, Marubeni Corp., and others.